❁ The Whispered Meanings

❁ The Whispered Meanings

Selected Essays of
Simon O. Lesser

Edited by Robert Sprich
and
Richard W. Noland

The University of Massachusetts Press   Amherst 1977

❖ Contents

❀ Preface

MANY people know Simon Lesser primarily as the author of *Fiction and the Unconscious*, the remarkable book that brought ego psychology decisively into literary criticism in 1957. In the context of his total work, that book is his *theoria*. These essays are the equally important *praxis* to complete and justify it.

In a larger context, the growth of psychoanalysis as a whole, Lesser challenged the early styles of psychoanalytic criticism in the best way, by invigorating them with the subsequent achievements of the parent discipline, clinical and theoretical psychoanalysis. Beginning with Freud's 1897 analysis of *Hamlet*, psychoanalysts understood literary works through the polarity between conscious and unconscious, demonstrated as general because of its presence across dreams, symptoms, jokes, and parapraxes. They thought of conscious and unconscious as systems or even physical locations in the mind. The early psychoanalytic critics found in literary works mostly variations on the two great divisions we face in the Oedipus complex: male and female, child and adult. Often, first-phase psychoanalytic critics relied on decodings into routinized anal, phallic, and oedipal themes, ingeniously creating a systematics of "Freudian symbolism" far beyond the limits Freud himself had set and common sense would confirm.

In the second phase of psychoanalysis, the structures of id, ego, and superego absorbed the old conscious-unconscious polarity, making it descriptive only. The psychoanalytic critic needed to do more than translate manifest content to latent. Lesser, in particular, found he could understand the reading and writing of literature as appeals to these three different agencies, and hence he could talk about the manifest content and its relation to the latent —a major move forward as well as a recapturing of Freud's early concern with latent and manifest as process rather than product. For his *praxis,* Lesser chose major texts and major writers. His style and insight merit no less than Homer, Sophocles, Dostoevsky, or Shakespeare.

Since Lesser's pioneering work, a third phase of psychoanalysis has evolved, in which the earlier conscious-unconscious and id-ego-superego are absorbed into a still larger psychology of the self in its relations to others. Yet just as these new theories (or better, perceptions) have grown around and by means of the earlier, so Lesser's ego-psychological criticism has become organic to all later psychoanalytic literary study.

From that later point of view, I place Lesser's understandings, not "in" the texts, but "in" his relation to them. Partly that relation includes his remarkable skill as a literary critic and his claim, therefore, to speak, not only for himself, but for the story and for a whole community of readers. More importantly, however, Lesser's reading rests on a fineness of intuition and expression which is distinctively his own: a psychoanalytically nurtured ability to bring out from his encounter with literary works perdurable human experience. It is this humanistic intuition, as much as his psychological innovation, that makes Simon Lesser a critic one wishes to know ever better.

Norman N. Holland

✿ The Whispered Meanings

☸ Introduction

Simon O. Lesser's *Fiction and the Unconscious*[1] is widely—and deservedly—regarded as a landmark in the application of psychoanalytic theory to literary criticism. The dynamic model of reader response to fiction which Lesser developed has formed a starting point for some of the most productive work in this field. As one critic put it, Lesser's book "posed the pragmatic and empirical questions that we are exploring today." It also "suggested a rational framework for the understanding of multiple readings of the same work."[2] Although the essays included in the present collection are self-contained and do not depend upon a knowledge of the theoretical formulations in *Fiction*, it is nevertheless useful to bring some understanding of Lesser's major work to a reading of these essays. More than half of them, after all, represent elaborations of brief interpretive comments in *Fiction*, and the essay on Hawthorne's "My Kinsman, Major Molineux" is reprinted *in toto* directly from the book.

Fiction and the Unconscious presents a remarkable synthesis of material from the writings of such psychoanalytic theorists as Freud and Ernest Jones with the aesthetic theories of such literary critics as I. A. Richards and Maud Bodkin. Less obviously, Lesser also draws upon psychologically oriented *fin de siècle* critics like Havelock Ellis, who, as early as 1896, had described the response to art as "the athletics of the emotions."[3]

Lesser published his first piece of psychological criticism in 1952— the short essay included in this volume entitled "A Note on *Pamela*." He

1. Boston: Beacon Press, 1957.
2. David Bleich, *Readings and Feelings* (Urbana, Ill.: National Council of Teachers of English, 1975), p. 112.
3. "Casanova," *Savoy* 7 (Nov. 1896): 48.

began his work in this field at a time when there was already a well-established tradition of psychological criticism which stretched all the way back to Freud's brief remarks on *Oedipus Rex* in *The Interpretation of Dreams* (1900). The development of psychoanalytic theory and psychoanalytic literary criticism are thus very much intertwined, and it is accordingly of great importance to understand some of the implications of this close relationship. In the first place, we should note that, in the development of Freud's thought, id psychology and ego psychology do not from the first constitute equal areas of interest. Broadly speaking, there are two main periods in this development: the period of id psychology (1900–1914) and the period of ego psychology (1914–1939).[4] In the earlier of these two periods, Freud's main concern was the nature of the repressed unconscious, the significance of infantile sexuality in normal and neurotic behavior, and the meaning of dreams, jokes, parapraxes, and neurotic symptoms. His orientation was still heavily biological—that is, he understood his work as the rediscovery of the role of instinct in human life.

As it happens, most of Freud's writings on art and the artist come from this period. Inevitably, then, his statements on art in general and on individual artists and works of art in particular reflect his main preoccupations during the period of id psychology. As we can see in such essays as "Delusions and Dreams in Jensen's *Gradiva*" (1906) and "Creative Writers and Daydreaming" (1909), he was naturally interested in the role of fantasy—especially repressed infantile fantasy—in the life and work of all artists. In addition, given his model of parapraxes, jokes, dreams, and neurotic symptoms as compromise formations between an unconscious impulse to express a wish and a conscious or unconscious attempt to defend against, to deny, that wish, it was a very easy step for Freud to assume that works of art are also compromise formations.

It does not take a very close reading of Freud's essays on literary subjects from 1900 to 1915 to realize that they are not primarily attempts at art criticism. They are, rather, efforts to validate or illustrate his developing theoretical ideas either in the whole of a given text, in the psychology of a character in a given text, or in the relationship between an artist's fantasy life and his work. As psychological evidence, this is a perfectly valid procedure, but it is hardly calculated to lead to an adequate theory of aesthetics. Nevertheless, Freud's general statements on art and artists and his comments on specific texts established the direction of psychoanalytic literary criticism for many years.

4.   This division follows the simplified version in Reuben Fine's *The Development of Freud's Thought: From the Beginnings (1886–1900) through Id Psychology (1900–1914) to Ego Psychology* (New York: Jason Aronson, Inc., 1973).

Following Freud, other psychoanalytic critics (usually Freudian psychologists, but also literary critics) continued to view the work of art as a compromise formation between an impulse and a defense against that impulse. In the early years of psychoanalytic criticism (1900–1927), there were two main questions: first, the question of whether or not the artist is neurotic; and second, the question of the relationship between art and the dream, which was in turn related to the issue of unconscious as against conscious creativity. We may take Hanns Sachs's 1942 book, *The Creative Unconscious* (a book which Lesser draws on in *Fiction*), with its idea of art as a communal or shared daydream, as an exemplary statement of the initial concern of psychoanalytic critics with unconscious creativity and fantasy in art.[5]

With the publication of *The Ego and the Id* (1923), Freud introduced into psychoanalysis a concept of the ego which, though tentative and very ambiguous in his own late work, was to lead to important new developments in psychoanalytic theory and psychoanalytic literary criticism. By the time Lesser began to publish, there was already a well-established tradition of psychoanalytic ego psychology. Two books in particular—Anna Freud's *The Ego and the Mechanisms of Defense* (1936) and Heinz Hartmann's *Ego Psychology and the Problem of Adaptation* (1939)—had established the ideas of ego defense and ego adaptation at the center of psychoanalytic thinking. The effect of this theoretical shift was an increasing interest in ego strength rather than ego weakness, in normal psychology rather than only psychopathology. With Ernst Kris's *Psychoanalytic Explorations in Art* (1952), ego psychology entered increasingly into psychoanalytic thinking about art and the artist. Leonard Manheim, a longtime friend of Lesser's and founding editor of the journal *Literature and Psychology* (in which some of Lesser's early work appeared), has commented on the importance of this development:

> It is now possible to find in psychoanalytic theory a justification for the judgment of the critic that there is such a thing as an "art impulse." It is possible to see the creative ego as one which is not limited to judging with the motive forces of the unconscious and presenting them in socially acceptable, palatable form; which does not deal solely with sublimations which are, after all, merely attenuated forms of crude drives. Nor, on the other hand, need we go along

5. This summary of early Freudian criticism is indebted to Claudia C. Morrison's *Freud and the Critic: The Early Use of Depth Psychology in Literary Criticism* (Chapel Hill: University of North Carolina Press, 1968). For another overview of psychoanalytic criticism, see also Morton Kaplan and Robert Kloss, *The Unspoken Motive: A Guide to Psychoanalytic Literary Criticism* (New York: The Free Press, 1973).

with those who insist that the artist is at his best only when he is completely under the domination of the unconscious. . . . Instead we see the artist as one who is endowed with the ability to permit material from the unconscious to enter into consciousness and to use it for the production of universal, humanly attractive products called works of art, without being dominated or destroyed by that material; one who can play with the forces that lead to neurosis and worse and tame them, without loss to himself and for the benefit of mankind.[6]

Manheim is undoubtedly correct in his estimate of the theoretical importance of ego psychology for literary criticism. Yet few critics have actually applied ego psychological theory in an even remotely adequate way to literary theory and analysis. Lesser is one of those few. *Fiction and the Unconscious* is a tribute to Lesser's knowledge of psychoanalytic theory and to his understanding of the nature of fiction. It is perhaps the first full-length work by a literary critic in which the id psychological and the ego psychological traditions of psychoanalysis are fused into a balanced, nonreductive examination of the art of fiction. That is no small achievement, and it accounts for the seminal importance of Lesser's work in *Fiction and the Unconscious.*

We do not intend to discuss *Fiction* in detail. By way of introduction to Lesser's essays, however, we will suggest a few of the major themes and accomplishments of this book so as to indicate the nature and scope of its achievement. It is worth noting, at the beginning, that Lesser defines fiction very broadly. By fiction, he means "every form of imaginative work basically concerned with telling a story—novels, novelettes and short stories; narrative poems; plays, whether in poetry or prose; and stories told through the various media of popular art, including magazines, motion pictures, comic books, radio and television."[7] Yet he identifies the basic subject matter of fiction—the "struggle between impulse and inhibition"—in a potentially narrow, reductive manner. The success of *Fiction* resides in the way in which Lesser manages to apply this traditional Freudian formula to the broad spectrum of literary types covered by his definition of fiction.

It is here that Lesser's debt to id and ego psychology comes into play. His definition of impulse and inhibition, accordingly, is broad, for he includes as impulse adult feelings as well as infantile instinctual ones,

6. Leonard and Eleanor Manheim, eds., *Hidden Patterns: Studies in Psychoanalytic Literary Criticism* (New York: MacMillan Company, 1966), p. 10.
7. Simon O. Lesser, *Fiction and the Unconscious* (Boston: Beacon Press, 1957), p. 11. All subsequent references are to this edition.

and as inhibition external as well as internal impediments. He thus avoids, in theory and practice, the traditional pitfall of psychoanalytic critics—the view that the basic drive behind all fiction is repressed infantile wishes. Lesser views fiction as responsive to both the pleasure principle and the reality principle. He also sees fiction as providing a forum for ego and superego as well as id.

In fact, the way in which fiction structures id, ego, and superego functions is central to his whole conception of the attitude of fiction. Like all Freudian critics, Lesser is fully responsive to the presence in works of fiction of emotional conflict, of fantasy and wish (both infantile and adult), and of forbidden sexual and aggressive impulses. But if fiction makes restitution to us for the instinctual deprivation demanded by civilization, it also seeks to speak for the other two psychic structures. Fiction, Lesser argues, "provides an outlet for idealistic and contemplative tendencies thwarted in our daily experience . . ." (p. 82). That is, it satisfies the superego. As for the ego, fiction represents this psychic structure in a variety of ways—in its recognition of reality (fiction always gives obstacles to the fulfillment of wishes as much weight as it does the wishes), in its urge toward form, and in its integrative capacity—that is, its ability to "heal intrapsychic tension" (p. 93). The greatest works of fiction, Lesser says, "give us the impression of having overlooked nothing, no relevant consideration, no possibility of harmonizing apparently incompatible elements" (p. 79). The balance and flexibility of Lesser's critical essays come in good part from his persistent attempt to show how, in each concrete narrative work, the claims of the entire adult psyche and of external reality receive their just due.

There is another remarkable theme in *Fiction and the Unconscious* which separates it from the bulk of Freudian criticism. This is Lesser's interest in form as well as content. Such an interest hardly seems unusual for someone concerned with the nature of art. But it is for someone concerned with the psychology of art. There are behavioral and gestalt psychological studies of form. But, by and large, psychoanalytic criticism has been interested in content, not form. Lesser is a conspicuous exception to the usual Freudian focus on content. He makes the function of form in fiction central to his whole argument. And, in fact, he devotes two substantial chapters to the subject.

Lesser identifies three essential psychological functions of form: the giving of pleasure (an id function), the avoiding or relieving of guilt (a superego function), and the facilitating of perception (an ego function). Like content, then, form synthesizes the often conflicting claims of the three psychic structures. In doing so, form guarantees the "communication of the expressive content in a way which provides a maximum amount of pleasure and minimizes guilt and anxiety" (p. 125).

In fiction, then, form and content support each other in representing the claims of inner and outer reality, of id, superego, and ego. Lesser's discussion of the various and complex modes of interaction in narrative structure among these psychic agencies is subtle and ample. It is further enhanced by aptly selected examples of fiction. Apart from its own intrinsic interest, Lesser's analysis of the textual structuring of id, ego, and superego demands by form and content leads to another important consideration. For, in Lesser's view, a text structures these demands for the satisfaction of a reader or an audience. Lesser, in other words, is not only interested in the text. He is also interested in the processes of conscious and unconscious perception by which a reader (or audience) responds to a text (or performance). He is concerned with what he calls the appeals of fiction to the parts of the psyche and with how this appeal can lead to the resolution of emotional conflicts and hence to ego integration.

Accordingly, Lesser devotes one whole chapter to a consideration of the appeals of fiction. He devotes three others to the conscious and unconscious processes of response (the second of which contains his by now classic reading of Hawthorne's "My Kinsman, Major Molineux"). As one would expect from a critic working in the Freudian tradition, Lesser is especially interested in unconscious perception in fiction. He identifies three unconscious perceptual processes: unconscious understanding (a kind of passive spectator reaction), unconscious identification with characters, and analogizing (an unconscious assimilation of the story to our own personal experience). Again, his discussion of these processes is lengthy, subtle, and always penetrating.

The remarkable thing about Lesser's analysis of reader/audience response to narrative works is its anticipation of what is now a major preoccupation in psychological criticism. Though the psychology of audience response is as old as Aristotle, and though Freud and other psychoanalysts were very much interested in the dynamics of literary response, the attention paid by Lesser to this subject in *Fiction* is clearly an important influence on recent psychoanalytic critics. In particular, the work of Norman N. Holland—whose last two books, *Poems in Persons* (1973) and *5 Readers Reading* (1975), are mainly about the nature of literary response—suggests the importance of this topic among contemporary psychoanalytic critics. But Holland has gone further than Lesser in this direction. However much interested he may be in the appeal of fiction or in how we assimilate a work of fiction to our own identity or our own fantasy, Lesser remains primarily interested in the meaning inherent in a given text. He prefers the role of literary critic to that of psychologist of the processes of fictional response. The essays collected in this volume clearly demonstrate Lesser's essential commitment to textual criticism.

Of the fourteen essays which appear in *The Whispered Meanings,* two are primarily theoretical, while the remaining twelve deal with particular literary works. Yet even in the latter group of essays Lesser frequently seizes the opportune moment to elucidate relevant aspects of psychoanalytic theory or of everyday human experience so that one senses an organic interplay between general remarks and practical criticism.

Lesser's two theoretical essays move in quite different directions: whereas "The Attitude of Fiction" concentrates on the factors which influence a reader's emotional involvement with a literary text, "The Role of Unconscious Understanding in Flaubert and Dostoevsky" remains almost entirely within the realm of depth-psychology. Based upon biographical evidence, Lesser notes that Dostoevsky and Flaubert manifested a similar pattern of psychosexual organization, namely a pronounced tendency toward bisexuality (and not merely in the trivial sense that Freud claimed every human being is bisexual: harboring characteristics of the opposite sex as latent potentialities). If both men had a similar character structure, Lesser then asks, why did Dostoevsky succeed so much more fully than Flaubert in expressing his unconscious understanding of bisexuality in his fiction? This essay thus remains focused upon the writers themselves rather than their works, on psychobiography and the psychology of artistic creativity.

Lesser's twelve essays which concentrate on the analysis of individual works are printed here in the order of their publication. These essays demonstrate convincingly that a consideration of the unconscious factors in the central conflict of a literary work deepens and enriches our appreciation of its subtleties. But the continuing interest of Lesser's criticism lies not only in his quest for "whispered meanings" but in his simultaneous close attention to the manifest verbal texture of a work.[8]

In *Fiction* Lesser remarked that the traditional grouping of literary works by genre and period tends to magnify differences while obscuring underlying similarities. The essays in this collection amply illustrate the

8. A good example of Lesser's attention to surface detail would be his analysis of Oedipus' shifts from plural to singular in speaking of King Laius' murderer(s).

breadth of literary materials which Lesser felt could be approached productively from a psychoanalytic perspective: they deal with works which
range in time from Homer to Harold Pinter and include novels, plays,
epic and lyric poems, short stories, and films. Because Lesser's essays
strive not merely to talk about literary works but to re-create and enhance
the reader's experience of them, any attempt at summary or paraphrase
would inevitably lose the sense of intimate dialectic which Lesser establishes with the texts. However, it might be useful to take a brief look at
the distinctive features of each essay.

Lesser's first published piece of psychoanalytic literary criticism—"A
Note on *Pamela*" (1952)—differs from his later essays in that it *is* a brief
note rather than a full-scale analysis. This essay not only sheds light on
Richardson's novel but also uses that novel as a case in point to illustrate
the power of psychoanalytic insights in explaining the continued popularity of a "dated" work. Although it is easy to poke fun at Pamela's stilted
protestations and Squire B.'s stereotyped role as the vile seducer, Lesser
asserts that Pamela's behavior—as distinct from her speeches—displays
the ambivalence of a girl who is genuinely in love, although she cannot
consciously admit it, even to herself. Hence a modern reader's enjoyment of the novel results, in part at least, from his ability to perceive intuitively the rightness of Pamela's actions, however archaic or priggish her
verbal pronouncements about sexual morality might seem.

The tone of the *Pamela* essay is light-hearted. Its structure follows
the pattern of Socratic discourse: the first third of the essay is devoted to
an enumeration of all the novel's faults, but just when the reader is ready
to agree with the prevailing modern critical opinion, Lesser comes to the
novel's defense: "The fact that *Pamela* has been read with pleasure for
two hundred years should suggest that it is not without appealing qualities." These qualities, as Lesser goes on to show, are apprehended for
the most part unconsciously. Yet, in spite of his emphasis on unconscious factors, Lesser avoids using psychoanalytic terminology, though
he does speculate playfully about what Pamela might have learned about
herself if she had had "the benefit of psychoanalysis." The essay thus
serves as a consciousness-raising exercise to suggest the value of applying depth-psychology to literary criticism. It concludes with a question
which foreshadows the central concerns of *Fiction* as well as most of
Lesser's other writings: "And is it not a tendency of modern criticism in
its hair-splitting preoccupation with moral issues and values to slight the
purely narrative and structural factors which account for the pleasure of
reading and deserve our chief attention?"

"Freud and *Hamlet* Again" occupies an important position in Lesser's criticism because, in it, Lesser not only reaffirms the essential validity of the Freud-Jones interpretation of *Hamlet*, but also defends Freudian psychology against the charge that it is intrinsically normative and conservative—in short, that it aims at the preservation of the status quo. Lesser notes that, as a therapeutic technique, psychoanalysis "seeks to help people see the world without distortion"—though it makes no guarantee that such a view will be pleasant. In relation to *Hamlet*, a psychoanalytic approach "provides at least one important clue to the almost universal appeal of the play, for it explains Hamlet's delay in terms of a conflict of intense moment to everyone." It was the neglect of unconscious dynamics which led such an astute critic as T. S. Eliot to judge *Hamlet* a radically flawed play.

Hawthorne's often-anthologized short story, "My Kinsman, Major Molineux," offers a case in point of a literary work which is virtually unintelligible without taking unconscious perceptions into account. The climax of the story occurs when the protagonist, Robin, seeing his kinsman in "tar-and-feathery dignity," laughs spontaneously. Robin's laughter seems both logically inconsistent and out of character unless one assumes, as Lesser does, that Robin's quest to find Major Molineux is half-hearted at best, that, to Robin, the Major is not only a potential benefactor but also, on another level, an extension of the repressive parental authority against which he ultimately rebels.

Lesser begins his analysis of Dostoevsky's *The Idiot* by stating that the main theme of the novel is "the inadequacy of mere goodness in the world of today." But he is quick to point out that Prince Myshkin's apparent saintliness masks an internal struggle between ego and superego. "His fatal flaw is an undeveloped ego: a sense of reality so deficient that it not only prevents him from doing good, but causes him to fail everyone, himself included, in the long run and to leave behind him . . . a trail of defeats and destruction." Maintaining a full awareness of the novel's narrative richness and hence avoiding the temptation to reduce Myshkin to a clinical case study, Lesser shows how Dostoevsky gradually reveals Myshkin's masochism and the passive-aggressive implications of his behavior so that the novel's final catastrophe seems believable and the title justified.

Kafka's *The Trial*, Lesser notes, resembles *The Idiot* in that it too deals with "the harm done by an overdeveloped and tyrannical superego, in a person with a deficient sense of reality." But its dreamlike atmosphere is very different from the complex social realism of *The Idiot*. Moreover, the abstractness with which Kafka's story is told and the many ambiguities which are left unresolved invite the reader both to identify with Joseph K. and to "analogize," that is, to supply autobiographical analogues to K.'s experiences. The title of Lesser's essay, "The Source of Guilt and the Sense of Guilt," suggests another reason for the relative ease with which readers empathize with Kafka's protagonist: *The Trial* embodies a quest for the source of the "abiding sense of guilt" which many people experience in ordinary life. But K. ultimately fails in his quest to come to terms with his sense of guilt, and this failure is symbolized by his willing submission to the executioners, who may be seen as representing his punitive superego. Lesser also devotes a section in this essay to reviewing approaches to *The Trial* from perspectives other than the psychoanalytic—ethical, religious, political—and shows how each makes a contribution to one's overall appreciation of the novel's artistry.

Michelangelo Antonioni's film, *L'Avventura*, also shares something of *The Trial's* "half-realistic, half-dreamlike quality" so that, when critics attempted to judge it on the basis of surface realism alone, they almost invariably found it lacking. In view of this general failure of respected film critics to make sense of *L'Avventura*, Lesser suggests that, with a few exceptions, "the knowledge of the unconscious now at our disposal has been largely ignored in the criticism of movies." This is especially ironic since movies "are 'written' in the very language of our dreams and fantasies" and hence "are in a better position than any other genre to bypass the conscious intelligence and communicate directly with the unconscious with little or no mediation." In *"L'Avventura*: A Closer Look" Lesser argues that the Antonioni film—which he regards as a "cinema masterpiece"—depicts a frustrating search for "love and the [ideal] beloved" which is doomed from the outset because it represents an attempt to recover the relationship with "the original love object, the mother." *L'Avventura* thus embodies one of the most universal and deeply repressed human longings, and, by implication, "makes a statement about the erotic life of modern man."

According to Freud, dreams express wish fulfillments and their successful interpretation provides significant clues to unconscious psychic processes. In his classic essay on *The Odyssey*, Lesser demonstrates that beneath the surface story of heroic adventures in Homer's epic poem, there lies a series of dreams which express what are perhaps the ultimate human wishes: to be omnipotent, to be immortal, and to be the center of one's own universe. Odysseus was gone so long from his homeland that, when he returned, it was as if he had survived death; moreover, his wife, his son, and his servants had ceased to live their own lives while he was away but had devoted themselves entirely to protecting his interests. Yet so skillfully are these threads of wish-fulfilling fantasy woven into the poem's narrative texture that it is generally regarded as quite "realistic." In *The Odyssey* the conscious and unconscious elements function synergistically to create an archetypal tale of triumph over the usual constraints of the human condition.

Lesser's essay on Yeats's "Sailing to Byzantium" questions Elder Olsen's interpretation of that poem as a joyous celebration of triumph over aging and death. Lesser sees the poem as basically "a sad poem—even a desperate one"—which arrives at a "negative resolution" of the problem it poses. Besides illuminating the subtle counterpoint which occurs between the manifest and latent content in this complex poem, Lesser chides critics such as Olsen who approach a lyric poem as if it were "a carefully reasoned philosophical treatise" instead of a product of primary process thought, the language of the unconscious. For, in attempting to paraphrase "Sailing to Byzantium," Olsen has remade it into a neatly symmetrical poem, but has lost sight of the tensions and ambivalences which, in Lesser's opinion, constitute its essential strengths.

To write about *Oedipus the King* is a task which most psychoanalytically oriented critics would approach with considerable diffidence, for Freud would seem to have given a definitive formulation of its unconscious dynamics. But, in fact, Freud gave only a schematic interpretation of the play, while Lesser, in "*Oedipus the King*: The Two Dramas, The Two Conflicts," presents a scene-by-scene analysis of Oedipus' ambivalent pursuit of his double goal: to learn the identity of the person responsible for the plague in Thebes and to establish the circumstances of his own birth. These two dramas, Lesser contends, are intricately related: "the background drama arises out of the foreground one: it is composed of what is repressed and wins its way to the light despite and against resistance." That both dramas involve an internal conflict for Oedipus becomes especially clear as the evidence begins to converge, pointing to him as the murderer of King Laius, and he shifts from a man on a quest for truth at all costs to a man on the defensive, fighting for survival. Many readers have found that Lesser's interpretation of *Oedipus the King* reveals psychological subtleties in Sophocles' play which go well beyond those noted by Freud and which make the play come alive with freshness and vigor.

In his criticism, Lesser frequently reminds us that our understanding of great literature does not depend upon how many graduate English courses we have taken but upon our ability to draw on our everyday life experience in order to become aware of how a literary character might feel in a given situation. It is in this way that Lesser approaches Act One,

Scene One of *King Lear*. In Lesser's view, Lear is primarily a frightened man erecting defenses against powerlessness and advancing age—and only secondarily a king dividing up his wealth. Moreover, Lear's rage at Cordelia's refusal to declare her love—as well as several remarks he makes—suggests that his relationship with his youngest daughter included unresolved sexual feelings. Thus Lesser concludes that this opening scene of *Lear*, far from being superfluous, as some critics have claimed, contains "the rest of the tragedy . . . in embryo" and that both Lear and Cordelia are among those greatest characters in Shakespeare who "transcend their role in a particular play . . . and come to have a quasi-independent existence in our minds."

Harold Pinter's *The Birthday Party* is the subject of Simon Lesser's only essay dealing with the Theatre of the Absurd, a genre particularly congenial to depth-psychological analysis. This play, Lesser says, in spite of its apparent objectivity and its setting in a room "too appallingly real to question," actually centers upon "subjective concerns, many of which go back to infancy." Pinter's thematic preoccupations resemble those of Kafka: both writers "share a conviction that the essential aspects of experience are ambiguous if not unknowable" and both concern themselves with "our fears—our anxieties really—rather than our hopes." In fact, Pinter goes beyond Kafka in creating situations which arouse our anxiety; for, whereas Kafka was explicit in describing K.'s execution, Pinter only hints at what Stanley's tormentors may do to him—leaving the audience free to fantasize about the particular horrors which await him after the curtain falls. Yet Lesser states that he finds it "peculiarly difficult to specify the meaning of *The Birthday Party* primarily or largely in psychological terms." More comprehensive is a "social reading" of the play in which Goldberg and McCann are seen as "exploiters—symbols both of the anonymous forces that control life and the managers, operators and decision makers who understand those forces well enough to use them for their own ends."

The final essay in this volume focuses on *Macbeth*, which Lesser calls the "most subjective" of Shakespeare's plays. Although much has been written about this play, Lesser points out that several "loose ends and apparent inconsistencies" have gone virtually unnoticed. So successful is Shakespeare in inducing a state of relaxation and regression that most readers of *Macbeth* accept without question the strange world into which the play projects them, a world in which each "objective" scene simultaneously expresses Macbeth's subjective wishes and fears. Having demonstrated the sense in which the play may be said to strike a balance between "drama" and "dream," Lesser goes on to challenge the notion that Macbeth is a "devil," a conscienceless monster. He contends that Macbeth remains "a moral man to the very end of the tragedy." Relentlessly tormented by his superego, Macbeth clings to the futile hope that, "by immersing himself more deeply in evil, he can make himself impervious to guilt." The *Macbeth* essay clearly illustrates one of the central paradoxes of psychoanalytic criticism: that the critic must frequently convince his readers that shortcomings do exist in the available interpretations of a given work before he can proceed to account for them. Here, as in all the essays in this volume, Lesser discovers that such critical shortcomings often exist because of a lack of awareness of just those whispered meanings which psychoanalysis helps us to hear more clearly.

☸ A Note on *Pamela*

IT is easy to jeer at this book, and men of wit have been jeering ever since Fielding satirized it in one of the finest parodies in the language. It is an especially tempting target for the "sophisticated" twentieth-century reader; to a considerable extent Krutch spoke for us all, and voiced our reactions more wittily and amusingly than we could have ourselves, in his essay on Richardson in *Five Masters*.

The sexual morality of *Pamela* seems either primitive and simpleminded, in which case we look down our nose a bit at author and heroine, or calculating and shrewd, in which case we feel free to be indignant. Sex is bad, bad, bad—except in marriage. Once a man has proposed this honorable condition for the fulfillment of his desires, no matter how he has behaved before, he may be regarded as the best of men and the addressee of his advances the most fortunate of women. Perhaps we are a little too insistent in seeing the indefensibility of such an external morality—our own breadth of view on sexual mores is an achievement rather than a birthright—but we are surely right in holding it suspect. We are justified too in feeling that Pamela is preoccupied with her virtue to the point of prurience.

The whole moral tone of *Pamela* is offensive to the modern reader, reminding him of everything pharisaical and prudential about bourgeois respectability. The letter form perhaps heightens one's feeling of revulsion. What twentieth-century reader can fail to find a girl priggish when she subscribes herself "your dutiful and honest daughter" or "your afflicted Pamela"? Nor are the parents to whom many of these letters are

Reprinted from *College English*, vol. 14, no. 1, October 1952. Copyright © 1952 by the National Council of Teachers of English. Reprinted by permission of the publisher and the author.

addressed much more likely to win our admiration when in reply they sign themselves "your truly loving, but careful, father and mother." "Careful" is indeed the word for all the characters in *Pamela*. Even Mr. B. never seems to get entirely out of control, and his pursuit of Pamela, though frightening to her and not lacking in ardor, seems more like a formal dance or a game of chess than the kind of passion which takes possession of characters in the novels of Tolstoy and Dostoevsky.

The emphasis on class distinctions in *Pamela* is also likely to exasperate the modern reader. In view of Richardson's sensitivity to social position, it is perhaps to be wondered at that the book is not worse than it is. Fortunately, his snobbishness was redeemed in part by his religious convictions—"My *soul*," Pamela protests, "is of equal importance with the soul of a princess, though my quality is inferior to that of the meanest slave"—and, perhaps more importantly, by what is one of Richardson's main contributions to literature, his stress on sensibility, on a refined analysis of each flutter of the heart. This emphasis, as Krutch has explained, was ultimately influential in destroying the fixed notion of what constitutes virtue on which Richardson set so much store and in paving the way for that highly fluid value system called "romanticism." For, if intensity of feeling is so important, is it not a better measure of the value of experience than conformity to a given code? It follows too that sensitivity is a better index than rank to the worth of an individual. But both of these implications of his writing Richardson would have rejected and deplored.

During the major portion of *Pamela* the emphasis on the difference in social position between the heroine and Mr. B. does not bother one; it is a *donnée* easy to accept. The emphasis the characters themselves put on that difference once the marriage is decided upon is a little harder to take. Mr. B., in his condescension, seems an insufferable prig. Pamela's scarcely disguised elation at her new position makes her a little suspect, however benevolently disposed to her we may have been before. At times her marriage seems less like the conclusion of a romance than it does the climax of a successful career—her elevation to the peerage, let us say, after a life of faithful service. Class matters also obtrude themselves unpleasantly at various less crucial places in the story. The etiquette Pamela feels she must observe in meeting the onslaught of Lady Davers makes that encounter mildly ridiculous. And one can only feel revulsion at the various incidental ways in which Pamela's sense of class distinction betrays itself during her hour of triumph: "My good master was highly delighted, generous gentleman as he is, with the

favourable opinion of the ladies; and I took the more pleasure in it, because their favour seemed to lessen the disgrace of his stooping so much
beneath himself."

There is a kind of ironic justice in devaluing *Pamela* because of its shoddy
morality: it seems only fair to approach the work in Richardson's terms.
But what if the novel has interest and value independent of and superior
to the instruction it was intended to provide? It is a commonplace of
modern criticism that a work need not be considered in terms of the
conscious intentions of its author; it may exceed, fall short, or simply dif-
fer from these. Whole periods have had aesthetics which failed to do
justice to their creative endeavor, sometimes describing it in what seem
to us quite misleading terms.

The fact that *Pamela* has been read with pleasure for two hundred
years should suggest that it is not without appealing qualities. It is one of
the duties of criticism to account for the pleasure the book gives, even if
in so doing one misses the opportunity to assert one's modernity and to
have one's share of fun with Pamela's profitable probity. One may dismiss the pleasure as an inferior one (Krutch invokes the word
"sentimental"), and it *is* inferior doubtless to the more bracing and elemental experience one has in reading tragedy. For all that, it is a reputable enough pleasure. *Pamela* admirably meets the two principal requirements of narrative art: it acquaints us with rounded, convincing
characters, about whom we come to care, and it tells an interesting,
well-conceived story in which each event is carefully prepared for and
develops in logical, satisfying fashion.

Not until we turn to the story can we begin to understand the book's
appeal. Analyzing *Pamela* is a little like reconstructing a gimcracky building which turns out to have essentially sound structure and good lines.
Indeed, once those lines are perceived, even some of the "gingerbread"
falls into place and becomes admissible.

Stripped of its occasionally nauseating moral coating, *Pamela* is that
perennial favorite: a love story. But, more, it is a Cinderella love story and
thus has special intensity. Since it is a Cinderella story, it is told, as it
should be, from the point of view of Cinderella, and it is not a defect that
Prince Charming, in this case Mr. B., is not so completely realized a
character as the heroine. It is essential that he be somewhat vague, for
there is always a faint incestuous quality to a Cinderella story: the Prince
is always to some extent the father and must not be too clearly seen.
Though Richardson would have been horrified had he known it, inces-

tuous overtones are quite evident, although unemphasized, in *Pamela*. Mr. B. is a kind of father figure not only because of his age and status; he is associated in Pamela's mind with the woman whom she served and who was so kind and generous to her that she undoubtedly became a kind of substitute mother. Nor does the incest thread lead only in one direction; it may be conjectured that Mr. B. was attracted to Pamela in part because of her relationship to his mother and that in his unconscious she was in part a daughter or younger sister.

Once we consider *Pamela* as a Cinderella love story, we see that most of the criticisms directed against it are not so much mistaken as irrelevant. Pamela's "hypocricies," for example, become rather complications which the reader understands and wants to see overcome. It is of the essence of the matter that she cannot acknowledge even to herself her love for Mr. B. and desire to win him. What more natural, then, that she finds herself enticing Mr. B. by her dress at the same time that she reproaches him for his advances, that she cannot bring herself to hate him despite his wickedness, that she cannot without regret leave either his Bedfordshire place or the house in Lincolnshire where he has kept her a virtual prisoner? Nor can she bring herself to become interested in the Reverend Mr. Williams, though he not only wishes to help her escape the wicked Mr. B. but offers her honorable matrimony. The list could easily be extended by the modern reader exposed to Freud. Pamela dreams of rape. She tries to escape by climbing a wall, not remembering until she falls and is quite stunned, her "shins" as well as her ankle broken, that there is a ladder near by which would have facilitated her flight. These actions are inconsistent and even reprehensible if we have our attention focused on her protestations, but they are quite understandable on the part of a troubled young girl in love. And the reader—at any rate, the unconscious of the reader—has, I suspect, taken them in this fashion all along.

The reader also perceives, even if Pamela herself does not, that it is not impossible that she may win her Mr. B. and so bring the story to a happy conclusion. There is a great deal of what might be called ambiguity throughout the novel: a sense that things may mean—or *also* mean—the opposite of what they appear to and that, if only things were slightly different, they might be very different indeed. *Pamela* is not only, or primarily, the slightly ridiculous story of a too-proper young girl resisting the importunities of her master; it is the story of a young girl hoping that seemingly insuperable obstacles can be overcome so that, legitimately and permanently, she can win the man she loves. As early as page 29 of the "Everyman's Library" edition of the novel we are informed of the possibility that Mr. B. may love Pamela. Mrs. Jervis, the "good" housekeeper, who in addition to being another mother surrogate acts as a kind of chorus, extols her master. He "is a fine gentleman; he has a great deal of wit and sense, and is admired, as I know, by half a dozen ladies, who would think themselves happy in his addresses. He has a noble estate.... And yet," she continues (the "And yet" of course sums up a good deal of what modern readers find objectionable), "I believe he loves you, though his servant, better than all the ladies in the land; he has tried to overcome it, because you are so much his inferior; and it is my opinion he finds he can't; and that vexes his proud heart." Mrs. Jewkes, the "bad" housekeeper, describes the ambiguity of Pamela's position rather more crisply. To the heroine's complaint that she is "a most miserable creature" she replies: "Mighty miserable indeed, to be well beloved by one of the finest gentlemen in England!"

Once we understand Pamela's situation, her actions no longer seem calculating or ridiculous. I stress the word "actions"; I would not deny that she puts it on pretty thick in her protestations. But I suspect that if Pamela had the benefit of psychoanalysis (and this is fun to imagine), while her analyst would tell her to stuff many of her pretty speeches and would set her straight on what she really felt about a number of matters, he could not but approve the basic course she followed. She could not have acted more unerringly to serve her wants if she had known consciously what they were. The reality situation, too, fully justified her behavior, on the basis of both moral and class considerations. However primitive, Pamela's morality ("It's wrong unless you're married") is not so different from that of our own age as we might like to suppose. Today, too, marriage sanctifies, and extramarital affairs are usually attended by guilt. To learn this we need only the evidence of literature; consider, for example, the instructive example of Anna Karenina or, to take a less clouded case, Miriam in *Sons and Lovers*. To be sure, there are exceptions. In casual affairs there is often no guilt, for moral considerations may be successfully sidestepped and the interests, integrity, and even nature of the partner disregarded; even in such affairs, however, guilt may be present, as Aldous Huxley among others has made us see, in the form of an impersonal, all-encompassing disgust. Relationships between people closely matched in all respects—including personal endowment, status, affection, and emancipation from conventional morality—perhaps represent a more serious type of exception; in such affairs responsibility is mutual, and there is little basis for either party looking down upon or feeling sorry for the other. Obviously, the relationship between Pamela and Mr. B. does not fit into this category; in view of her strict bringing-up and the very real importance of class distinctions not only in eighteenth-century England generally but in her eyes and Mr. B.'s specifically, it was necessary to legitimatize the relationship if it was not to take the form of a casual and relatively brief sexual affair. It is beside the point that such an outcome would not have been as horrendous as it seemed to Richardson and to Pamela. What matters is that the reader, aware of the social situation and the love of these young people for each other, hopes that Pamela's conditions can be met, that Mr. B. will not prove too unregenerate, and that all the obstacles to a happy and permanent consummation of their relationship can be overcome. The pleasure the novel affords comes from seeing this brought about.

It can give this pleasure even to readers "vexed" by the moral coating which Richardson thought was the adornment of his book. That coating is so obtrusive that one can understand why critics have focused their attention upon it. In so doing, however, they have neglected the story which gives *Pamela* its vitality and its appeal. And is it not a tendency of modern criticism in its hairsplitting preoccupation with moral issues and values to slight the purely narrative and structural factors which account for the pleasure of reading and deserve our chief attention?

✿ Freud and *Hamlet* Again

THE controversies about *Hamlet* have a way of repeating themselves generation after generation. But they are worth refighting not only because the play itself seems forever new but because—another tribute to its vitality—discussion of it so often raises exciting collateral issues.

An article by John Ashworth in the *Atlantic,* denouncing the Olivier movie version of *Hamlet,* provides a case in point. The article could be dismissed as no more than a restatement of the view that Hamlet's difficulties in avenging his father are entirely objective—a view given definitive expression more than forty years ago by the German Shakespearean scholar, Karl Werder. But the disciple at least takes cognizance of a view of which his predecessor knew nothing—the Freud-Ernest Jones thesis that Hamlet's delay stems from an internal unconscious conflict experienced, in some degree, by all men in our culture. To call attention to this thesis even in negative fashion is something of a service, for despite the interest it might be expected to have for our psychologically oriented age it has been conspicuously ignored in contemporary Shakespearean criticism and honored by the general reader more in the breach than in the observance.

Not content with refuting Freud's views of *Hamlet,* the article challenges his right to have any—on the ground that he did not know enough about the cultural history of the Elizabethan age to stand any chance of reading Shakespeare "accurately." Is it really true that one needs a Ph.D. —preferably acquired under Kittredge, who did not have one—to read Shakespeare with comprehension? The very success of the movie version of *Hamlet* casts doubt upon the assumption. Year after year thousands of people with no special literary training read Shake-

Reprinted from *The American Imago,* vol. 12, no. 2, Summer 1955.

speare, or respond to revivals of one or another of his plays, with un-
feigned enjoyment. Evidently Shakespeare has something to say to *us*.
Most fair-minded critics recognize this. Says L. C. Knights, in his essay,
"Shakespeare and Shakespeareans" in *Explorations*: "The true Shakespeare critic will be concerned to make himself, as far as possible, a contemporary of Shakespeare's. . . . But, more important, he will also be
concerned to make Shakespeare a contemporary, to see his particular
relevance for our time." Intruders from such fields as psychoanalysis
aside, most of the creative critics of today are primarily concerned with
the second of these objectives, the search for the enduring values of literature, those least subject to the decaying influence of time. In strict
logic we would have to repudiate almost the entire body of work loosely
lumped together as "the new criticism" if we decided that the task of
criticism is simply to reconstruct the meaning works of art had for their
own age and denied psychoanalytic interpretations a hearing.

2

The nub of Ashworth's argument is that Freud is foolish to explain Hamlet's delay in killing Claudius, for there is no delay. Hamlet must first obtain airtight proof that Claudius has really murdered the previous King,
Hamlet's father. Once Hamlet has secured this proof, through the play
within a play, he proceeds expeditiously about his business. Only external obstacles and the fear of losing his own life keep him from killing
Claudius sooner than he does.

According to this interpretation, Hamlet cannot accept the word of
the Ghost about Claudius' guilt because—though like nearly all
Elizabethans he believed in ghosts—he also shared the prevalent notion
that demons can masquerade as ghosts. Now it may be that Shakespeare
also believed in ghosts, but what seems quite certain is that he didn't
believe in them in simple-minded fashion. In Act I the Ghost is seen by
Horatio, Marcellus, Bernardo and Hamlet, but speaks only to his son.
When he reappears in the Queen's closet, he is seen and heard by Hamlet but not by the Queen. These facts at least suggest the possibility that
the Ghost has some relation to the psychic state of those to whom he
appears—that he may be a projection of their unconscious suspicions
and fears. He would be seen by the watch and Horatio because they felt
vaguely troubled about conditions in their land. "Something is rotten in
the state of Denmark." But his message, as Horatio predicted, was for
Hamlet's ears alone. So when he appears *in his nightgown* ("Shakespeare's stage directions are explicit, if brief") in the Queen's closet he is

seen only by Hamlet because, as Hamlet knows, he has come to rebuke him:

> Do you not come your tardy son to chide,
> That, laps'd in time and passion, lets go by
> Th' important acting of your dread command?

(Act III, Scene 4, lines 106–8)*

The fear that the Ghost may be a demon fits in with the theory that he is a projection of the mental state of those who see him. It is natural that Horatio, Marcellus and Hamlet would be apprehensive about the revelation they feel the Ghost has for them. One of the important things psychoanalysis has taught us is that we spend a great deal of psychic energy in the endeavor not to see certain things. But this initial doubt is overcome. Despite his own fears and the warnings of Marcellus and Horatio, Hamlet follows the Ghost and hears him. What he hears confirms suspicions he tells us he has already held:

> O my prophetic soul!
> My uncle?

(I, 5, 40–41)

After this speech it does not matter whether we regard the Ghost as "subjective" or "objective." Either way Hamlet is now consciously aware of his uncle's guilt. And he assumes the burden of avenging his father:

> And thy commandment all alone shall live
> Within the book and volume of my brain,
> Unmix'd with baser matter.

(I, 5, 102–4)

3

Neither these lines nor the entire speech in which they occur suggest that Hamlet has the slightest doubt about the authenticity of the Ghost or his own clear duty to avenge his father. Later, to be sure, Hamlet conceives the idea of *confirming* (not really deciding) his uncle's guilt† by the play within the play, *but the need for additional proof, for absolute certainty is itself part of Hamlet's neurotic hesitancy* in connection with this

---

*All references are to the Kittredge edition of Shakespeare (Ginn and Co., Boston, 1936).

† I'll observe his looks
I'll tent him to the quick. *If he but blench,*
I know my course. (II, 2, 624–26)

particular action. One does not have to understand the intricacies of psychoanalysis to know about rationalization—to be aware that the reasons we give for our actions do not always reveal our real motives.

If Hamlet does not delay, what is the basis for the self-reproach which is so continuous and conspicuous a feature of the play? How can one account for the famous monologue in Act II, Scene 2—before the play within a play:

> What's Hecuba to him, or he to Hecuba
> That he should weep for her? What would he do
> Had he the motive and the cue for passion
> That I have? . . . .
>
> . . . It cannot be
> But I am pigeon-liver'd and lack gall
> To make oppression bitter, or ere this
> I should have fatted all the region kites,
> With this slave's offal. Bloody, bawdy villain!
> Remorseless, treacherous, lecherous, kindless villain!
>
> O, vengeance!
> Why, what an ass am I! This is most brave,
> That I, the son of a dear father murther'd,
> Prompted to my revenge by heaven and hell,
> Must (like a whore) unpack my heart with words
> And fall a-cursing like a very drab . . .

Assuming, however, that Hamlet's need for further proof is justified, not just an excuse for further delay, *why doesn't he proceed with his task when he has the proof*—when the "frighted" King starts up before the end of the play, revealing his guilt to the assembled court? Or, if there were any conceivable reason for letting such an opportunity slip by, why doesn't he kill the King later, perhaps waiting until he finishes his prayers, then setting upon him?

I deliberately omit the possibility that he might have killed the King while he was praying, because Werder and his followers think that Ham-

---

If his occulted guilt
Do not itself unkennel in one speech,
It is a damned ghost that we have seen . . . (III, 2, 85–87)

Italics mine. The assumption behind both speeches is that his uncle is guilty, that only a small amount of additional evidence is needed, and that it will undoubtedly be forthcoming.

let's inaction on this occasion can be explained by the convention that the soul of one killed at prayer would go to Heaven. But here again, I would maintain, Hamlet is simply taking advantage of the convention to justify his inability to act. If conditions had been reversed, would Claudius have hesitated to kill Hamlet? We do not have to speculate about the matter; the answer is in the play. In Act IV, Scene 7, the King is testing Laertes to make sure he can still use him to get rid of Hamlet:

> What would you undertake
> To show yourself your father's son in deed
> More than in words?

Laertes replies:

> To cut his throat i' th' church.

And the King answers:

> No place indeed should murther sanctuarize;
> Revenge should have no bounds.

But Hamlet is also deterred, Ashworth argues, by the fear of death. "Even if he succeeded [in killing the King before being stopped], he would immediately lose his own life. Does that matter?"

Now the question is certainly a spurious one; as we shall later see, there is every reason to believe that Hamlet could have won the populace to his side and avenged his father without being killed. But granting the legitimacy of the question for the moment, the answer to it assuredly is "No":

> O that this too too solid flesh would melt
> Thaw, and resolve itself into a dew!
> Or that the Everlasting had not fix'd
> His canon 'gainst self-slaughter! O God! O God!
> How weary, stale, flat and unprofitable
> Seem to me all the uses of this world!

(I, 2, 129–34)

And later when the hated windbag, Polonius, asks to humbly take his leave, Hamlet replies: "You cannot, sir, take from me anything that I will more willingly part withal—except my life, except my life, except my life." Nothing seems more clear than Hamlet's *desire* for death as a way out of the insoluble conflict in which he finds himself. And by proceeding in such a way as to arouse the King's suspicions he brings about his own death, as certainly as if he had committed suicide.

"The Elizabethan," Ashworth writes, "was accustomed to seeing royalty well 'attended' both in life and in plays." Perhaps so: but what matters is not the actuarial probabilities, what usually obtained, in life or in literature, but the actual situation in this particular play, *Hamlet*. In *Hamlet*, Claudius is not always well attended. Hamlet chances upon him while he is alone at prayer. In Act IV, Scene 1, Claudius and the Queen are able to confer privately simply by dismissing Rosencrantz and Guildenstern. There are no attendants about. The evidence of the play suggests that the castle at Elsinore was much less densely populated than Ashworth makes out; Hamlet could walk "four hours together" in its lobby, presumably without company or interruption. The assumption that the King was always well attended seems to me a clearcut example of the harm the possession of historical knowledge can lead to when it is used as anything more than a guide and not complemented by a careful study of a text.

But one does not have to study *Hamlet* to perceive that its hero never acts like a man concerned about the objective difficulty of his assignment. He is troubled first and last by the mysterious force within him which keeps him from executing it:

> I do not know
> Why yet I live to say "This thing's to do,'
> Sith I have cause, and will, and strength and means
> To do't.

(IV, 4, 43–46)

Hamlet was not a man to be easily deterred from his purpose by external obstacles. The deftness with which he handles the plot against his life, sending Rosencrantz and Guildenstern to the death intended for him, would alone teach us this, but the fact is that Hamlet shows skill and decision in *everything except the execution of the task laid on him by his father's ghost.*

This, by the bye, is the Freud-Jones thesis. Freud wrote, in *The Interpretation of Dreams*, "Hamlet is able to do anything but take vengeance upon the man who did away with his father and has taken his father's place with his mother—the man who shows him in realization the repressed desires of his own childhood. He is inhibited in accomplishing this by conscientious scruples, which tell him that he himself is no better than the murderer whom he is required to punish." At times Ashworth seems aware that this is the Freud-Jones position, but at other times he lumps them with Goethe and other critics who have seen Hamlet as a neurasthenic intellectual, whose will is paralyzed by excessive thought. The least one can say is that this is unscholarly: brief as Freud's discussion of the play is, he finds space specifically to disavow the Goethe viewpoint. Jones marshals the extensive evidence for Hamlet's general decisiveness and quotes with approval the famous Bradley dictum that Hamlet was "a man who at any *other* time and in any *other* circumstances than those presented would have been perfectly equal to his task. . . ."

Hamlet's general capacity for action and his own attitude toward his mission should be sufficient to dispose of the argument that he is held back by external difficulties. But it is refuted by an important secondary strand of the plot as well. In the belief that Claudius has killed Polonius, Laertes easily recruits a mob of followers ready to proclaim him king, and overcoming the King's Switzers, breaks into the palace. How much more easily might not Hamlet have done the same thing—the Prince who has a legitimate claim to the throne and is so beloved by the public that the King dared not denounce him for having killed Polonius. As Ernest Jones writes, ". . . the whole Laertes episode seems almost deliberately to have been woven into the drama so as to show the world how a pious son should really deal with his father's murderer, how possible was the vengeance in just these particular circumstances, and by contrast to illuminate the ignoble vacillation of Hamlet whose honour had been doubly wounded by the same treacherous villain."

But, says Ashworth finally, Hamlet does try to kill the King twice. Hearing someone behind the arras, he immediately sticks his sword into him. "There's Freud's 'hesitation' for you. Hamlet *thinks* the 'eavesdropper' whom he does kill without any hesitation whatever *is* the King. How can such an incredible blind spot in Freud be explained?" Now in the first place precisely the point to be noted is that Hamlet here acts impulsively and precipitately; as Freud says—Freud who, remember, is well aware that in general Hamlet is *not* hesitant—he acts "in a sudden outburst of rage." Even the law distinguishes between such an act and one done in cold blood. Furthermore, there is no evidence that Hamlet thinks the eavesdropper behind the arras is Claudius. *After* the murder, perhaps already penitent for having killed an unknown man, he asks "Is it the King?" But immediately before the deed he has seen the King in another room, kneeling at prayer. Furthermore, before he strikes, he hears the unseen man behind the arras cry for help. Did he cry with the King's voice?

Of course, Hamlet finally kills Claudius. But it could be argued that *he never avenges his father's death.* He kills Claudius in the despair and bitter anger that follows his mother's poisoning and Laertes' disclosure that he, Hamlet, will die of his "envenom'd" wound—and that "the King, the King's to blame." Now whether Hamlet kills Claudius to avenge his father, or to avenge his mother and himself, what is indisputable is that he kills him at the last possible minute. Those who maintain that he needed the confirmatory evidence of the play within the play tend to forget that this is obtained in Act III, Scene 2. Hamlet's hesitation continues long enough thereafter to be responsible, directly or indirectly, for the deaths of Rosencrantz and Guildenstern, Polonius, Ophelia and Laertes, the Queen, and Hamlet himself.

It is this hesitation, which is the central problem of *Hamlet*, that Freud and Jones have explained. The explanation does not "account" for the greatness of Shakespeare's play. Jones specifically disavows any intention of dealing with the play's poetic and literary qualities. However, at the very least, he and Freud have performed a negative service to literature of no small value. For if there were no satisfactory explanation of Hamlet's delay—if we felt that his inaction made no sense and was dramatically "wrong" —we would have to conclude that *Hamlet* is not a great play; and in fact T. S. Eliot, who sees Hamlet "dominated by an emotion which is . . . in excess of the facts as they appear," and is unwilling or unable to allow for the unconscious source of the emotion, regards *Hamlet* as an artistic failure.

But most people do not; and the Freud-Jones interpretation provides at least one important clue to the almost universal appeal of the play, for it explains Hamlet's delay in terms of a conflict of intense moment to everyone. The Werder interpretation, in contrast, would not even permit *Hamlet* to qualify as a good fairy story. No great emotional interest could be expected to attach to a story of a cautious hero who spends half his time verifying his mission and then proceeds to execute it in bungling fashion.

4

As one would expect, most of the efforts of psychoanalytic critics of *Hamlet* have been devoted to elucidating the psychology of the characters, and in particular, the unconscious sources of emotion when these can be inferred. Admittedly Freud and Jones have not done full justice to the play's esthetic aspects or its religious, cultural and moral values. These values are brilliantly dealt with by Francis Fergusson in his essay on *Hamlet* in *Idea of the Theatre*. But Fergusson errs, it seems to me, in maintaining that "the main action of Hamlet may be described as the attempt to find and destroy the hidden 'imposthume' which is poisoning the life of Claudius' Denmark." Is it not because Hamlet is sick at heart that he searches, almost greedily, for evidence of disorder in that macrocosm, the world? He does not, of course, fail to find it: it is always there. But the play's political happenings and allusions are intended to heighten and echo the personal tragedy.

Space does not permit me to document this conclusion, which to some extent, in any case, rests on one's entire reading of the play. But a belief which Ashworth mentions in the course of his article should be discussed if only because so many share it; this is the belief that in its treatment of social issues psychoanalysis is fundamentally and necessarily conservative. Analysis has shown that certain people are radical as a result of unconscious conflicts. In dealing with individual neurosis it tentatively assumes the "normality" (the quotes are Freud's) of the environment. Thus, many conclude, psychoanalysis tends to align itself with the defense of the *status quo*.

The difficulty of combatting this belief is compounded by the fact that there are good grounds for regarding Freud as a conservative. As we see in particular from *Civilization and Its Discontents,* he was dubious of all panaceas, including communism. Most reforms, he appears to have believed, would create some new difficulty for every old one they eliminated. Or they would simply shift the conflicts which make life burdensome to new arenas. If people do not struggle about private property, they will struggle about "prerogatives in sexual relationships," power and other things. Like Shakespeare, Freud was a pessimist, with a tragic sense of human destiny. He saw the extent to which man's difficulties arise out of his own instinctual drives, which can be modified but not fundamentally changed by altering social conditions. Above all, he knew that "there are certain difficulties inherent in the very nature of culture which will not yield to any efforts at reform." Any society must seek to curb man's aggressive and sexual impulses, and such curbs cannot fail to produce difficulties, tension and unhappiness.

However, neither Freud's pessimism nor his conservatism should be exaggerated. If he saw the limits beyond which reforms could not hope to be effective, within those limits he favored doing everything possible. Opposed to communism because of its extravagant claims, he was willing to concede the enormous benefits which would flow from "an actual change in men's attitude to property." Aware of the need for controlling man's sexual impulses, he was sharply critical of the extreme restrictions which have been imposed by Western European civilization. In a 1925 paper which is too little known ("The Resistances to Psychoanalysis," *Collected Papers*, vol. 5) he speaks out with the zeal of a reformer against the unnecessary severity with which the instincts generally are curbed in our culture:

> . . . On the whole . . . [the individual] is obliged to live psychologically beyond his income, while the unsatisfied claims of his instincts make him feel the demands of civilization as a constant pressure upon him. Thus society maintains a condition of cultural hypocrisy, which is bound to be accompanied by a sense of insecurity and a necessity for guarding what is an undeniably precarious situation by forbidding criticism and discussion. This line of thought holds good for all the instinctual impulses, including, therefore the egoistic ones. . . .
>
> Psychoanalysis has revealed the weaknesses of this system and has recommended that it should be altered. It proposes that there should be a reduction in the strictness with which instincts are repressed and that correspondingly more play should be given to truthfulness. Certain instinctual impulses, with whose suppression society has gone too far, should be permitted a greater amount of satisfaction; in the case of certain others the inefficient method of suppressing them by means of repression should be replaced by a better and securer procedure. . . .

Comment by analysts linking revolutionary propensities to infantile conflicts seems to be one important source of the impression that psychoanalysis harbors a conservative bias. In particular the *apercu*, "the origin of all revolutions is the revolution in the family," has become well known. But if there is any bias in this remark, it is one in behalf of the formative influence of infantile experiences. Psychoanalysis not only believes but has empirically verified the fact that patterns of later attitudes are laid down in childhood. But of course this applies as every analyst recognizes, to patterns of submission, conformity and conservatism as much as to patterns of revolt.

Common observation reveals how frequently an emotional inclination to believe one thing rather than another warps our judgment. But no analyst would be naive enough to believe that it *necessarily* has this effect. If it did, the human situation would be hopeless indeed, for there are few subjects of any importance which we can approach with complete objectivity. When we feel that a person's unrecognized emotional needs have determined his ideological position, we are fully justified in holding it suspect. But we are not justified at all in assuming that it is mistaken. The only test of the rightness or wrongness of a belief—one in practice of course not always easy to apply—is the way it corresponds to external conditions, to what psychoanalysis calls the reality principle. Though in general our objective judgments are the more reliable, an opinion to which we are inclined by our personality may be correct and one which reflects no bias may be mistaken. Indeed, a person may originally adopt a certain position, such as radicalism, in response to neurotic needs, free himself from his neurosis, and maintain the same position because his more objective appraisal of the facts confirms its correctness. This is in part the theme of a much misunderstood modern novel, Koestler's *Arrival and Departure*.

The worth of an individual or the value of his achievements cannot be decided, any more than the correctness of his opinions, on the basis of genetic considerations. Freud's various biographical studies show that he fully recognized this. They reveal too that his yardstick for measuring people was a liberal and enlightened one. He tracked down Leonardo's passion for investigating nature to its source in an unusually intense infantile sexual curiosity, but this did not lessen his admiration for him as the first modern natural philosopher and a man who achieved a great measure of religious emancipation in an age when that was not easy. In contrast, Freud is scornful of Dostoevsky's submission to temporal and spiritual authority, his narrow nationalism and grovelling before God—a position, Freud says bitterly, "which lesser minds have reached with smaller effort." Freud saw that Dostoevsky was probably condemned to these views by his neurosis, but neither this realization nor Freud's admiration for Dostoevsky as a writer softens his indictment of the Russian's orthodoxy. "Dostoevsky threw away the chance of becoming a teacher and liberator of humanity and made himself one with their gaolers."

As a system of therapy, psychoanalysis seeks to help people see the world without distortion. To see it as it is is not necessarily calculated to make one like it as it is. Nor does the goal of "adjustment" (which in any case is far less emphasized in analysis than in other forms of psychotherapy) imply either uncritical acceptance of existing social arrangements or submissiveness before their demands. There are, fortunately, many worlds within the large world—many different patterns of life and many different ways of expressing dissent. Every reputable analyst seeks to *minimize* the coerciveness of reality—to help each of his patients find the kind of occupational, sexual and general life adjustment which is congenial to his personality and likely to develop his powers. The most undeviating nonconformity would probably not be discouraged where a person was willing to face the consequences. Only if one's radicalism were neurotically grounded—in which case it would crumble under any severe test—would it be likely to be disturbed by psychoanalysis. Since analysis releases energy which has previously been wasted in internal conflicts, its usual result is to make those it helps more effective fighters for the kind of world in which they believe.

❧ The Attitude of Fiction

FICTION is too large a subject to be seen in the same fashion by different minds, but there is one point on which nearly all studies are agreed: conflict is its perennial theme; almost every story centers around some struggle, internal or external. The observation is not likely to be challenged, but how much does it tell us? Like many purely descriptive characterizations, it seems to raise questions more important than any it happens to answer. In life itself conflict is not a source of pleasure but rather of pain. Why should the fictional presentation of our conflicts afford us pleasure or satisfaction?

Interestingly, when we attempt to answer this question we are more likely to think of explanations connected with what we call form than of explanations connected with subject matter. After a little reflection it will occur to us that when our conflicts are represented in fiction, they can be projected upon others, the characters in the story. They can also be disguised and "distanced." These alterations are unquestionably of the greatest importance. They permit fiction to depict our conflicts in such a way that we do not have to acknowledge them as our own. We may not recognize that there is any connection whatever between what we read and our own experience. Because of this one difference, for which form is responsible, when we read we can deal with our most troublesome problems without undue fear. We can leisurely and securely examine aspects of our emotional situation which under other conditions we could not consider at all.

However, the most secure examination of our conflicts imaginable would not automatically generate pleasure. If fiction gives us deep satisfaction, as of course it does, it must be because *what* it shows us is to our liking: it must depict our conflicts in a way we find peculiarly satisfying.

Reprinted from *Modern Fiction Studies*, May 1956.

And in fact, I believe, there are two crucial differences in the way conflicts are likely to be treated in fiction and in life. The differences are worth the most careful scrutiny. They bring us close to what seems to me the basic attitude characteristic of fiction, an attitude of cardinal importance in explaining its appeal.

Fiction, to begin with, ventilates our conflicts much more thoroughly than we ordinarily do. It confines its attention to a single action, but it tries to give us all the information we need to understand that action. Directly or indirectly, for example, it tries to represent every essential consideration which might be advanced to justify or oppose the satisfaction of a given impulse. It seeks to give the impulse its full measure of attraction and at the same time remind us of everything which whispers that we should not yield to it. With scrupulous impartiality it tries to consider the claims of our entire being, the kind of claims we are likely to neglect as well as those we take into account and, it may be, overemphasize.

Even if fiction went no farther than this, we would have reason to feel grateful to it. We have all had the experience of feeling the continued pull of some desire, though we have marshaled impressive arguments against gratifying it and perhaps reached a decision we thought of as final. Almost as common is a persistent feeling of uneasiness about some course of action which every logical consideration appears to recommend. Evidently we find it very difficult to dredge forth all the factors we should consider in resolving our conflicts and to give each its just due. But fiction not only brings all the claims into the open; as we shall see, it seeks actively to reconcile them. Moreover, in keeping with its willingness to hear all sides, it strives for resolutions based upon maximum fulfillment rather than the illusory kind achieved by denying or slighting certain claims; it seeks resolutions which, to use a happy word of Robert Penn Warren's, are "earned" rather than forced. Obviously such resolutions are more richly satisfying and more stable than the provisional solutions of our difficulties with which we must so often be content in life.

Of course, such ideal resolutions are only occasionally achieved. Only the very greatest narrative works give us the impression of having overlooked nothing, no relevant consideration, no possibility of harmonizing apparently irreconcilable elements. I am describing a tendency discernible in fiction rather than something which is always perfectly realized. It should be noted, too, that in life itself we may experience moments of illumination in which we see ourselves and our dilemmas with sudden clarity, and perhaps even find solutions of problems which until then appeared to admit of none. But while fiction characteristically achieves a broad view, such moments of revelation, and usually of more complete self-acceptance, are rare in life; some people never experience them.

In a general way we know why our consideration of our own conflicts is likely to be partial in both senses of the word: incomplete and dishonest. We are afraid to see our more vexing problems clearly. A searching examination is almost certain to involve tension and strain and make us aware of our limitations. In a general way we also know the kinds of things we prefer not to take into account: they are things which would make us anxious, for example, ideas which would stir feelings of self-reproach or jeopardize an adjustment to life which we may fear to upset even though it makes us unhappy. What may surprise us is the range of the ideas which can arouse anxiety. Of course we do not wish to be reminded of impulses we find it difficult to cope with or of selfish and malicious motives. But we may be no more willing to face anything which will remind us of relatively trivial shortcomings, of peevishness, let us say, or stinginess. Even ideas which it might be expected we would welcome, or at any rate regard with indifference, may be rejected because in some roundabout way they mobilize anxiety. For example, we may try to discount some generous and idealistic action because, to excuse our own corruption, we are trying to convince ourselves that no one acts unselfishly. Or we may try to disavow feelings of revulsion towards life because they call for a more searching examination of our society than we feel prepared to make.

Under the most favorable conditions there are many facets of human experience, many kinds of situations, many surmises about why people act and feel as they do, which we are unable to consider objectively. When we are involved in a conflict which could disrupt our life, the situation is still worse. A certain degree of blindness and a certain amount of distortion are almost inevitable. It is worth illustrating this, although any example, presented in expository terms, must seem sketchy and crude.

Let us take a case which arises frequently enough in life and will also suggest parallel instances in fiction, the case of a man involved in a serious extramarital relationship. How likely is he to see either the relationship or any of the people involved in it with any clarity? He may not even admit that a problem exists, however unhappy everyone may be, for any resolution of the situation involves a danger and possible loss. What is more certain is that, to justify his own conduct or to escape the full force of the conflict, he will alter the facts this way or that. He may try to disparage his mistress and his feeling for her, acknowledging only those qualities in her about which he is ambivalent, such as her physical beauty, and denying that he is drawn to her by anything but sexual attraction. In keeping with this he may pretend that his marriage is better than it is and stifle complaints against his wife he would be justified in making. Or he may endow his mistress with qualities she does not possess and deny his wife her virtues.

It is our fears which lead us to evade and falsify issues. And in reading of the imaginary doings of others we do not have to be afraid. By the roundabout route of immersion in fiction we can attain to that profound and honest understanding of our situation we crave but can seldom achieve by direct attack. In fiction we know we will find our problems imaged in their full complexity, the desires and fears we have slighted drawn as distinctly as anything else.

How much we prize fiction on the basis of this one characteristic I believe it would be impossible to say. Unconsciously we want to see justice done to the considerations we neglect—they are a part of us too. Fiction redresses balances. It tries to annihilate the unctuous lies we live by—the lies which other forms of communication, incidentally, from newspaper editorials to political oratory, tire us by trying to sustain. It exposes, sometimes of course too indecorously, the backside of life. In words of which the hero of Dostoevsky's Notes from Underground seeks to justify himself, it carries to an extreme what we have not dared to carry halfway, and it does not mistake cowardice for good sense or tolerate self-deception. A phrase Edward Bullough used to describe art in general seems particularly applicable to fiction: it gives us a "sudden view of things from their reverse, usually unnoticed side."

In terms of content this means most obviously that fiction makes restitution to us for some of our instinctual deprivations. It emphasizes "sex" to augment the meagre satisfactions available through sanctioned channels and to allay our guilt feelings about our frequent transgressions of these sanctions, either in deed or in desire. It gives expression and outlet to aggressive tendencies which we are expected to hold in strict leash though they are covertly encouraged by our competitive culture. The present vogue of detective stories and melodramas has here its explanation. It is equally important to realize that fiction provides an outlet for idealistic and contemplative tendencies thwarted in our daily experience; in a phrase of Kenneth Burke's, it is a "corrective of the practical."

Fiction makes good certain omissions in our lives. It serves as a dev-

il's advocate for tendencies in ourselves we may be afraid to defend; it
depicts precisely those aspects of experience our fears cause us to scant.
Out of the vast body of fiction available to us, from the past and the present, we choose those works which we believe will best perform this service for us, and our search is no less purposive because in large part it is
pursued unconsciously.

In its zeal to do justice to our repressed tendencies fiction is in constant danger of overstating the case for them. Particularly if it does this
too directly, with a minimum of disguise and control—we think at once
of such a writer as Henry Miller—it is likely to arouse aversion rather than
pleasure. But it is not always easy to say whether a work of fiction or the
reader is responsible for a failure of this sort. A work which in the
perspective of time appears well balanced may cause us to recoil because
it insists on telling us more of the truth, above all more of the truth about
ourselves, than we are prepared to accept. As Havelock Ellis declares in
the preface to *The Dance of Life,* certain books "may have to knock again
and again at the closed door of our hearts. 'Who is there?' we carelessly
cry, and we cannot open the door; we bid the importunate stranger,
whatever he may be, to go away; until, as in the apologue of the Persian
mystic, at last we seem to hear the voice saying: 'It is thyself.' "

Fiction not only takes account of considerations we ordinarily neglect,
thus giving us a more complete and accurate representation of our problems than we can ordinarily achieve; it seeks actively to harmonize all
claims. It tries to see whatever problem it focusses upon from a number
of opposed points of view. It is this characteristic which we must now
examine more closely. It lies close to the very heart of fiction. Perhaps
even more than the trait we have already considered, it explains fiction's
capacity to deal with our problems in a way which so often leaves us profoundly satisfied.

First let us attempt to describe the characteristic more exactly and
more fully, utilizing the help of various critics who have been aware of it.
It is a product of what Keats meant by Shakespeare's "negative
capability"—his willingness to tolerate uncertainty and doubt, to take
cognizance of viewpoints directly at variance with those being pro-
claimed. In John Dewey's terms, it is an outlook which "accepts life and
experience in all its uncertainties, mystery, doubt and half-knowledge
and turns that experience upon itself to deepen and intensify its own
qualities." It is what F. Scott Fitzgerald had in mind when he declared
that "the test of a first-rate intelligence is the ability to hold two opposed

ideas in the mind at the same time, and still maintain the ability to function." Lionel Trilling, who recognizes the importance of the tendency in fiction generally, has explained why it is invaluable in the novel of social purpose: the novelist who takes sides, who shows for example that an excluded group has a different and better ethic than the excluding group, may not be able "to muster the satirical ambivalence toward both groups which marks the good novel even when it has a social *parti pris.*"

The tendency we are seeking to understand has perhaps been most beautifully described by Yeats in *Per Amica Silentia Lunae.* The search of the poet, Yeats maintains, must be not so much for the self as for the anti-self, the antithetical self, for poetry arises out of a kind of quarrel with ourselves. "We must not make false faith by hiding from our thoughts the causes of doubt. . . . Neither must we create, by hiding ugliness, a false beauty as our offering to the world."

In a brilliant literary essay, "Pure and Impure Poetry," Robert Penn Warren has explained why a false beauty achieved by concealing the ugly cannot satisfy a mature intelligence. Exponents of pure poetry assume that poetry inheres in some particular essence from which a long (but varying) list of elements—meaning, complicated images, narrative, irony, subjective elements—must be excluded; it seeks to "overspiritualize nature." Impure poetry, in order to be faithful to the complexities of any subject with which it deals, admits anything in human experience which is relevant. Indeed, it deliberately takes cognizance of a variety of attitudes—including, perhaps, even cynical ones—toward whatever experience it celebrates, so that the finished poem will not be vulnerable to attack from some disregarded point of view; in Robert Penn Warren's phrase, it tries to "come to terms with Mercutio." The impure poem "arises from a recalcitrant and contradictory context." It invites resistances and achieves its goodness by overcoming them; its goodness is "earned." We can see at once why a resolution achieved in this manner would be more likely to satisfy us than one achieved by ignoring the perverse voice in us which so often objects, "No! It's just the other way around." We prefer impure to pure poetry for the same reason that we feel that no virtue can be regarded as trustworthy and no conviction as durable until they have been tested.

Fiction is perhaps more "impure" than poetry. Lionel Trilling's statement about the novel, that it is "the literary form to which the virtues of understanding and forgiveness [are] indigenous" can perhaps be applied to fiction in general. The virtues Mr. Trilling names make themselves felt, often despite the conscious intention of writers, in some of the great verse narratives which antedate the flowering of the novel form. The classical example is Milton's treatment of Satan in *Paradise Lost*. But Milton vacillates also, Maud Bodkin points out, in his treatment of Eve, picturing her now as innocent victim, now as a culpable agent. Indeed, "the whole course of *Paradise Lost*," Miss Bodkin writes, "seems to indicate a profoundly felt tension of the soul between loyalty and revolt—loyalty to an ideal, thought of as the will of God expressed both in conscience and in the history of the world, and on the other hand, a revolt of passion and sensibility against this ideal." Throughout *Archetypal Patterns in Poetry* Miss Bodkin reminds us of many similar examples—of Virgil's justice to Dido despite his loyalty to the patriarchal ideal, of Dante's sympathy with Paolo and Francesca.

Many additional examples of the same general character will immediately occur to any reader of fiction—Cervantes's treatment of Don Quixote, Richardson's incapacity to deny Lovelace and his most persuasive heroine, Clarissa, their vitality and appeal. "That complicated balance of elements which is necessary for good fiction," writes Joseph Wood Krutch, "seems usually to have been achieved by the imagination of a writer whose mind was to some extent divided against itself." All the examples given so far would tend to suggest that the balance stems from a conflict between the conscious intention of the writer and his unconscious sympathies. But we do not know, nor does it matter, whether the balance always arises in this fashion. Probably a great deal of conscious vacillation helped determine Shakespeare's attitude toward his tragic heroes, Tolstoy's toward Anna Karenina, James's toward Isabel Archer, Joyce's toward Gabriel Conroy. What is certain is that these characters are presented to us from many different, and opposed, points of view. When a single viewpoint predominates, particularly if it is a conscious and narrowly moralistic one, the fiction writer is likely, in Krutch's phrase, to win "a lugubrious triumph over his own art."

The most passionate affirmations of literature, it appears, show an awareness of all the considerations which can be urged against them. The awareness may be implicit rather than explicit, sketched in rather than developed—in Shakespeare's Sonnet 116 it is crowded into a single cry, "O, no!"; but unless the awareness is there a work will lack tension and excitement and its affirmations will carry little conviction. The characterizations, the value systems of great literature, certainly of great narrative art, are all pervaded by what I like to think of as *a sense of the opposite*. The underlying attitude is one of poised and sustained ambivalence.

❁

Let us see how this attitude manifests itself in a particular story, using for purposes of illustration "The Birthmark" by Nathaniel Hawthorne. This is not a simple story, for Hawthorne was not a simple man, yet Cleanth Brooks and Robert Penn Warren seem justified in calling it a parable—a kind of story, according to their definition, "which makes an obvious point or has a rather obvious symbolic meaning." Hawthorne himself says that the tale has "a deeply impressive moral."

"The Birthmark" is the story of a brilliant scientist, Aylmer, who became obsessed with the idea of removing a birthmark, which rather resembled a tiny crimson hand, from the cheek of his beautiful young wife, Georgiana. Aware of her husband's abhorrence of this flaw, of his desire to have her perfect, Georgiana agrees to let him attempt to remove the birthmark, an attempt which he feels is certain to succeed. But it develops that the crimson stain, superficial as it seems, has clutched its grasp into Georgiana's being with a strength of which Aylmer had no conception. Nevertheless, he persists, and develops a draught which to his "irrepressible ecstasy" removes the birthmark from his wife's cheek. But his ecstasy lasts but for a second, for "as the last crimson tint of the birthmark—that sole token of human imperfection" fades from Georgiana's cheek, she dies. "The fatal hand had grappled with the mystery of life, and was the bond by which an angelic spirit kept itself in union with a mortal frame."

The most obvious meaning of "The Birthmark," the "deeply impressive moral," is implicit in the story; in fact, so that we cannot possibly fail to see it, it is heavily underscored. We cannot have perfection. Georgiana's birthmark represents "the fatal flaw of humanity which Nature, in one shape or another, stamps ineffaceably on all her productions, either to imply that they are temporary and finite, or that their perfection must be wrought by toil and pain." By refusing to resign himself to "the limitations and imperfections of nature," Aylmer rejects, in the words of his dying wife, "the best the earth could offer."

The story has a second meaning, which is also so heavily emphasized that it is hard to believe that it was not consciously intended. What can be the specific symbolic significance of this crimson mark, which sometimes called to mind a tiny bloody hand—a mark which some of Georgiana's lovers had found attractive and which Aylmer, more spiritual than they, only became aware of after his marriage? Hawthorne does not leave us in much doubt. "The crimson hand expressed the ineludable grip in which mortality clutches the highest and purest of earthly mold, degrading them into kindred with the lowest, and even with the very brutes, like whom their visible frames return to dust." The crimson mark symbolizes sexuality, and Aylmer is one of those men, described by Freud, who sharply dissociate heavenly and earthly love, the tender and the sensual. Such men strive "to keep their sensuality out of contact with the objects they love." Just so, Aylmer rejects his wife's sexuality, ultimately with physical revulsion; and she regards his attitude as an affront.

What sort of man is this, who in his pride insists on perfection and in his refinement recoils from his wife's femininity? In reaching a judgment it might be helpful to get outside the frame of the story for a minute and, accepting the story as a true account, try to imagine in what terms Aylmer's character and conduct would have been described by the gossips of the town. But we do not have to do this; the adverse judgments appear in the story itself. Aylmer's laboratory assistant, Aminadab, who, "with his vast strength, his shaggy hair . . . and the indescribable earthiness that incrusted him . . . seemed to represent man's physical nature," declares that if Georgiana were his wife he would "never part with that birthmark." And Georgiana herself, though docile and unembittered, bitingly indicts her husband's restless spirit. She could not, she says, hope to satisfy Aylmer for "longer than one moment . . . for his spirit was ever on the march, ever ascending and each instant required something that was beyond the scope of the instant before."

These viewpoints are present in the story, *but they are not the only viewpoints and they are not Hawthorne's.* They are kept in poised tension with other viewpoints which show, as Brooks and Warren put it, that "the author is sympathetic to [Aylmer], and obviously sees in his ruinous experiment a certain nobility." The very speech of Georgiana's from which I have already quoted contains other statements that, though not without a tinge of irony, predominately express understanding and admiration of her idealistic husband. "Her heart exulted, while it trembled, at his honorable love—so pure and lofty that it would accept nothing less than perfection nor miserably make itself contented with an earthier nature than he had dreamed of." It is clear, furthermore, as Brooks and Warren also point out, that if Aminadab provides a sort of measuring stick for Aylmer's folly he provides one also for his nobility. Despite his shortcomings, Aylmer, the intellectual and spiritual man, is the hero of the tale. It is difficult to resist the surmise that he represents certain aspects of his creator. Perhaps Hawthorne, too, found it hard to accept sensuality in woman. We may be sure in any case that he knew what it meant to strive for perfection and find himself miserably thwarted. There are unmistakable autobiographical allusions in the story. "Perhaps every man of genius in whatever sphere might recognize the image of his own experience in Aylmer's journal."

But Hawthorne does not attempt to excuse the folly of Aylmer's course either; on the contrary, he mercilessly exposes it and shows its disastrous consequences. His attitude is not a condemnatory one, but neither is it indulgent. If it were, we may be sure, we would not be pleased: we would regard the story as a form of special pleading, perhaps for some weakness of Hawthorne's, acknowledged or unacknowledged.

It is clear enough that Hawthorne was both attracted and repelled by Aylmer; his attitude reflects a delicate balance. But why we should place a high value upon such an attitude is not immediately clear. There is still something a little puzzling about the attitude itself.

In life itself, it immediately occurs to us, the kind of interested impartiality which is indigenous to fiction is extremely rare. By a very indirect route the greatest religious and moral leaders—Hosea, for example, and Jesus—achieve judgments which are no less perfectly balanced. Aware of tendencies in themselves over which they have triumphed, they refuse, even when those tendencies have spent their force, to condemn those who succumb to them. But the attitude of fiction is not a judging attitude at all. It has so little in common with the kind of moral evaluations one commonly encounters that, in trying to describe it, one is tempted to search for some antonym of the word "moral." But then the attitude is uncommon in every area of our experience. It represents a balance of forces which is evidently extremely hard to achieve or maintain. When there is a narcissistic investment in another person, we tend to overestimate his virtues and capacities and deny or minimize his faults. When we are antagonistic, we do just the opposite—overlook good qualities and exaggerate weaknesses. We are correct in assuming that the kind of exposure of a person's failings which is characteristic of fiction is usually in the service of aggression.

In trying to clarify my understanding of the balanced attitude of fiction, I kept returning again and again, at first without perceiving why, to what is perhaps the most beautiful of all Freud's papers, the six-page note on "Humour." In that special form of the comic called humour, which Freud distinguishes sharply from wit, the humorist, he suggests, "adopts toward the other the attitude of an adult toward a child, recognizing and smiling at the triviality of the interests and sufferings which seem to the child so big." The humorist identifies himself to some extent with the father. In that very important form of humour "in which a man adopts a humorous attitude towards himself in order to ward off possible suffering," the situation is not so very different: the superego, the internal representative of the parental function, strives to comfort the ego. " 'Look here!' it says in effect. 'This is all that this seemingly dangerous world amounts to. Child's play—the very thing to jest about!' "

In fiction no such comforting takes place, nor is there usually any attempt to minimize the issues, but all the same we sense some sort of parallel. It is evident, in the first place, that the same two institutions of the mind are concerned: the ego and superego share an interest in the remorseless facing of truth which fiction insists upon, and it is of course the superego which requires that transgressions be punished. We suspect too that some sort of communication is taking place between the superego and the ego. Only one thing prevents us from divining its nature immediately: our tendency to think of the superego as stern and punitive. But the example of humour reminds us that the superego inherits the kindly as well as the harsh aspects of the parents. Once we realize this, we can readily reconstruct the nature of the intrapsychic interchange which the attitude of fiction stimulates: it is a kind of confession based upon acceptance and love. The ego withholds nothing and it asks for nothing, neither for extenuation of punishment nor even for forgiveness. The superego voluntarily gives the ego something it evidently values even more than these, understanding and the assurance of continued love. It notes the strivings of the ego which have gotten it into difficulty, but without revulsion or censure. Like a fond parent, the superego assures the ego: "I see your faults very clearly. But I do not condemn you. And I love you still."

Literature itself suggests how much such an attitude means to us. With his dying breath Othello beseeches precisely the kind of justice fiction tries to render:

> I pray you, in your letters
> When you shall these unlucky deeds relate,
> Speak of me as I am. Nothing extenuate,
> Nor set down aught in malice.

We want the truth about ourselves to be known by those who love us. We long to be accepted as we are, *to tell the bad and still be loved.* Perhaps because it carries overtones of experience in which, after estrangement, we were embraced by a beloved parent, such an attitude produces in us a rapturous tranquility, in which there is a faint erotic element. This response, like the attitude which engenders it, has been precisely described in fiction itself. It is incarnated in Melville's *Billy Budd.* Although the relationship between Billy and Captain Vere has definite sexual implications, at the deepest level *Billy Budd* is a legend of reconciliation between an erring son and a stern but loving father-figure. No less instinctively than he had recoiled from Claggart's hostile assault, Billy submits to his sentence because he feels that Captain Vere has decreed it in love. Billy's expression as he sleeps before his execution makes the Chaplain who has gone to comfort him realize that he "had no consolation to proffer which could result in a peace transcending that which he beheld"; and Billy goes to his death saying, "God bless Captain Vere!"

Our own reaction to the "punishment," physical or verbal, the world inflicts upon us is seldom like Billy Budd's, but that is because we sense the hostility which ordinarily underlies it; it is against this that we recoil. We can accept censure, even punishment, from those of whose love we feel assured, and the attainment of accord with them brings us a rich kind of peace. *And this entire process can be recapitulated within the self.*

In trying to understand why the fictional depiction of conflict affords us pleasure, we have, I believe, chanced upon one of the most valuable kinds of satisfactions narrative art is capable of providing. In addition to satisfying various component parts of the personality, as punishment, for example, satisfies the superego, fiction can heal intrapsychic tension. The characteristic of fiction we are considering is integrative. The facets of experience and variety of viewpoints fiction strives to take into account can be conceived as representing the conflicting claims of the several parts of the psyche. In trying to balance those claims fiction is engaging in one of the enterprises which occupy the ego itself. And fiction works under ideal conditions. In consequence it may take account of factors and perceive possibilities of achieving harmony which the ego might overlook. Through reading, these additional possibilities become available to us. In view of the mind's capacity for analogizing it is reasonable to suppose that they will often be of value not only when the problems dealt with have some clearly defined relationship to our own but in many additional cases. The reading of fiction may be of considerable help to the ego in its own integrative activity.

❋ Hawthorne's "My Kinsman, Major Molineux"

THE scene of Hawthorne's story "My Kinsman, Major Molineux" is a New England colony; the time, like the place, not too precisely fixed, a "moonlight" night during that period before the Revolution when Great Britain "had assumed the right of appointing the colonial governors."

To prepare us for certain occurrences in the story, Hawthorne tells us at once that those governors could not look forward with assurance to untroubled reigns. "The annals of Massachusetts Bay will inform us, that of six governors in the space of about forty years from the surrender of the old charter, under James II, two were imprisoned by a popular insurrection; a third . . . driven from the province by the whizzing of a musket-ball; a fourth . . . hastened to his grave by continual bickerings with the House of Representatives. . . ."

A young boy of eighteen, named Robin, has come to the capital to seek his relative, Major Molineux. The Major is either governor of the colony or a subordinate of high rank—just which is not made clear. The boy has good reasons for wanting to find him. He is the second son of a poor clergyman. His elder brother is destined to inherit the farm "which his father cultivated in the interval of sacred duties." The Major is not only rich and influential but childless, and, during a visit paid his cousin the clergyman a year or two before the story opens, has shown an interest in Robin and his brother and hinted he would be happy to establish one of them in life. Robin has been selected for the honor, handsomely fitted out in homespun, and, to cover the expenses of his journey, given half the remnant of his father's salary of the year before.

Reprinted from *Fiction and the Unconscious*, © Copyright 1957 by Simon O. Lesser. All rights reserved. Published 1957. Midway reprint 1975. Printed in the United States of America. Published by the University of Chicago Press, Chicago.

Just before reaching the town Robin has had to cross a river, and it occurs to him that he should have perhaps asked the ferryman to direct him to the home of his kinsman or perhaps even accompany him as a guide. But he reflects that the first person he meets will serve as well.

To his surprise, however, he experiences rebuff after rebuff, difficulty upon difficulty. He asks an elderly gentleman to direct him, but the man not only disclaims any knowledge of the Major; he rebukes Robin so angrily—the youth has impulsively gripped the old man's coat—that some people nearby roar with laughter. Robin now wanders through a maze of deserted streets near the waterfront. Coming to a still-open tavern, he decides to make inquiry there. He is at first cordially received, but as soon as he asks to be directed to his relative, the innkeeper begins to read the description of an escaped "bounden servant," looking at Robin in such a way as to suggest that the description fits him exactly. Robin leaves, derisive laughter ringing in his ears for the second time that night.

Now the youth loiters up and down a spacious street, looking at each man who passes by in the hope of finding the Major. Hearing sounds which betoken the approach of the elderly gentleman with whom he has had such an unpleasant encounter, he turns down a side street. He is now so tired and hungry that he begins to consider the wisdom of lifting his cudgel and compelling the first passerby he meets to direct him to his kinsman. While toying with this idea, he enters an empty and rather disreputable-looking street. Through the half-open door of the third house he passes he catches a glimpse of a lady wearing a scarlet petticoat and decides to address his inquiry to her. His appearance and voice are winning, and the lady steps outside to talk to him. She proves both attractive and hospitable. She assures the youth that the Major dwells there, but is asleep. Intimating that she is his housekeeper, she offers to welcome the youth in his stead. Though Robin only half believes her—he is not oblivious to the meanness of the house or the street—he is about to follow her when she is startled by the opening of a door in a nearby house and leaves him to run into her own.

A watchman now approaches, muttering sleepy threats. They are perfunctory, but sufficient to discourage Robin temporarily from inquiring for his kinsman. He shouts an inquiry just as the watchman is about to vanish around a corner, but receives no reply. Robin thinks he hears a sound of muffled laughter. He quite clearly hears a pleasant titter from an open window above his head, whence a round arm beckons him. Being a clergyman's son and a good youth, Robin flees.

He now roams through the town "desperately, and at random, . . . almost ready to believe that a spell was on him." In most of the houses of the town the lights are already out. Twice, however, Robin comes upon little parties of men, including some dressed in outlandish attire. In each case the men pause to address him, but saying nothing he finds intelligible and perceiving his inability to reply, they curse him and pass on.

Encountering a solitary passer-by in the shadow of a church steeple, Robin insists on being directed to the home of his kinsman. The passerby unmuffles his face. He proves to be a man Robin had noticed earlier at the tavern, but now half of his face has been painted a livid red, the other half black. Grinning at the surprised youth, the man tells him that his kinsman will pass that very spot within the hour.

Robin settles down on the church steps to wait. As he struggles against drowsiness, strange and extraordinarily vivid fantasies flit through his mind. He dozes but, hearing a man pass by, wakes and inquires, with unwarranted peevishness, if he must wait there all night for his kinsman, Major Molineux. Despite the rather objectionable way in which the stranger has been addressed, he stops and, seeing a country youth who is apparently homeless and without friends, offers to be of help. After hearing Robin's story he offers to keep the youth company until the Major appears.

Shortly a mighty stream of people come into view. Robin gradually makes out that some of them are applauding spectators, some participants in a curious procession. It is headed by a single horseman, who bears a drawn sword and whose face is painted red and black: he is the man who has told Robin that his kinsman would pass that way within the hour. Behind the horseman come a band of wind instruments, then men carrying torches, then "wild figures in the Indian dress, and many fantastic shapes without a model, giving the whole march a visionary air, as if a dream had broken forth from some feverish brain, and were sweeping visibly through the midnight streets."

Robin has a feeling that he is involved in this procession, a feeling which is quickly confirmed. As the torches approach him, the leader thunders a command, the parade stops, the tumult dies down.

> Right before Robin's eyes was an uncovered cart. There the torches blazed the brightest, there the moon shone out like day, and there, in tar-and-feathery dignity, sat his kinsman, Major Molineux!

The Major is a large and majestic man, but now his face is pale, his forehead contracted in agony, and his body "agitated by a quick and continual tremor" he cannot quell. The encounter with Robin causes him to suffer still more deeply. He recognizes the youth on the instant.

Staring at his kinsman, Robin's knees shake and his hair bristles.

Soon, however, a curious change sets in. The adventures of the night, his fatigue, the confusion of the spectacle, above all "the spectre of his kinsman reviled by that great multitude . . . [affect] him with a sort of mental inebriety." In the crowd he sees the watchman he has encountered earlier, enjoying his amazement. A woman twitches his arm: it is the minx of the scarlet petticoat. Among the noises he distinguishes the laugh of the initially courteous innkeeper. Finally, from the balcony of the large house across from the church comes a great, broad laugh which momentarily dominates everything: it is the formidable old man of whom Robin made his first inquiries and whom he later went out of his way to avoid.

> Then Robin seemed to hear the voices of . . . all who had made sport of him that night. The contagion was spreading among the multitude, when all at once, it seized upon Robin, and he sent forth a shout of laughter that echoed through the street, —every man shook his sides, every man emptied his lungs, but Robin's shout was the loudest there.

When the laughter has momentarily spent its force, the march of the procession is resumed. Robin asks the gentleman who has been sitting beside him to direct him to the ferry. The Major, the boy realizes, will scarcely desire to see his face again. In the friendliest possible way the gentleman turns down Robin's request. He tells the youth that he will speed him on his journey in a few days if he still wants to leave. But he suggests another possibility. " '. . . if you prefer to remain with us, perhaps, as you are a shrewd youth, you may rise in the world without the help of your kinsman, Major Molineux.' "

2

"My Kinsman, Major Molineux" belongs, I believe, among Hawthorne's half-dozen greatest short stories. But unexpected difficulties arise when one attempts to account for the spell the story casts. Although it seems clear enough as it is read, it resists analysis. Above all, its climax is puzzling. "Mental inebriety" is hardly an adequate explanation for a youth's barefaced mockery of an elderly relative for whom he has been searching, whose ill-treatment might have been expected to inspire feelings of compassion and anger.

Of the half-dozen critics who have discussed the story, surprisingly, no more than two seem aware that it presents any difficulties. The rest accept Hawthorne's explanation at face value. They regard "My Kinsman,

Major Molineux" as the story of an ignorant country youth who, happening to wander upon the scene at an inopportune time, is first frustrated in his search as a result of the preparations the colonists are making and then becomes a reluctant and confused spectator at their humiliation of his kinsman. Such an interpretation not only fails to explain many aspects of the story; it hardly suggests why the story should interest us. It is perhaps significant that the critics who recognize that the story is by no means so one-dimensional as this, Malcolm Cowley and Q. D. Leavis, also show the keenest awareness of its greatness. Unfortunately, even these critics have not succeeded, in my opinion, in penetrating to the story's richest veins of meaning.

Malcolm Cowley describes the story as "the legend of a youth who achieves manhood through searching for a spiritual father and finding that the object of his search is an impostor" (Editor's Note to "Tales," *The Portable Hawthorne*). Leaving aside the question of whether Robin is searching for a spiritual father, it may be said at once that there is no evidence that Major Molineux is an impostor. The first paragraph of the story tells us that the colonial servants appointed by Great Britain were likely to be resented even when they carried out instructions with some lenience; and we are later told that the Major's head had "grown gray in honor."

Mrs. Leavis regards "My Kinsman, Major Molineux" as a "prophetic forecast of . . . the rejection of England that was to occur in fact much later."[1] This is by no means as far-fetched a reading of the story as it may at first appear. It has the merit of calling attention to a rebelliousness in Robin for which, as we shall see, there is a great deal of evidence. But as I think will become clear, Mrs. Leavis has perceived a secondary implication of that rebelliousness; it has a much more intimate source and reference. To account for certain events in the story, furthermore, her interpretation would have to be painfully strained.

The remaining critics who have commented on "Major Molineux" have evidently based their remarks almost entirely on their conscious reactions to the story's manifest level of meaning. At best, I believe, such criticism is of limited value; in connection with such a work as this it is sometimes actually misleading. Like some other stories by Hawthorne and by such writers as Melville, Kafka, Dostoevsky and Shakespeare, "My Kinsman, Major Molineux" is Janus-faced. It says one thing to the conscious mind and whispers something quite different to the unconscious. The second level of meaning is *understood* readily enough, immediately and intuitively. Our acceptance of Robin's behavior—which, as we shall

1.   "Hawthorne as Poet," *Sewanee Review*, 59, 1951.

see, is bizarre not only during his ultimate encounter with his kinsman but throughout the story—is only explicable, I believe, on the assumption that we understand it without difficulty. To respond to the story, to find Robin's behavior not only "right" but satisfying, we must perceive a great many things which are nowhere explicitly developed. These hidden implications are not meant to come to our attention as we read; they would arouse anxiety if they did. Even to get at them after one has read the story requires a deliberate exertion of will. There is still another difficulty. To deal with these implications at all systematically, one is almost compelled to make some use of depth-psychology. This is a kind of knowledge most critics are curiously loath to employ.

3

As soon as we look at "My Kinsman, Major Molineux" more closely, we discover that it is only in part a story of baffled search: Robin is never so intent on finding his illustrious relative as he believes he is and as it appears. The story even tells us why this is so. To some extent we understand from the very beginning; the explanations offered serve basically to remind us of things we have experienced ourselves.

As Robin walks into the town, it will be remembered, he realizes that he should have probably asked the ferryman how to get to the home of Major Molineux. Today we have scientific evidence for what Hawthorne, and we, understand intuitively—the significance of such forgetting. In the paragraph before this we have been told something equally significant. Robin walks into the town "with as light a step as if his day's journey had not already exceeded thirty miles, and with as eager an eye as if he were entering London city, instead of the little metropolis of a New England colony." This though he has momentarily lost sight of the reason for his visit! As early as this we begin to suspect that the town attracts the youth for reasons which have nothing whatever to do with finding his influential relative. The intimation does not surprise us. Robin is eighteen. The ferryman has surmised that this is his first visit to town. In a general way we understand why his eye is "eager."

Robin makes his first inquiry for his kinsman with reasonable alacrity. But a considerable time appears to elapse before his second inquiry, at the tavern, and he is evidently spurred to enter it as much by the odor of food, which reminds him of his own hunger, as by any zeal to find the Major.

After his rebuff at the tavern it perhaps seems reasonable enough that Robin should drop his inquiries and simply walk through the streets looking for Major Molineux. If our critical faculties were not already somewhat relaxed, however, it might occur to us at once that this is a singularly inefficient way of looking for anyone. And Robin does not pursue his impractical plan with any ardor. He stares at the young men he encounters with as much interest as at the old ones; though he notices the jaunty gait of others, he never increases his pace; and there are many pauses "to examine the gorgeous display of goods in the shop-windows."

Nor does his lack of success make him impatient. Only the approach of the elderly gentleman he had first accosted causes him to abandon his plan and turn down a side street. He is now so tired and hungry that he *considers* demanding guidance from the first solitary passerby he encounters. But while this resolution is, as Hawthorne puts it, "gaining strength," what he actually does is enter "a street of mean appearance, on either side of which a row of ill-built houses was straggling toward the harbor." It is of the utmost importance that Robin continues his "researches" on this less respectable street, although no one is visible along its entire extent. If we were not by now so completely immersed in the concealed story which is unfolding itself, we might begin to wonder consciously whether Robin is seriously searching for his kinsman.

The encounters with women which follow explain the attraction of the street. They show that unconsciously Robin is searching for sexual adventure. The strength of his desire is almost pathetically betrayed by his half-willingness to believe the cock-and-bull story of the pretty young "housekeeper." Here, if not before, we identify one of the specific forces which is inhibiting Robin in his search for his kinsman: he would like a greater measure of sexual freedom than it is reasonable to suppose he would enjoy in the home of a colonial official.

The encounter with the watchman furnishes additional evidence of Robin's ambivalence. The youth could scarcely hope to find a better person of whom to ask directions. It is likely that he is also held back in this case by guilt about what he has just been doing, but the ease with which he has permitted himself to be diverted from his search is probably one of the sources of that guilt.

After further wandering Robin finally detains the passer-by who tells him that the Major will pass that very spot within the hour. In talking with the kindly gentleman who joins him to await the arrival of the Major, Robin is unable to restrain himself from boasting of his shrewdness and grown-upness. These boasts help us to understand another of the forces which has been holding him back: he wants to succeed through his own efforts and his own merits. His departure from home has evidently caused him to dream of achieving economic as well as sexual independence. When at the end of the story the gentleman suggests that Robin may decide to stay in town and may prosper without the help of his kinsman, he is simply giving expression to the youth's unvoiced but readily discernible desire.

The gentleman has an opportunity to observe how half-hearted Robin is about finding his kinsman. When the sounds of the approaching procession become more clearly audible the youth comes to the conclusion that some kind of "prodigious merry-making" is going forward and suggests that he and his new-found friend step around the corner, to a point where he thinks everyone is hastening, and partake of their share of the fun. He has to be reminded by his companion that he is searching for his kinsman, who is supposed to pass by the place where they now are in a very short time. With insight and artistry to which any tribute is inadequate, Hawthorne spreads the evidence of Robin's irresoluteness of purpose from the very beginning of the story to the moment of Major Molineux's appearance; but so subtle is the evidence, so smoothly does it fit into the surface flow of the narrative, that its significance never obtrudes itself on our attention.

4

By this point in the story we unconsciously understand Robin's vacillation more completely than I have been able to suggest. We see that, unbeknown to himself, the youth has good reasons for *not* wanting to find Major Molineux: when he finds him, he will have to re-submit to the kind of authority from which, temporarily at least, he has just escaped. At some deep level the Major appears anything but a potential benefactor; he symbolizes just those aspects of the father from which the youth so urgently desires to be free. As an elderly relative of the father and an authority figure, he may be confused with the father. In any case, however undeservedly, he has now become the target of all the hostile and rebellious feelings which were originally directed against the father.

Hawthorne tells us these things, it is interesting to note, by means of just the kind of unconscious manifestations which twentieth-century psychology has found so significant. While Robin sits on the steps of the church, fighting his desire to sleep, he has a fantasy in which he imagines that his kinsman is already dead! And his very next thought is of his father's household. He wonders how "that evening of ambiguity and weariness" has been spent at home, and has a second fantasy of such hallucinatory vividness that he wonders if he is "here or there." Nor is this an idle question. His father and Major Molineux are so inextricably linked in his mind that in a sense the drama in which he is involved is being played out "there"—at home—as well as in the town where bodily he happens to be.

The climax of this drama, so puzzling to the conscious intellect, is immediately comprehensible to that portion of the mind which has been following the hidden course of developments. It is comprehensible although Hawthorne describes Robin's feelings, as is right, in vague terms. Robin never understands those feelings and the reader would find it disturbing if they were too plainly labeled.

The youth's initial reactions can, of course, be consciously understood. They express the emotions any decent young lad might be expected to have in the circumstances. Robin's knees shake and his hair bristles. He feels pity and terror and, it may be, an impulse to strike back at the tormentors of his elderly relative.

The feelings which then begin to assert themselves would probably never have secured open expression except under circumstances as out of the ordinary as those the story describes. But now everything conspires not simply to permit but to encourage Robin to give in to tendencies which, as we know, he was finding it difficult to control. To everyone present Major Molineux is overtly what he is to the youth on some dark and secret level—a symbol of restraint and unwelcome authority. He is this even to the elderly gentleman, the watchman, the man by his side—people whose disapproval of the crowd's behavior might have had a powerful effect upon him. Without a voice being raised in protest, the crowd is acting out the youth's repressed impulses and in effect urging him to act on them also. The joy the crowd takes in asserting its strength and the reappearance of the lady of the scarlet petticoat provide him with incentives for letting himself go.

And so Robin makes common cause with the crowd. He laughs—he laughs louder than anyone else. So long as he himself did not know how he would act he had reason to fear the crowd, and the relief he feels at the easing of the immediate situation is one of the sources of his laughter. But his decision resolves still deeper and more vexing conflicts. The relief he feels that he can vent his hostility for his kinsman and abandon his search for him is the ultimate source of his "riotous mirth." It is fueled by energy which until then was being expended in repression and inner conflict.

Although Hawthorne uses figurative language which may keep his meaning from being consciously noted, he is at pains to let us know that murderous hate underlies the merriment of the crowd of which Robin becomes a part. When the laughter momentarily dies down, the procession resumes its march.

> On they went, like fiends that throng in mockery around some dead potentate, mighty no more, but majestic still in his agony. On they went, in counterfeited pomp, in senseless uproar, in frenzied merriment, trampling all on an old man's heart.

Symbolically and to some extent actually the crowd has carried out the fantasy Robin had on the steps of the church.

To the conscious mind "My Kinsman, Major Molineux" is a story of an ambitious youth's thwarted search for an influential relative he wants to find. To the unconscious, it is a story of the youth's hostile and rebellious feelings for the relative—and for the father—and his wish to be free of adult domination. To the conscious mind it is a story of a search which was unsuccessful because of external difficulties. To the unconscious— like *Hamlet*, with which it has more than one point in common—it is a story of a young man caught up in an enterprise for which he has no stomach and debarred from succeeding in it by internal inhibitions.

From one point of view the unacknowledged forces playing upon the apparently simple and candid central character of "My Kinsman, Major Molineux" are deeply abhorrent. Our sympathy for the character should tell us, however, that there is another side to the matter. The tendencies which assert themselves in Robin exist in all men. What he is doing, unwittingly but flamboyantly, is something which every young man does and must do, however gradually, prudently and inconspicuously: he is destroying an image of paternal authority so that, freed from its restraining influence, he can begin life as an adult.

✿ Saint and Sinner: Dostoevsky's "Idiot"

THE theme of *The Idiot* is the inadequacy of mere goodness in the world of today. *The Idiot* is the modern morality story in the same sense that *Hamlet* is the modern rendition of the Oedipus situation.

It is easy to miss the point of the novel entirely because it has, with one conspicuous exception, no great analogues. The exception is *Don Quixote*; and it is not by accident that references to the poor knight find their way into the Russian version of the same story. The perennial theme of modern fiction is that of a great man being torn and finally overcome by some one emotional weakness: lust, ambition, jealousy. Whatever the external situation, the fundamental internal conflict is always between what Freud would call the id—the emotional, instinctual, unsocialized part of our personality—and either the superego, which embodies our ideals and values: our conscience; or the ego, the directing, rational part of our personality, the prudent little judge who mediates between the id and superego and reconciles the demands of both with the demands of reality. In *The Idiot*, as in *Don Quixote*, the fundamental conflict is between the superego and the ego. Myshkin suffers from the noblest and most endearing of all possible weaknesses: an excess of goodness. His fatal flaw is an undeveloped ego: a sense of reality so deficient that it not only prevents him from accomplishing good, but causes him to fail everyone, himself included, in the long run and to leave behind him during his brief encounter with nineteenth-century Russian society a trail of defeats and destruction. As Freud—and Dostoevsky—knew, the unbridled superego can be as dangerous as the id. Many of our notions of right and wrong are accepted early and uncrit-

Reprinted from *Modern Fiction Studies*, vol. 4, no. 3, Autumn 1958.

ically. They are no safer a guide to the complicated problems of life than our instinctual impulses. Both those impulses and the instructions from the superego must be weighed by the conscious intelligence and related to the objective situation. It is amazing, in a way, that there are not more novels along the lines of *Don Quixote* and *The Idiot*—our own century has of course added *The Trial*—for the harm done by an overdeveloped and tyrannical superego, in a person with a deficient sense of reality, is a familiar phenomenon in life.

So weak is Myshkin's sense of reality that in the last analysis he *is* an idiot. There are of course ironies on ironies in calling him that. He is morally so superior to, and in many respects so much wiser and more penetrating than, the characters who think of him as an idiot that our first tendency is to laugh at them. But if we set up the simplest operational definition of intelligence—self-knowledge and a capacity to appraise people and situations accurately enough so that one can thread one's way safely through the jungle of the world—we see at once that Myshkin is indeed an idiot. A second irony is the literalness of the title; we balk at perceiving Myshkin's "idiocy" because his intellectual weaknesses are weaknesses we admire. We are aware of our own malice and envy, our tendency to do less than justice to the qualities of almost all other human beings—all, indeed, but a handful whose accomplishments in some curious way feed our own narcissism. How then can we despise a man who suffers from an excess of generosity, who "sees the good" in everyone and everything? Or, hating ourselves for our concessions to expediency, how can we despise a man who is invariably honest and candid?

We face the same difficulty in taking a critical view of Myshkin's actions. We know our own timidity and cowardice. How can we despise a man who acts spontaneously and, though frail, even rashly, manifesting no fear? We know how incapable we are of accepting the words of Jesus about the lilies of the field; an anxious, wizened old man possesses our soul and keeps even our charities within bounds. How can we feel contempt for a man who is unfailingly and excessively generous? Nothing blocks us perhaps from perceiving the childishness of Myshkin, his probable sexual impotence; but even this deficiency, particularly since it has a physical cause, we tend to judge indulgently.

Yet Dostoevsky wants us to see the stupidity and shortcomings of Myshkin: *The Idiot* is the story of the tragedy they cause. To understand the novel, we must shed our illusions and view Myshkin's character and conduct with our everyday eyes. In our hearts we know the futility of pure goodness and the stupidity of naive generosity. There is a level, as we shall see, on which Myshkin's "goodness" is immoral and cruel. It is admirable perhaps but also foolish to accept everyone and everything. The *appropriate* reaction to something hateful is hatred. We should shrink from the potential murderer, not welcome him to our circle of friends. We should be on guard against involvements with neurotic people, for example, women whose neurosis feeds our own. We should be sensible enough not to permit our generous and admirable tendencies—kindness, let us say, or candor—to carry us away. There are times when it is prudent to be silent or even to lie—perhaps even do things of dubious propriety, for example, open letters not intended for our eyes but which may contain information it is essential for us to have if we are to act wisely. So much Dostoevsky is saying, it might be maintained, explicitly. One other equally important thing is implied. This is the wrongness of completely repressing our instinctual needs. Myshkin is doubly crippled by his sexual innocence: he is incapable in the end of satisfying either of the women with whom he becomes involved—this is a failure of response—and he has no healthy guiding impulse to give order to his own life.

The complete man would perhaps be an amalgam of the three men whose destinies become interlocked in the first chapter of the novel—idealistic, sensual, prudent. The amalgam is unlovely, but it is man. Anyone who, like Myshkin, tries to deny, or simply lacks, some of the components is doomed, more surely than the mixed and imperfect ordinary man, to defeat and destruction by society.

Of course, there is a final, mocking irony in Dostoevsky's title: in a more perfect world the prince's "idiocy" would be something else again. Before the story proper opens, Myshkin has scored his one notable triumph. He has brought peace and ultimate happiness to the wronged and despised Marie. But, significantly, he has achieved this idyllic victory by influencing the hearts of children, and the woman he helps is herself childlike, making no demands on life; she is surprised and satisfied by pity.

Only in a world of children and Maries, or as Aglaia perceived, in a world where he did not get involved in action at all, could Myshkin possibly succeed and his "idiocy," his unrealistic acceptance of everything, be regarded as entirely admirable.

2

In writing *The Idiot*, Dostoevsky faced the, it would seem, insuperable problem of dramatizing pure goodness and certain *failures* of response—failure, for example, to react adequately to the cruelty perceived in Rogozhin. Now for fictional purposes these qualities have a dubious value, for they seldom lead to action. They suggest the spectator rather than the participant, the person acted upon rather than the person setting a chain of events in motion; and neither of these roles is adequate for the central character of a novel. Making a completely faultless character believable also presented difficulties—and difficulties which had to be solved if *The Idiot* was to be a flesh-and-blood novel, not a bodiless allegory. Perhaps Dostoevsky divined very early during the gestation of the book that his hero's goodness would have to be alloyed with weakness or evil. Otherwise the ultimate failure and even destructiveness of the goodness would possess no narrative significance, would seem unrelated to character; it would represent a basically expository comment on the wickedness of the world.

Dostoevsky's difficulties were resolved when, in developing the eighth plan for *The Idiot*, he selected a Christ-like character for his protagonist and proceeded to endow him with his own variety of masochism. In retrospect it is easy to see that no other kind of hero could have fulfilled Dostoevsky's narrative and thematic purposes. Myshkin's goodness is based upon masochism, and the masochistic man *invites* reactions and involvements; he has a principle of action, albeit a neurotic one; his passivity is only apparent. Myshkin's goodness, his moral masochism, rests on a denial of his lusts and hatreds; it is an extension of his personal or, using the term broadly, his sexual masochism. A man whose goodness has this kind of underlying structure can be an active and wholly credible agent of destruction.

Inevitably, the people with whom such a character would become most closely involved would be sadistic, full of the passion and hatred he represses. He would be attracted by such people and they by him. The masochistic person seeks people who will use him cruelly; the sadistic, people he can torture. There is even more to it than this. According to Freud, neither masochism nor sadism is ever found in isolation. While one characteristic may be dominant, every masochist or sadist has some element of the opposite tendency in his makeup, so that he is drawn to other sadistic-masochistic people not only by his needs but by his ability to identify and sympathize with them.

Thus we have Rogozhin, Nastasya Filippovna, and Aglaia, the only kind of people with whom Myshkin could have established deep emotional relationships. The nature of the other principal characters in *The Idiot*, and the prince's relation with them, is inherent in his personality structure. The dominant traits of the three principal characters have an almost formal symmetry. Myshkin is apparently an example of pure masochism; in Rogozhin sadism is dominant; Nastasya, vindictive to all men but bent on self-destruction, has both qualities in equal proportion.

There is nothing mechanical about the actual working out of the relationships, however. The relationship between Myshkin and Nastasya is underscored and echoed by the relationship between him and Aglaia. Aglaia is a genteel bourgeois counterpart of the fiercer Nastasya. The relative breadth of Nastasya's reaction to Myshkin, as compared with Rogozhin's, is another asymmetrical factor. She reacts to his moral as well as his sexual masochism, in this respect serving as a link with the novel's minor characters. In the proposal scene which ends Part I, for example, she thrice rebukes Myshkin for regarding her, unrealistically, as an innocent. Rogozhin, the sensual man of instinct, is almost completely oblivious to the prince's moral masochism. From the time he first meets him, and expresses distrust of his disclaimer of interest in women, to the time he expresses his fear that Myshkin's "pity" may prove a more powerful weapon than his own passionate, sadistic love, he is almost wholly concerned with the prince as a sexual rival.

Rogozhin's reaction to Myshkin makes up in intensity for anything it lacks in breadth. The relationship between the two men frames the book dramatically and cuts to its heart psychologically. When it is fully understood, The Idiot has yielded its ultimate secrets. The most deeply buried parts of Myshkin's personality come to light in his relationship with Rogozhin.

The dominant traits of Rogozhin and Myshkin, and the nature of the relationship which is to bind them together, are brought out in the short initial chapter of the novel. The first word Rogozhin addresses to Myshkin—he of course does not then know his name—reveals his cruelty. Myshkin's masochism is disclosed almost as promptly by his willingness to answer any question, however impertinent or inappropriate. As the two men part after this first meeting, Rogozhin extends a patronizing invitation to Myshkin and offers him aid; and the prince—though we later find he possesses considerable means—abjectly accepts the offer.

In this initial chapter we are also given a wealth of information about the woman for whom these men will soon be bitterly competing, who will serve to ripen the relationship between them. By the end of Part I of the novel Myshkin and Rogozhin are destined to be implacable rivals for the hand of this woman. By the end of Part II, in her cruelty, confusion, and vacillation, she will have twice run away from each of them, feeding their hatred for one another at the same time that she enmeshes each of them more deeply in a sadistic-masochistic relationship with her. By the end of the novel, every possibility of a nontragic solution of the affair exhausted, the two men—themselves on the verge of destruction—are destined to be reunited over the corpse of this woman. She, Nastasya Filippovna, has of course been murdered by Rogozhin. It is indicative of the rapidity with which Dostoevsky develops his plot that by the end of chapter 3, the probability of this murder has been consciously foreseen by Myshkin.

The relationship between Myshkin and Rogozhin reaches its climax in Part II of the novel. The dramatic focus of chapters 3 to 5 of this part is on the impulse the prince and Rogozhin feel to kill one another. The prince, of course, represses his murderous impulses, but they are revealed to us none the less, once our eyes are open, with unmistakable clarity. Rogozhin's impulses are more obviously revealed and are of course confirmed in the end by his actual attempt to kill Myshkin.

The section which brings the relationship of the two men to a head begins with the prince seeking out Rogozhin in his gloomy home. In the ensuing conversation the motives each man has for hating the other—as well as the motives each has for hating Nastasya—are clearly revealed. With what anguish we can imagine, Rogozhin tells Myshkin that he is the one Nastasya loves and that if she marries him, Rogozhin, it will only be as a way of seeking her own destruction. Rogozhin also shows an awareness of Nastasya's sadism and of the contempt she feels for him. Nor does he attempt to deny the sadistic nature of his love for her: he accepts Myshkin's charge that he wants to marry Nastasya only to pay her back for the torment she has caused him, just as he had previously accepted the charge when it was made by Nastasya herself. At the end of chapter 4, he announces the decision against which he is fighting and which is the ultimate source of his hatred of the prince: he offers to surrender Nastasya to him. How incapable he is of this renunciation his subsequent attempt to kill Myshkin reveals.

But the prince is no more capable of finally renouncing Nastasya than is Rogozhin. He has come to see his friend to assure him that if it is true, as he has heard, that Rogozhin and Nastasya have been reconciled and are to be married, despite his own feeling that the marriage will be ruinous for her, he will not interfere. Yet that very evening he finds himself irresistibly drawn to the house on the "Petersburg Side" where he believes Nastasya to be staying. It is a stroke of genius that his compulsive desire to see her asserts itself at this time, for his impulse to kill Rogozhin also reveals itself most clearly on this same day, and it is psychologically and artistically right that his libidinal and aggressive repressions should crumble simultaneously. Myshkin's thoughts while he is walking to Nastasya's also show that no one has surpassed Dostoevsky as a psychologist. The prince keeps reassuring himself about the purity of his intentions. He tells himself that he wishes he could see Rogozhin, so that the two friends could visit Nastasya together. In fact, he does see him a few minutes later—Nastasya, it turns out, has gone to Pavlovsk—and is so guilt-ridden he cannot speak to him at all.

Myshkin's desire for Nastasya is of course also the primary basis of his repressed hostility toward Rogozhin. In the scene where the prince visits his friend it emerges very clearly that, just as Rogozhin is suspicious of Myshkin's "pity," so Myshkin is jealous of Rogozhin's passionate love, a kind of love of which he feels himself incapable. The scene at Rogozhin's house also reminds us that Myshkin has a more legitimate reason for wishing Rogozhin out of the way—his desire to protect Nastasya against the laxly curbed violence he perceives in his friend.

Myshkin's murderous impulses toward Rogozhin must of course be revealed to us by unconscious manifestations. Myshkin cannot become aware of them; a principal purpose of his epileptic fits, one of which he feels impending, is to keep such an "idea" from consciousness. Two other factors may keep a hurried reader of *The Idiot* from becoming aware of the murderous rage against which Myshkin is struggling. The first is his apparent innocence of such impulses. The second is our conscious and sympathetic awareness of the prince's fear of Rogozhin. Our initial impulse is to assume that the prince's preoccupation with knives and the subject of murder stems from this fear, from the need he feels to defend himself. But on closer examination it becomes clear that Myshkin's awareness of Rogozhin's desire to kill him—an awareness for which he reproaches himself—is screening the still more terrible idea that he, Myshkin, wants to kill his friend. He is probably as sensitive as he is to what Rogozhin is feeling because of the murderous hate in his own heart.

The evidence for this hate, when we open our eyes to see it, is unmistakable; as though compensating for the fact that he could not be more explicit, Dostoevsky has piled clue upon clue. It is Myshkin, not Rogozhin, who *twice* unconsciously, in a state of extreme agitation, picks up a knife which is lying on his friend's table. Later that afternoon the prince realizes that for some hours previously "he had at intervals begun suddenly looking for something." The "something" proves to be an item he had seen in a hardware store window—a knife with a staghorn handle. It materializes that he has been haunted all day by thoughts of murder. He has been thinking of Lebedyev's nephew, whom he has confused with the murderer of whom Lebedyev spoke at the time he introduced his nephew to the prince. During dinner he has discussed the crime committed by this murderer with his waiter.

The fact that Myshkin is guilty of the same murderous and erotic impulses which are more nakedly revealed in Rogozhin is of the greatest structural importance. It explains his ability to forgive Rogozhin's attempt upon his life—forgive him, it might almost be said, in advance of the attempt. It is a key to understanding the entire relationship between the prince and Rogozhin. It is basic to our emotional acceptance of the overwhelming final scene of *The Idiot*. Myshkin cannot find it in his heart to reproach Rogozhin for the murder of Nastasya for very much the same reason that Hamlet cannot bring himself to kill Claudius: he is himself filled with guilt. Even consciously he has cause to reproach himself: not only has he failed to protect Nastasya, but his inability even at the very last, at Pavlovsk, to give her up has set in motion the final chain of events leading to her death. Unconsciously he knows that his complicity is far deeper and more encompassing than this. Through his identification with Rogozhin he has acted out the sadism and lust for Nastasya he tries so desperately to deny. Through his identification with her he has responded to those feelings, thus satisfying unacknowledged passive and feminine tendencies. In his own person he has felt homosexual love and murderous hate for Rogozhin and irresistible desire for Nastasya. Though these feelings have been repudiated and repressed, at the core of his being Myshkin knows that he is guilty of lusts and hatreds no less terrible than those to which his passionate companions have yielded.

3

Except for the chapters which have been discussed and much of chapter 1, which summarizes what has happened between the time of the proposal scene and Myshkin's reappearance in St. Petersburg six months later, Parts II and III of *The Idiot* are concerned with Myshkin's efforts to extricate himself from the neurotic triangular situation in which he is involved and make a reasonably normal adjustment to Russian society. Only failure to perceive this, it seems to me, can account for the charge, in part baseless and in part irrelevant, that this middle section of the novel is diffuse and structurally deficient. It is, of course, less intense than Part I. But this loss of intensity is inevitable, for it is of the essence of Myshkin's efforts to achieve stability that Rogozhin and Nastasya must tend to disappear from his life. Some diffuseness is also inevitable, for Dostoevsky is trying to show us the prince's ability to cope with a wide variety of people and problems, of the sort that a man in his position would not fail to encounter. In this section of the book Dostoevsky is giving his hero his chance. Not until we are convinced that he is incapable of taking advantage of it are we fully prepared for *The Idiot*'s tragic conclusion. Considering the prince's position in society, it is essential that he be given a broad test. Considering the nature of the relationships he is attempting to escape and establish, it is essential that the test extend over some period of time.

As a matter of fact, the technical skill and economy with which this portion of the novel are developed cannot be passed by without some comment. The loss of intensity is fully compensated for by an accrual of richness which is the despair of anyone trying to write about the book. We not only see Myshkin's relationships with many characters, but we see those characters live and breathe apart from him—see them in their setting, see their vanities, ambitions, intrigues. *The Idiot*'s minor characters are without exception interesting in their own right—so interesting that we may fail to observe the structural role they play. But our knowledge of them, and of the way they treat one another, provides indispensable background information for judging Myshkin's responses. The way Lebedyev tortures General Ivolgin to punish him for his theft shows us, for example, how far the prince goes in the other direction in his indulgence of the old man. The interrelationships of the secondary characters, which are also casually and, it appears, effortlessly revealed to us, are also used to advance the action of the novel; consider, for example, the use made of the relationship between Ganya and Ippolit, and between each of them and Aglaia.

On examination we find that Dostoevsky achieves the rich, realistic, peopled texture of the middle part of the book by focussing on just four families—the Epanchins, Lebedyevs, Ivolgins and Ptitsyns—and Mrs. Ptitsyn is the already introduced Varya Ivolgin. Even the "Burdovsky incident," while perhaps spun out too much in length, is developed with great economy so far as use of characters is concerned. Burdovsky is—apparently—the bastard son of Myshkin's benefactor, Pavlishtchev, and we have already been introduced to Lebedyev's nephew. The two characters who do not stem from the past, Keller and Ippolit, are used extensively in the further development of the story, and the latter is a friend of Kilya Ivolgin. The Burdovsky affair can by no means be regarded as simply an interpolated incident designed to show Myshkin's attitude toward social problems and ability to handle affairs. All of the characters involved in it have links with the larger movement of the novel.

A final brilliant technical achievement of the middle part of *The Idiot* is the way in which Dostoevsky makes the presence of Nastasya and Rogozhin felt, even though it is essential that their actual appearances on the scene be held to a minimum. The presence of Nastasya in particular is felt with cumulative intensity toward the end of Part III, even though she and Myshkin do not encounter one another face to face until the section's final pages. Without bringing her on the scene often, Dostoevsky, in preparation for the final catastrophe, shows how deeply she and Myshkin are still involved with one another. Her interest in the prince is revealed by their one encounter, the testimony of Rogozhin, and, as Aglaia realizes, in inverted fashion by the several letters she has written Aglaia and her effort to eliminate Yevgeny Pavlovitch as a suitor for that young lady so that she will be free to marry Myshkin. His interest in Nastasya is shown by his intervention to protect her during the altercation at the band concert and, even more portentously, by his dreaming of her while awaiting Aglaia's arrival for their early morning rendezvous.

The main focus of the middle section of *The Idiot*, however, is on Myshkin's efforts to make a normal adjustment to society. These efforts center on his relationship with the Epanchin family, and, above all of course, with Aglaia. Though the Epanchins constitute Myshkin's bridge to the ordinary life of his time and place, it is to be noted that they are by no means a typical bourgeois family. If only because of the warm, impulsive character of Lizaveta Prokofyevna, they have a touch of eccentricity about them and are fully aware of it themselves. Aglaia is no run-of-the-mill specimen of the well-brought-up upper-middle-class young lady. She is not only the most remarkable and beautiful of the three sisters, but in any group, however large, would stand out for her intelligence, high spirit and intrepidity. In the character of the Epanchins and Aglaia, Dostoevsky has tilted the scales in Myshkin's favor. If he cannot achieve satisfactory relations with them, his case, it is clear, is hopeless.

Like Nastasya, Aglaia is what Freud would call a castrating type of woman—a type encountered frequently enough in modern fiction and modern life. Her sadism is revealed by her treatment of Yevgeny Pavlovitch and Ganya as well as by her treatment of Myshkin himself. It is recognized by her not too perceptive father. Her mother comments on her daughter's cruelty at the time she drags Myshkin to the Epanchin home when she finds he has misinterpreted a note from Aglaia and again a little later on:

> "She is exactly, exactly like me, the very picture of me in every respect," the mother used to say to herself. "Self-willed, horrid little imp: Nihilist, eccentric, mad and spiteful, spiteful, spiteful! Good Lord, how unhappy she will be!"

Aglaia's sadism, however, is tempered and redeemed by her intelligence and her deep and growing love for Myshkin. It may be, too, that only a woman possessed of a certain masculine firmness could take the prince seriously as a suitor. Aglaia is compelled to arrange rendezvous, to make Myshkin face his relationship with herself and Nastasya realistically, to reveal her own love with a nakedness that must have shamed her, to maneuver the prince into proposing to her. Her tendency to tease and torment her "suitor" is understandable enough. Aglaia errs only once, and this error is one we cannot fail to admire: in her determination to clear up the matter of Myshkin's relation with Nastasya once and for all she overreaches herself and sets the stage for *The Idiot*'s crushing reversal.

Just as Myshkin's sexual masochism keeps us doubtful, throughout the middle section of the novel, about his ability to establish a good relationship with Aglaia, so his moral masochism makes us question his ability to adjust to society. His behavior in handling the Burdovsky affair is so meek that, on one level, it outrages the Epanchins. He is so lenient in his judgment of Ippolit that even the kindly Prince S. chides him for his lack of realism. He shows no ability to protect himself—does not know when he is being chaffed, readily forgives Keller and Lebedyev for exploiting him, is unwilling to accept reports about intrigues even when there is every reason to credit them. A curious and more disturbing fact is that Myshkin frequently provokes the attack of the very people he tries to help. His motives are mistrusted and his ingenuousness makes it difficult for him to attain his idealistic ends. Without being sure of our ground, we are inclined to wonder if there is not some truth in the charge levelled against him by Lebedyev's nephew:

> "Yes, prince, one must do you justice, you do know how to make use of your . . . well, illness (to express it politely); you've managed to offer your friendship and money in such an ingenious way that now it's impossible for an honourable man to take it under any circumstances. That's either a bit too innocent or a bit too clever. . . . You know best which."

While we are troubled by this charge and by the recurring evidence of Myshkin's ineffectuality, on the whole, throughout the middle section of the novel, we are inclined to give him the benefit of the doubt. By and large his relations with people seem to be going along well enough and, as has been mentioned, his shortcomings are amiable ones. Dostoevsky dramatizes this fact: we are inclined to judge the prince in kindly fashion not only because *we* cannot condemn such faults as he reveals, but because we see him much of the time through indulgent and admiring eyes—Kolya's and Vera Lebedyev's, for example, and Madame Epanchin's and Aglaia's. It is the judgment of the latter two, above all, that is decisive. While we have some forebodings, our dominant feeling, at the end of Part III of *The Idiot,* is that we are on the eve of the prince's engagement to Aglaia—and this engagement does in fact become a reality early in Part IV. Seeing Myshkin through the hopeful, loving eyes of his intended and her mother—who so much resembles her that, like Aglaia, she continues to feel warmly toward him even when her mind tells her he is impossible—we begin to believe that somehow he may "make out" despite his unworldliness. At the end of this middle section of the novel the prince's affairs are apparently prospering.

4

But of course his situation is really precarious. We have been prepared openly in the first part of the novel and subterraneously throughout the middle part for the possibility that the prince will not be able to free himself from Nastasya or cope with his other problems. He has still hardly demonstrated his capacity for affairs, and what success he has had may be attributed in part to the happiness and confidence he feels as a result of his relationship with Aglaia. And her indulgence softens and extenuates his failures.

Thus Myshkin's worldly success and the solution of his personal problems both pivot around Aglaia. Ironically, the consummation of his relationship with her is jeopardized by the very growth of his love and his partial success in freeing himself from Nastasya. The compulsive attraction he feels for Nastasya undoubtedly fades in intensity during the middle portion of the novel. However, simultaneously, his pity for her grows; he comes to the conclusion that she is mad and desperately in need of help. At this point in the story there is no doubt for which woman Myshkin feels the more normal, complete love. But with his fatal flaw of masochism there is no doubt either that, in any showdown, he will choose the woman he loves least, the woman for whom he feels deepest pity, the woman who will bring him most pain.

Myshkin's showdown occurs in chapters 6 to 8 of Part IV. His ability to make an adjustment to society, being the matter of lesser intensity, is disposed of first. The decisive test comes during the party which the Epanchins have planned to introduce Myshkin, now formally engaged to Aglaia, to society. In particular they are eager for him to make a good impression on Madame Epanchin's influential friend, Princess Byelokonsky. The party is planned with some apprehension and, even though it pains her to do so, Aglaia does not hesitate to brief her fiancé about how he should conduct himself.

There is a shift of focus here which permits Dostoevsky to show us

Myshkin's shortcomings magnified. Whereas before we have seen him much of the time through the clement eyes of the Epanchins, in this scene we see them watching his conduct anxiously. Still another technical device is employed to disclose Myshkin's ineptness. In previous scenes, we have seen the prince in relation to people whom we knew and for whom we felt some sympathy. If he judged them too charitably, we were inclined in turn to be charitable toward him. But most of the people at the Epanchin party we do not know or have met only casually. We have no emotional investment in them, and when Myshkin's judgment of them is absurdly overgenerous, nothing prevents us from perceiving the fact. It is even easier to perceive the stupidity of his view of the party as a whole and of his willingness to whitewash the Russian aristocracy en masse.

Even in this scene, there are some residual traces of ambiguity. Within limits the prince's sincerity and intensity seem admirable precisely because he is with a group that takes nothing very seriously and has long since forgotten the meaning of simple honesty. It is significant, too, that despite the prince's fiasco and the pain he has caused them, both Aglaia and her mother continue to feel warmly toward him. Even at the end of chapter 7, his position is not completely hopeless.

But on the whole Dostoevsky does not spare Myshkin in this scene. In addition to dramatizing his failure, and giving us the negative reactions of such a kindly observer as Adelaida, Dostoevsky intervenes as omniscient novelist at a half-dozen points to call attention to the prince's ineptness. In this scene, too, we finally come to see why Myshkin's readiness to forgive defeats its apparent purpose. In judging the Epanchin's guests, he is so indulgent that his ingenuousness has precisely the effect of irony. His appraisal of the aristocracy is so at variance with the facts that it makes his listeners more keenly aware of their shortcomings. Instead of providing expiation, it increases their sense of guilt.

It may be that Dostoevsky is saying that one is not in a position either to blame or forgive another unless one first understands him. It is clear in any case that many of the people drawn to Myshkin want understanding as well as forgiveness, and are disappointed when they receive only the latter.

Perhaps the most obvious example is General Ivolgin. In contrast to Lebedyev, who has tortured Ivolgin in reprisal for his theft and ridiculed him for his lying, Myshkin says nothing about the former and accepts the most outrageous lies with no show of incredulity. At first Ivolgin is delighted and feels a rush of affection for the prince. But that evening he writes him a letter in which he informs him that "he was parting with him, too, forever, that he respected him, and was grateful to him, but that even from him he could not accept 'proofs of compassion which were derogatory to the dignity of a man who was unhappy enough without that.' " On reflection it is easy enough to understand this later reaction. Although the course Myshkin follows is apparently dictated by kindness, what he is doing is playing make-believe with the General. Ivolgin is aware of his tendency to lie; he would probably respond either to a serious analysis of the tendency or the sort of chaffing which suggests that his being found out in a lie has not led to any diminution of affection. The prince's course of disregarding the General's lying is not without a trace of malice, for it implies that it is hopeless to talk to him, that he is beyond redemption. Madame Epanchin's treatment of the General dramatizes the fact that there is a sensible middle course between the deliberate cruelty of Lebedyev and the unsatisfactory form of forgiveness offered by Myshkin: she is critical but at the same time tolerant and, above all, perfectly straightforward.

Even after the fiasco of the engagement party, it is still theoretically possible for Myshkin to make some sort of adjustment to society, for he still has Aglaia's love. But one of the purposes of that scene is to prepare us for Myshkin's graver failure in the climactic scene of the novel where for the first time he, Nastasya, Aglaia and Rogozhin come together to work out their destiny. It is one of the ironies of the book that Aglaia, the most likable of the four central characters, plays so prominent a part in this catastrophic meeting. She has suggested the meeting and it is her harshness to Nastasya which stings her into attempting to prove her continued power over Myshkin. But of course the decisive failure is his. It is not a moral failure in the usual sense of the term. It is a neurotic failure, the final triumph of his masochism. He chooses the woman he most pities, not the one he most loves.

Once that choice is made, the triangular situation of Part I is reestablished—with one decisive difference. Every possible solution of the situation of Myshkin, Nastasya and Rogozhin which does not involve their destruction has now been eliminated. We are reconciled to a tragic liquidation of their relationship and even prepared for the specific series of events which now follow so swiftly—Nastasya's final recoil from Myshkin, her murder by the tormented Rogozhin, the prince's forgiveness. It is a measure of Dostoevsky's greatness that horrible as the final scene of *The Idiot* is—it is a scene that few writers would attempt—we do not balk at accepting its truth for a minute.

❀ The Source of Guilt
and the Sense of Guilt:
Kafka's *The Trial*

1

THERE are two miraculous things about *The Trial* and the other stories of Franz Kafka. Such fantasies could only occur to an exceptionally rare kind of person: one disturbed almost to the point of psychosis and yet sufficiently integrated, sufficiently courageous, to face, indeed to want to capture, precisely the most unpleasant truths about himself and his world—to be willing "to cross the supersonic thresholds of the mind"[1] in quest of them. The second miracle is that the fantasies were not only faced, permitted to register on the mind, but worked out to completion or virtual completion and written down. It is not surprising that Kafka left some of his works unfinished and wanted most of them destroyed after his death. The marvel is that he accomplished as much as he did. This frail, short-lived man, who did not feel free to give his whole time to writing and dealt with material from which most writers would recoil, produced three novels, two of them of the very first rank, and many short stories, fables, meditations, and parables, some of them indubitably great. Kafka was a dedicated man. At a cost in loneliness and suffering which if it were not for some of his own stories, such as "A Hunger Artist," we could perhaps not even comprehend, he made explorations in terrifying realms. His discoveries have enormously enlarged the world of experience open to us through prose fiction.

The plot of *The Trial* has become well known. The novel opens with

Reprinted from *Modern Fiction Studies*, Spring 1962.
1. *Time*, 49 (April 28, 1947), 106.

a sentence at once as colloquial and as captivating as a good news story lead: "Someone must have been telling lies about Joseph K., for without having done anything wrong he was arrested one fine morning."[2] K. is a bank official and a bachelor. The arrest takes place on his thirtieth birthday in his room at the boarding house of Frau Grubach. A preliminary hearing is held in an adjacent room, which has recently been occupied by a Fräulein Bürstner, a typist to whom K. is attracted. K. has a fugitive desire to dismiss the whole business as a practical joke; he blusters a good deal, and protests his innocence. He seeks—in vain—to find out just what authority it is which is arresting him and the nature of the crime with which he is charged. He is destined never to learn the answers to these questions or to acquire an understanding of the laws, procedures, and ultimate meaning of the mysterious Court before which he is summoned to appear. K. becomes progressively more absorbed in his case until practically all his time and energies are devoted to it; he becomes less and less able to give his attention to his work at the bank. He retains an advocate, and exerts himself to prove his innocence or at any rate reach some sort of understanding with the merciless tribunal by which he is being judged. Yet, for all his efforts, he becomes increasingly convinced of his own guilt and reconciled to the need for being punished. When on the eve of his thirty-first birthday two men in frock coats come to his lodgings, K.—though he has not been informed of their coming—is waiting for them. He is also dressed in black. He goes with the men, not seeking help, indeed pulling his companions away from a policeman who, it seemed, was about to question them. In a deserted stone quarry on the outskirts of the town, the group comes to a halt. While one of the partners holds K., the other thrusts a knife into his heart.

Even in broad outline the story seems at once meaningful and baffling, and the outline gives no sense of the richness of the novel. Each detail of *The Trial*, and not simply, as with some other novels, the legend as a whole, seems charged with meaning. The immense literature which has grown up about *The Trial* since its posthumous publication in German in 1925 and in English in 1937 is proof of the significance the book possesses for at least the present generation of readers. A sampling of this literature may help both to illuminate this particular work and to enlarge our understanding of the kind of communication which may occur in reading any moving and meaningful story.

2. *The Trial*, trans. Willa and Edwin Muir (New York: Knopf, 1945), p. 3. All subsequent references to *The Trial* are taken from this edition.

2

Among the many interpretations of *The Trial* which might have been considered, I have tried to select a few which seem to me to be representative of the *kinds* of response the novel has provoked. There are difficulties in dealing with even this handful of interpretations adequately, for most of them are elaborately developed. Since I shall have to indicate what I regard as acceptable and what mistaken about each of these interpretations, perhaps the best procedure is to start by indicating what *The Trial* means to me. Some circularity, however, may be unavoidable: my own reading of the novel may have been shaped in part by the natural tendency to extend, qualify, or quarrel with the points made by other critics.

On the deepest level, *The Trial* seems to me a quasi-abstract story of a man's mental and spiritual collapse—of what is sometimes loosely called a nervous breakdown, but can be more accurately described as a psychotic episode.[3] More schematically, it is the story of the disintegration of an initially none too strong ego under the onslaught of a suddenly angry and implacable superego. This onslaught is caused by certain instinctual impulses which are unacceptable and which reactivate the emotional turmoil, the tabooed desires, and, above all, the fears and guilt feelings associated with the Oedipus conflict.

Though they sometimes fuse, there are two distinct strands to the story of *The Trial*. There is, first, the story of certain *specific* conflicts faced by Joseph K., in the present and in the past. It is to be noted, however, that—quite deliberately, I think—this phase of the story is only lightly and incompletely developed. For Kafka is simultaneously telling the story of another struggle which is in some ways even more bitter than the Oedipal conflicts which are recalled and relived, in memory and in terms of actual experiences, in the course of *The Trial*. This is the struggle against generalized authority, generalized guilt—in short, against the superego, the "Court" whose jurisdiction can never be escaped this side of death or madness because it is part of our personality itself.

The fact that *The Trial* has at once this specific and abstract reference accounts for its peculiar power and appeal. If Kafka had patterned the novel more closely and exclusively on his own love for F. (who is undoubtedly the prototype of Fräulein Bürstner in *The Trial*),[4] he could still

---

3. Paul Goodman is more specific still. In *Kafka's Prayer* (New York: Vanguard, 1947), p. 142, he describes *The Trial* as "a paranoic dream."
4. See Max Brod, *Franz Kafka* (New York: Schocken Books, 1947), especially p. 146.

have produced a moving story, for this love, which he could never con-
summate by marriage, threw him into agonizing conflict and, as one can
see more clearly in "The Judgment," mobilized the whole cluster of feelings associated with the Oedipal situation. But in *The Trial* Kafka goes
farther than he did in "The Judgment" in disguising the autobiographical
material. The father, *in propria persona*, is omitted and Fräulein Bürstner
and K.'s feeling for her are only lightly sketched in, so that the abstract
strand of reference can receive simultaneous development. Though by
itself this strand might have been less compelling than the first, it is also
fertile material for a novel. As indicated, it too has a significant "objective
correlative" in the world of our emotional experience: it mirrors the
never-ceasing struggle with the superego.

We regard *The Trial* as a masterpiece because it fuses and permits us
to deal simultaneously and economically with these two basic emotional
preoccupations. Many of the characters and incidents in the novel are
overdetermined; in responding to them we simultaneously act out our
feelings toward individual authority figures and toward authority in the
abstract. Besides the obvious contribution this makes to the richness and
intensity of our response, this double strand of reference heightens our
reaction in a more subtle way: it cues two different, and complementary,
kinds of response. The specific strand encourages us to identify with K.;
the abstract strand, to project ourself into the novel in our own person,
to "analogize."[5] Since, for example, the causes of K.'s guilt are only
faintly indicated, we tend to supply the explanation for it out of our own
knowledge and experience. We fill in the blank spaces with reminis-
cences of the things which cause us guilt; we evoke our own conflicts,
our own "trial." *The Trial* furnishes an unexcelled example of the kind of
story which permits us to deal with our own problems while ostensibly
(and so far as we ourselves know) we are "just reading."

One final point: the degree of abstractness in *The Trial* corresponds
to the situation which usually prevails in life itself. Like Joseph K., most of
us know our own suffering, but we know ourselves less well. Though we
may be aware of some of the weaknesses in ourselves against which we
must struggle, we can seldom track down the original weaknesses, the
more remote failures, which may have burdened us with such an abiding
sense of guilt that even hard-won victories over temptation in the present can relieve it only temporarily. Nor are we any more successful in
identifying the institutional arrangements which oppress and thwart us
so cleverly that, except in occasional flashes of lucidity, we tend to be-

5. See my book, *Fiction and the Unconscious* (Boston: Beacon, 1957), pp. 241–
247 and *passim*, for a discussion of this seldom-noted but highly valued component of reader response.

lieve that in some mysterious way we rather than they are responsible for all the deprivations and suffering to which we are subjected.

Of the fact that *The Trial* is concerned with internal conflicts there is more evidence than can or need be cited. The point receives continuous stress. During his first interrogation K. says: "You may object that it is not a trial at all; you are quite right, for it is only a trial if I recognize it as such" (p. 51). In the cathedral scene, toward the end of the book, the priest reminds K. of the same thing: ". . . the Court makes no claim upon you. It receives you when you come and relinquishes you when you go" (p. 279).

Whole scenes of the novel bear the mark of being born of K.'s wishes and fears, of being dramatizations of half-desired, half-dreaded events. The arrest scene which opens the novel and the execution scene which closes it are the most conspicuous examples, but in between there are many others: the whipping scene (which perhaps because of its peculiar vividness seems almost like a dream within a dream), the arrival of K.'s uncle, and the meeting and discussion with Block. Though not always so obviously as in these instances, the entire novel may be said to be composed of such scenes: it is a series of objectified dreams mirroring K.'s thought processes at particular times and tracing his gradual disintegration.

In the same way, most if not all of the characters in *The Trial* can be regarded as projections—as evocations of the father, the mother, siblings, splinters of K. himself. At the same time they have sufficient objective validity, as have the dramatized representations of K.'s thoughts and problems. In form *The Trial* is always a story, not an interior monologue.

Kafka's capacity to write objectively without ever losing sight of the essentially subjective nature of his material is most triumphantly shown in the way he dramatizes K.'s struggle with his superego. Critics have seen the "Court" as a symbol of social convention, the bureaucratic or Fascistic state, capitalism, even God. It is each of these and all of these; and, because it is, on one level *The Trial* is a tale of man versus oppressive and inadequately understood external authority. But beyond any question the Court is also a projection of the persecuting superego. The whole novel bears witness to the psychical validity of this, and in Kafka's depiction of the Law-Court offices, the only fixed and visible locus of the Court's authority, the superego may even be said to receive physical representation. The offices occupy an indefinite number of (one feels) mostly small cubicles; they are invariably situated in low-lying attics; they are poorly lighted so that whatever people happen to be present and whatever activities are taking place are usually perceived, if at all, in a confused, ambiguous way. Kafka's description seems to echo an archetypal way of imaging an institution of the mind. Rounding out the representation, the qualities attributed to the Court mirror, in condensed fashion, both the functions of the superego of which K. is most painfully aware and his own defensive reactions, past and present, towards it and towards the parental figures whose aspirations and decrees it inherited: the Court is stern, judicial, punitive—and unwarrantedly so because it itself is irrational, lustful, and corrupt. With a kind of knowledge almost too comprehensive and systematic to be called intuitive, Kafka lets us know that, whatever else it was, K.'s trial was an internal struggle also.

Before exploring the meaning of *The Trial* in greater detail, we must take cognizance of two important aspects of Kafka's art which are closely related but distinguishable: his exploitation of ambivalence and of ambiguity. The qualities are never stressed, as in some of Kafka's imitators, for decorative effect. They are an integral part of the understanding of human behavior and the human predicament Kafka is seeking to convey and they have important narrative functions.

K.'s ambivalence is stressed either to explain his behavior in full or to account for what might otherwise seem an excessive or inadequate response. It is K.'s compulsive desire for Fräulein Bürstner which precipitates the superego onslaught that in the end demolishes his ego. Since the desire reactivates such deep guilt feelings and fears that it cannot be faced, it is not surprising that it has devastating effects. Nevertheless, for it to destroy K. as it does, it must be assumed that in a sense he wants to be destroyed. From the very beginning he feels a desire to submit to some strong and protective, albeit castrating, authority; his ego is looking for an opportunity to abdicate its precarious sovereignty. This desire might be regarded as K.'s tragic flaw, the weakness which leads ultimately to his defeat and death. The central conflict of the novel is whether this desire or the integrative forces of the ego will prevail.

The dependency wishes manifest themselves very early in the novel; they gradually gain complete sway. When Franz, one of the warders who arrests K., shouts that the inspector wants to see him, K. finds that "the command . . . was actually welcome to him" (p. 13). K. is summoned to his first interrogation, but the following Sunday he reports to the Court without having been summoned. While in the empty interrogation chambers, he gets so weak that he practically has to be carried out. Finally he hears a voice saying, "First he wants to go, then you tell him a hundred times that the door is in front of him and he makes no move to go" (p. 90). In the Cathedral scene, K. hears himself called. He wavers: he knows that he is still free, but that "if he were to turn round he would be caught, for that would amount to an admission . . . that he was really the person addressed, and that he was ready to obey" (p. 264).

In addition to securing representation in such ways as these, at various points the dependency wishes express themselves through self-defeating tendencies, for example by some form of defiance which at once masks and reveals the wish to be overcome. In every major episode of the novel K. vacillates between submissiveness and the protection of his own autonomy. Thus ambivalence lies at the very heart of *The Trial*. The book is a legend of our confused feelings toward ourselves, our own impulses, authority figures, and social institutions.

More consistently perhaps than any other prose writer, Kafka also exploits the ambiguity characteristic of our experience. The ambiguity is related to the ambivalence: in a sense is its intellectual analogue. Compulsives[6] —and among other things, Joseph K., like his creator, is a compulsive—develop alternative explanations of events to express their ambivalence and to avoid decisions; their thinking is a mechanism of defense. Thus it is not surprising that ambiguity rules in Kafka's world, where the meaning of everyone and everything—the Court, the whipping continually going on in the lumber room at the Bank—seems ultimately lost in mist. Sometimes the ambiguity is a direct expression of emotional ambivalence. "Was the Advocate seeking to comfort him or to drive him to despair?" (p. 158) Later K. wavers among various explanations of the Advocate's conduct. Two of these are hostile, but one would suggest the desirability of retaining the Advocate, the second of giving him up: "Was it personal affection for K.'s uncle, or did he really regard the case as so extraordinary that he hoped to win prestige either from defending K. or—a possibility not to be excluded—from pandering to his friends in the Court?" (p. 235)

At other times the ambiguity simply reflects K.'s inability to determine the real meaning of something. "The Inspector was possibly of the same mind, K. fancied, as far as he could tell from a hasty side-glance. But it was equally possible that the Inspector had not even been listening . . ." (p. 19). And there is a moment of tremulous hope before his execution:

> His glance fell on the top storey of the house adjoining the quarry. With a flicker as of a light going up, the casements of a window there suddenly flew open; a human figure, faint and insubstantial at that distance and that height, leaned abruptly far forward and stretched both arms still farther. Who was it? A friend? A good man? Someone

6.   The most important features of the compulsive character are "inflexibility . . . the inability to abandon or alter a course of action or thought in order to avoid suffering, and excessive indecisiveness." Ives Hendrick, *Facts and Theories of Psychoanalysis* (New York: Knopf, 1939), pp. 346–347.

who sympathized? Someone who wanted to help? Was it one person only? Or were they all there? Was help at hand? Were there some arguments in his favor that had been overlooked? (pp. 287–288)

A moment's reflection will convince us that this sort of ambiguity, like the kind which expresses our ambivalence, is a pervasive if neglected characteristic of our everyday life. Whether we are trying to understand the ultimate source of authority, the laws which govern human life, or the basis of our friends' actions, we can arrive at absolutely unequivocal explanations only if we are fools. Kafka is the dramatist of the inescapable uncertainty of our experience.

3

"Ever since I can remember," wrote Kafka in his famous Letter to his Father, "a deep anxiety about safeguarding my mental existence has made me indifferent to everything else."[7] There is evidence that Joseph K., like his creator, expended a great deal of psychic energy in preventing just such a mental crisis as he goes through in *The Trial*.

If immediately on wakening I had got up without troubling my head about Anna's absence [he explains to Frau Grubach] . . . all this would have been nipped in the bud. But one is so unprepared. In the Bank, for instance, I am always prepared, nothing of that kind could possibly happen to me there, I have my own attendant, the general telephone and the office telephone stand before me on my desk, people keep coming in to see me, clients and clerks, and above all my mind is always on my work and so kept on the alert. (pp. 26–27)

But one cannot always keep busy, and those last minutes in bed are a natural time for day-dreaming and, on the morning of one's thirtieth birthday, for stock-taking.

A natural time, too, for thinking of the typist in a nearby room, whose appearance and actions may have suggested to K. that she was not inaccessible.[8] The fact that K. is "called" to her room may have more than one meaning. Though he can never acknowledge his desire for Fräulein Bürstner, it is made unmistakably clear. K. feels compelled to discuss his "case" with her and waits up for her until half past eleven, in

7. Quoted in *Kafka's Prayer*, p. 134.
8. She regularly comes home late. Note also Frau Grubach's report on Fräulein Bürstner and K.'s over-indignant reaction to it, pp. 28–29.

his fear of missing her postponing his dinner and a visit to Elsa, a prostitute whom he is accustomed to seeing once a week. His talk with Fräulein Bürstner ends up with compulsive love-making. " 'I'm just coming,' K. said, rushed out, seized her, and kissed her first on the lips, then all over the face, like some thirsty animal lapping greedily at a spring of long-sought fresh water" (p. 38).

Fräulein Bürstner's connection with K.'s "case" is made clear to us in many other ways—for example, by K.'s hostile feelings toward the other male boarder, Captain Lanz, and by his asking for someone by that name on his first visit to the Interrogation Commission. When K. tells his Uncle about his case, he mentions the Fräulein only once, because, he assures himself, she has no connection with it. One does not need to be aware of Freud's observation that in situations like this the negative can be disregarded to realize that Kafka has introduced the denial only to remind us of the connection.

The most dramatic evidence of the connection is the reappearance of Fräulein Bürstner in the concluding scene of the novel. K. has a momentary impulse to resist and escape from the men who are leading him to his death.

> And then before them Fräulein Bürstner appeared, mounting a small flight of steps leading into the square from a low-lying side-street. It was not quite certain that it was she, but the resemblance was close enough. Whether it was really Fräulein Bürstner or not, however, did not matter to K.; the important thing was that he suddenly realized the futility of resistance. (p. 284)

He is reminded, that is to say, of his own guilt. Perhaps Fräulein Bürstner resembled his mother. But for anyone as inhibited as K. that would not have to be the case. It would be enough that, for whatever reason, he felt strongly attracted to her, so that he dreamt, however fugitively, of winning her for himself—of marriage or at any rate of something better than his relationship with Elsa. Ironically, a desire K. tried to deny was powerful enough to mobilize the whole cluster of Oedipal feelings: envy and hatred of the father, guilt, and talion fears.

The Trial moves simultaneously forward and backward in time. The story of K.'s struggle to remain sane, to resist the onslaught of his punitive superego, carries us forward. We see how a paranoid fantasy which K. at first feels he can throw off at will gradually gains control of him until all his energies are absorbed in a losing struggle against it, until he can think of nothing else even at the Bank, where he had once felt so secure. This strand of the story ends in K.'s execution, which may be taken literally or regarded as a symbol of his mental collapse—it does not matter, for in any case the execution means the death of his ego. But at the same time that K.'s struggle against abstract authority carries us forward, he is regressing to childhood, recalling and reliving the original experiences which account for his desire for Fräulein Bürstner being so laden with guilt. And here the execution stands for the final submission to the strong and castrating father, a submission K. has struggled against but longed for from the first.

This two-way movement is another source of *The Trial*'s richness and strange half-realistic, half-dreamlike quality. Many of the incidents, like the execution, have a place both in K.'s "trial" and in his unconscious evocation of his past. But there is no attempt to work out this double movement of the story in complete detail; in particular, K.'s unconscious recall of the infantile source of his conflict is only lightly sketched in. Any attempt to give each element in the story dual significance would almost certainly have interfered with the narrative flow and given *The Trial* a mechanical quality. It would have been psychologically wrong as well: the recapture of the past is neither an orderly process nor one that can ordinarily aspire to completeness.

Nevertheless, there is copious evidence of regression, of "the return of the repressed." Twice, for example, K. struggles with a father figure— and to a lesser extent with a brother—for the favor of a woman. There is, first of all, the scene with the wife of the Law-Court Attendant. She finds K. attractive and K. finally overcomes his fears and begins to dream of winning her: ". . . some night the Examining Magistrate . . . might come to the woman's bed and find it empty. Empty because she had gone off with K., because the woman now standing in the window, that supple, voluptuous warm body under the dark dress of rough material, belonged to K. and to K. alone" (p.70). But in the end K. loses out both to the Examining Magistrate and to the student Bertold. The fear of the father is so great that even in dreams K. cannot at this point permit himself a victory. We begin to understand why K. is so frightened by his feeling for Fräulein Bürstner and why, at thirty, he has not achieved a satisfactory heterosexual adjustment.

In this scene, as in the previous one ("First Interrogation"), K. is also searching for evidence of the sexuality of adults. This is the significance, for example, of his discovery that the "law books" contain indecent pictures and erotic stories. It is the *tu quoque* defiance of the child for the adults who judge him though they are no better than he is. But the very fact that he feels compelled to reassure himself in this fashion shows how guilty he feels.

K. also relives his Oedipus conflict in his fight with the Advocate for Leni's favors, and this series of scenes provides a brilliant illustration of the way Kafka handles the two-way progression of his plot. On one level the scenes advance the story of the trial, of K.'s effort to defend himself against his punitive superego. It is a losing fight: K.'s position steadily deteriorates. He defeats himself, and a second level of the story reveals the infantile source of this tendency. Most of the people and incidents in these scenes have a two-edged reference. For example, the Advocate has a realistic place in the trial story and reveals K.'s attitude toward authority in general. K. vacillates between leaning on the Advocate and dispensing with his services altogether, just as in his appearance before the Court he alternates between self-defense and defiance. At the same time, the Advocate is a father figure, with whom K. relives all his infantile struggles. His castrative tendencies toward the old man are revealed by his effort to persuade himself that the Advocate is ineffectual and, above all, by the constant emphasis on his age, illness, and weakness. In the meetings with the Advocate which are dramatized, the old man is in bed—just as in "The Judgment" the son puts his father to bed, symbolically murdering him. But there is the same fear which reveals itself in that story that the aggressive act is, after all, unsuccessful. The Advocate, like the father, asserts his superior strength at the critical moment.

The compulsive sexual episode with Leni is a defiance and momentary triumph over three authority figures: the Advocate, the Chief Clerk of the Court who is visiting him at the time of K.'s first call, and K.'s uncle. But of course the episode also reveals K.'s self-defeating tendencies: it confirms his guilt and immeasurably weakens his position.

Leni is clearly a mother figure; more specifically, she is the "bad" mother; the connecting web of skin between the two middle fingers of her right hand symbolizes her animality. "What a pretty little paw!" exclaims K. (p. 139). His experience with Leni reflects the small boy's distorted belief that he is taking the mother away from the father and enjoying some sort of guilty intimacy when he is alone with her. One penalty of the distortion is sibling jealousy—thus K.'s immediate suspicion that Block is also enjoying Leni's favors. Block is a brother figure and at the same time a projection of what K. fears he will become if he gives in to his dependency wishes.[9]

9.   Chapter VIII contains many amusing indications that the Advocate, Leni, K., and Block comprise a family in which Block is the less favored son. "Yes, one becomes very dependent on one's Advocate in the course of time," he says (p. 228). "He's just pretending to complain," Leni puts in, "for he likes sleeping here, as he has often told me." She shows K. his bedroom, which is a small, low-roofed chamber off the kitchen. After a time K. can no longer stand the sight of

While the specific anxieties which trouble K. have their roots in the past they cause him to recall and re-experience, and are triggered by his lust for Fräulein Bürstner, they are probably fed also by dissatisfaction with the way he is living at the time the story opens and by fears about the future. It is not without significance that the onset of his illness occurs on his thirtieth birthday. The thirties are a critical period for most men. It is a time when one may feel compelled to face the fact that one has not built a satisfactory life for oneself—and the terrifying possibility that this may be because of some inner weakness, not easily to be overcome. At thirty a man is no longer young; it is not enough simply to be promising. About this time most men begin quite soberly to take stock of their goals and their resources for reaching them, of external obstacles and the competition one faces not only from those on about the same level but from younger men fighting their way up. (This may be one of the explanations for the appearance of the three clerks on the morning of K.'s arrest.) We may begin to worry about our health, about old age and even death. The will to live may become less keen.

At about this time, too, we begin to realize that other people are taking our measure, professionally and personally, that we are being judged not only by friends, but by people whom we do not even know. We have grown accustomed to talking about others, not always without malice. Suddenly we realize that others have been talking about *us,* that without our knowledge we have acquired that frightening thing, a reputation. We may fear, not without reason, that we have been judged too harshly—dismissed as cold when we feel ourselves to be warm, held guilty for failures for which we feel others are primarily responsible. Particularly if something happens to upset our lives, we may begin to feel that we are on trial and be as puzzled as K. was about who is trying us and how to conduct our defense.

4

In order to round out the interpretation which has been offered and to define certain facets of it more clearly, I should like to turn now to Paul Goodman's psychoanalytic study of *The Trial* in his *Kafka's Prayer.* [10]

Block. "Put him to bed," he cries to Leni (p. 229). Later the Advocate asks for a report of Block as though he were a child: "How has he been behaving today?" Leni gives a favorable report: "He has been quiet and industrious" (pp. 242–243).
10. Charles Neider has also written a psychoanalytic study of Kafka, *The Frozen Sea* (New York: Oxford, 1948). But Neider scants the abstract quality of *The Trial* and makes a number of basic errors. For example, he constantly tends to equate the unconscious with the id, overlooking the superego, though in *The Trial* it

Though I believe that at times Goodman searches too hard for specific symbolic meanings, he is well aware of the abstract quality of *The Trial*. He errs, however, it seems to me, in accounting for it. "Psychologically the abstraction indicates the withdrawal of affect, anesthetizing the perceptions of ordinary experience" (p. 149). This is good psychological theory, but does not seem to me to have relevance for *The Trial*, where there is relatively little withdrawal of affect. The affect is admitted to consciousness, but disassociated from what occasions it; it is this which is repressed. K. is aware of his turbulent feelings but not of what causes them.

The point is unimportant in itself, but worth mentioning because it is typical: most of what few errors Goodman makes are due to his getting outside the framework of the novel. Repressed homosexuality is clinically associated with paranoia and as I have suggested is present in *The Trial*, but not, in my judgment, to anywhere near the extent Goodman maintains. Similarly, when (perhaps simply out of carelessness) Goodman refers to K.'s "falling in love" with Fräulein Bürstner, I feel sure that he is thinking, not of *The Trial*, but of Kafka's feeling for F. A final, and more important, error comes from considering the novel in terms of an extrinsic philosophical standard. Goodman begins his book by assessing Kafka's thought, particularly as it reveals itself in his aphorisms. But, unlike an aphorism or an essay, a novel cannot be profitably dealt with in terms of its truth or falsity; it is not so much a statement of the writer's beliefs as it is a projection, by means of character and situation, of his wishes and fears. When Goodman talks of the importance of the "willful ego [relaxing] to the instincts," and of "the right use of the ego: open to the soul and the world . . ." (p. 173), I believe that he is once again thinking of Kafka, or of Kafka's thought, rather than of *The Trial*. There is never any chance that K. will use his ego in this desirable fashion. The question—if there is *any* question; the falling action of the novel starts almost at once—is whether K. will be able to maintain the weak ego organization he has to begin with or whether he will go to pieces completely.

These errors do not loom large in comparison with the many insights Goodman offers us. For example, there is the brilliant surmise that the two warders who arrest K. are brother-figures—the two younger brothers of Kafka who died in infancy. "He hated them. They die. He is

---

plays the more immediately important role. He assumes that Kafka "applied Freud's dream findings deliberately" (p. vii). In general his study is less valuable than Goodman's.

guilty of it" (p. 157). This seems to me an example of the legitimate use of biographical material. Whatever prompted the surmise, the evidence for its accuracy is in the novel. The warders eat K.'s breakfast and take his body linen. The brothers turn up again, Goodman points out, as K.'s executioners. Witness the "fat double chins . . . painful cleanliness of their faces. One could literally see that the cleansing hand had been at work in the corners of the eyes . . ." (*The Trial*, p. 283).

Goodman is particularly persuasive when he writes of the novel in social terms. Here is his interpretation of the abstractness of the Court:

> . . . these traits accurately describe the atomization of natural groups into mass-men alien to each other; the loss of meaningful productive work in the subdivision of labor; the impersonality of exchange value and bourgeois financial relations; the loss of function of the family; the distant, indirect, but all-pervasive coercion of centralized states; the lapse of individual responsibility in corporate action; the puzzlement of the little man when his life is ruled by powers he knows only by name, never face to face; the sterilization of city life from all biological experience; the discouragement of initiative by remote planning; the substitution of actuarial probabilities for proximate causes. The anonymity and mystery of the Court is little deeper than the anonymity and remoteness of every part of our economy, politics, pedagogy, entertainment—*and nevertheless the blow falls.* (p. 176)

5

A number of interpretations of *The Trial* are too superficial or confused to reward analysis. Of those which seek to probe the meaning of the book and possess internal consistency we shall consider three more, one religious, one ethical, one socio-economic. Besides giving us new perspectives for understanding *The Trial*, a glance at these interpretations may shed light on the general question of multiple response to fiction. To what extent should we accept different glosses of the same story? When are we justified in dismissing an interpretation as mistaken?

John Kelly offers a religious interpretation of *The Trial*.[11] It is an eschatological novel, he argues, as indebted to Kierkegaard's theology of crisis as is the religious thought of Karl Barth. There is an infinite distance, an incommensurability between God and man. "God is tran-

11. "*The Trial* and the Theology of Crisis," in Angel Flores, ed., *The Kafka Problem* (New York: New Directions, 1946), pp. 151–171.

scendant and absolute. . . . Any quest for Him on the part of man is point-
less, for there is no way up to Him" (p. 157). At his moment of crisis,
Joseph K. accepts his trial. From that moment, "Bit by bit, the continuity
of his life is broken down, and all his reliances, habits, and safeguards
cease to operate" (p. 158). He is in the grip of the Law.

> What is the Law? What must a man do to be saved? Kafka works out
> his hero's problem by basing his allegory on the prophetic writings
> of the Old Testament, and on Calvin's Pauline Christianity, absorbed
> through Kierkegaard. The most bewildering problem which con-
> fronts Joseph K. after his arrest is that of his 'guilt.' In the court of-
> fices, K. encounters some other 'claimed' men. 'They did not stand
> quite erect, their backs remained bowed, their knees bent, they
> stood like street beggars. K. waited for the Law-Court Attendant,
> who kept slightly behind him, and said: "How humbled they must
> be!" "Yes," said the Law-Court Attendant, "these are accused men,
> all of them are accused of guilt." "Indeed!" said K. "Then they're col-
> leagues of mine." ' Thus sarcastically, humorously, tentatively, K.
> fumbles with the notion of his own 'guilt' for a time; but, in the end,
> he is so convinced of it that he wills his own destruction in expia-
> tion. He evolves into a Pauline Christian. (pp. 158–159)

"Guilt," it is to be noted, is a key word in this interpretation, and
Kelly tends to accept guilt as an absolute. But Kafka does not simply describe K.'s guilt; he explains it, albeit in symbolic and elliptical fashion.
The analytically oriented critic cannot fail to feel that his first task is to
decode and piece out the explanation. K.'s guilt is to be understood, not
taken for granted. Nevertheless, I can see no basis for rejecting Kelly's
interpretation. Though he makes one or two mistakes—e.g., "Women
cease to concern [K.]"—he provides a key by which most of the major
happenings in The Trial can be explained. The key leads to some beautiful insights: "The final scene is . . . conceived in an atmosphere of ritual:
the ceremonial attitude of the executioners, the questions of prece-
dence that arise between them, the pains taken to find a suitable sacrifi-
cial stone" (p. 169).

In Man for Himself[12] Erich Fromm offers a superficially psychological
but basically ethical interpretation of The Trial, which is further elabo-
rated in The Forgotten Language.[13] Fromm's interpretation rests upon
the belief that there are two consciences. The first, the authoritarian

12. Man for Himself, An Inquiry into the Psychology of Ethics (New York:
Rinehart, 1947), pp. 167–171.
13. The Forgotten Language (New York: Rinehart, 1951), pp. 249–263.

conscience, is the same as the Freudian superego: it is "the internalized voice of an authority whom we are eager to please and afraid of displeasing."[14] There is also a humanistic conscience. It is "the reaction of our total personality to its proper functioning or disfunctioning . . . knowledge of our . . . success or failure in the art of living."[15] K.'s guilt feeling, Fromm maintains, is to a considerable extent a reaction of his humanistic conscience. It expresses his dissatisfaction with his sterile and unproductive life.

Now there is no doubt that K.'s life was sterile and unproductive, if judged from the perspective of someone poignantly aware of the potentialities of an ideal and ideally adjusted human being. Nor is there any doubt that K. himself felt some degree of dissatisfaction about his life and some anxiety about the future, and that these contributed to his collapse. But there is no evidence that his dissatisfaction was so acute as to have precipitated his collapse, or that his work was an important source of such dissatisfaction as he felt. In picturing K. as a person who had creative abilities and impulses which he felt were being thwarted, Fromm seems to me to be using *The Trial* to substantiate certain of his own theories. Judged in K.'s own terms, or in the terms of his immediate associates, he was not unproductive. A paragraph Fromm quotes to demonstrate the opposite tells us that K. was usually at his office until nine and that the Manager of the Bank "highly valued his diligence and ability." To be sure, one of the reasons K. worked as long and as hard as he did may have been to ward off anxiety. But until the Bürstner affair the device served its purpose; indeed, the security he felt at the Bank was one of the last of his defenses to crumble. In the area of work, it can be maintained, K. had found an adjustment which enabled him to make the most of his meager psychological resources.

It was a reaching out of an altogether different sort, not for greater productiveness, or increased autonomy, but simply for a more satisfactory love object, that was responsible for K.'s collapse. In terms of his psychosexual organization, Fräulein Bürstner satisfied "higher," that is, more mature, needs than the prostitute, Elsa. Ironically, that is why K.'s desire for her aroused deep guilt and an ultimately overpowering need for punishment. I cannot refrain from adding that I believe this is something Fromm would have seen at an earlier stage of his career, before his zeal for grafting ethical tenets upon psychoanalysis caused him to slight more primitive drives and conflicts.

Hannah Arendt sees *The Trial* as the legend of a man's forced sub-

14. *Man for Himself,* p. 158.
15. Ibid.

mission to a world " of necessity and injustice and lying."[16] His feelings of guilt are exploited to make him adapt himself to existing conditions. On one level, the novel is a critique of the bureaucratic regime of the pre-war Austrian government, from whose "senseless automatism" no man might expect justice. More broadly, it is a critique of an entire society "which has established itself as a substitute for God," a world in which the laws of men are looked upon as though they were divine laws. According to Miss Arendt, behind all of Kafka's work there is an ideal image of the man of good will, the (Hegelian-Marxian) *fabricator mundi*, a man who wants to remake the world "in accordance with human needs and dignities, [to create] a world where man's actions are determined by himself and which is ruled by his laws and not by mysterious forces emanating from above or from below" (p. 421). K. dies like a dog, feeling that the shame of his death will outlive him, because he submits instead of attempting to build such a world.

There is much in *The Trial* which Miss Arendt's interpretation leaves unexplained. She does not tell us, for example, why K. was suddenly overcome by guilt, nor attempt to account for the novel's sexual episodes and imagery. But she enriches our understanding of the abstract objective meaning of the novel. It is certainly possible to include the state and capitalism among the anonymous forces against which K. struggles.

6

It is not, however, *necessary* to include them. Miss Arendt makes the opposite assumption—that her reading of *The Trial* is the only correct one. She expresses impatience in particular with religious and psychoanalytic interpretations. Now the belief that one reading of a literary work invalidates all others is certainly not unusual. What amounts to a theoretical defense of the belief appears in *Theory of Literature* by Rene Wellek and Austin Warren:[17] "The real poem," they maintain, "must be conceived as a structure of norms, realized only partially in the actual experience of its many readers"—a *complex* system of norms, to be sure, "made up of several strata," but nevertheless a single fixed thing. Wellek and Warren compare a work of art to a system of language. Just as a language has a "fundamental coherence and identity," even though this is realized only imperfectly in any individual speech act, so, they argue, a work of art has

16. "Franz Kafka: A Revaluation," *Partisan Review* (Fall 1944), p. 413.
17. *Theory of Literature*, New York: Harcourt Brace, 1949. The quotations are from pages 151, 152 and 153.

one correct meaning which no individual experience of it can hope to realize completely.

What makes Miss Arendt's position interesting is that she seems on the verge of discovering another possibility. The search for religious significance in *The Trial* began, she feels, because "to the public of the twenties, bureaucracy did not seem an evil great enough to explain the horror and terror expressed in the novel."[18] If she had asked herself why it *did* seem great enough to explain the horror in the novel to her, she would have discovered, I believe, that it was because of her particular political orientation—an orientation which is clearly grounded on deep feelings as well as intellectual convictions. She might then have made the still more significant discovery that other people, with different backgrounds, might have read the novel in different, but perhaps equally valid, ways.

In fact, a great work of narrative art, quite unlike a system of language, can never be reduced to a single "correct" meaning; it is a symbolical structure admitting of many different interpretations. Some of these, to be sure, may be superficial or otherwise inadequate, incomplete, or altogether erroneous. But others may be of approximately equal validity and worth—as incommensurate as different imaginative works of relatively equal stature.

A corollary of the fact that a story says different things to different readers is that its meaning does not remain fixed: it changes with the experience readers bring to bear upon it, and that experience includes the broad historical developments which affect our lives. Many readers of *The Trial* have been struck by the resemblance between the Court which persecuted K. and the fascist state. The resemblance does not mean that Kafka was a prophet. It is simply a striking example of the fact that upon completion a story acquires an autonomous existence and through time may gain levels of meaning and reference its author could not have anticipated.

18.   "Franz Kafka: A Revaluation," p. 414.

❀ The Role of Unconscious Understanding in Flaubert and Dostoevsky

NORMAL jealousy, Freud observes, is "by no means completely rational . . . it is rooted in the unconscious, it is a continuation of the earliest stirrings of the child's affective life. . . ."[1] Moreover, he continues, "it is noteworthy that in many persons it is experienced bisexually; that is to say, in a man, besides the suffering in regard to the loved woman and the hatred against the male rival, grief in regard to the unconsciously loved man and hatred of the woman as a rival will add to its intensity."

As Freud elsewhere rather ruefully acknowledged, writers of fiction had frequently been vouchsafed an understanding of psychological mechanisms earlier (and he felt more easily) than he and his colleagues. A half-century before Freud wrote, Dostoevsky displayed full unconscious understanding of normal jealousy experienced bisexually in several of his works, most especially *The Idiot*.

Some twelve years before the appearance of *The Idiot* in 1868, Gustave Flaubert published *Madame Bovary*, parts of which revolve around triangular situations. But neither of the triangles is developed in a way which shows more than a trace of the kind of knowledge Dostoevsky unconsciously possessed and communicated.

It is interesting to compare the way Flaubert and Dostoevsky handle these triangular situations because, as I shall try to show, they had quite similar psychosexual organizations. Both were bisexual; both firmly re-

Reprinted from *Daedalus*, Spring 1963.
1. Sigmund Freud, "Certain Neurotic Mechanisms in Jealousy, Paranoia and Homosexuality," in *Collected Papers*, vol. 2 (London: Hogarth, 1924), pp. 232–233.

pressed or sublimated their homosexual feelings. Might not Flaubert, then, have "known" at some level all that Dostoevsky knew and, if he did, would he not have tended to endow Charles or one of the other male characters with some glimmering of his own unconscious understanding? If he didn't know or, knowing, withheld the knowledge from his characters or for some other reason was unable to make use of it, what accounts for this? And how does it happen that Dostoevsky *was* able to use his knowledge, though he, too, it must be emphasized, was never able to confront his homosexual tendencies?

If we can answer these questions even in part, if we can identify at least some of the factors which inhibited Flaubert and which explain Dostoevsky's unconscious understanding and his ability to make such good use of it, our knowledge of the creative process will be importantly enhanced.

In *The Idiot,* the three principal characters—Prince Myshkin, Rogozhin, and Nastasya Filippovna—are locked in an intense and highly complex relationship which for all of them, though in different ways and on different levels of awareness, gratifies deep-seated libidinal and sado-masochistic needs. From the time the two male characters meet in the opening chapter of the novel, they are drawn to one another—in part because Rogozhin's sadism meshes perfectly with Myshkin's masochism but also, we come to see, because of repressed homosexual feelings. However, they quickly become involved in a to-the-death struggle for Nastasya; the most dramatic portions of the novel focus on this struggle and the way the confused and tormented heroine vacillates between her two unlike lovers, fanning their jealousy and hatred—for *her* as well as for one another. At the same time we see that she is a link between the rivals, each of whom acts out some of his feelings for the other through her. No more than occasional hints are needed to make us realize that their mutual jealousy is based in part on "grief in regard to the unconsciously loved man and hatred of the woman as a rival."

Since Myshkin represses his unsanctioned impulses even as he acts some of them out through his more passionate companions, all of his stronger feelings, including his jealousy, must be conveyed to us by means of unconscious manifestations or other forms of indirect evidence. There is abundant evidence of this sort for both Myshkin's inability to give up Nastasya and for his enmity toward Rogozhin. In the nature of the case, the evidence of the bisexual component of his jealousy is still more carefully hidden. The hatred we would expect to find for Nastasya is completely denied: it is, as it were, taken care of by Rogozhin and replaced in Myshkin by feelings deriving from it—fear and pity. In the long middle section of the novel, the Prince's grief and unextirpated feelings for Rogozhin have to be conveyed by small indications of continuing interest, for Rogozhin is seldom on-scene; but the business of that section of the novel is Myshkin's effort to make a reasonably normal adjustment to Russian society and to free himself from the neurotic triangular relationship with Nastasya and Rogozhin, which despite his efforts continues to hold him.

For the most part Rogozhin's jealousy, unlike Myshkin's, is revealed quite openly. Even his hatred of Nastasya is directly expressed, though we may tend to assume that it stems solely from the suffering she has caused him. But if there is any doubt that she is hated also *as a rival,* and that to the very end there is a strong homosexual bond between Rogozhin and Myshkin, it is dispelled in the stunning climax of the novel. In that scene, there is no hatred or jealousy; the books have been closed on both emotions. Nastasya Filippovna has been killed by the tortured Rogozhin. The Prince has been looking for him, and in due time Rogozhin goes out, looks for and finds the Prince. Speaking only in whispers he leads Myshkin to a gloomy, darkened room in his gloomy home and shows him the corpse of the woman who had been at once a bond between them and the cause of their separation and rivalry. Even though Rogozhin is now half-demented, his homosexual feelings, like the Prince's, remain unacknowledged. Still, one idea obsesses him: he and his friend must sleep together, keep vigil over the dead Nastasya and not let anyone take her away:

> It was clear that he had thought of the bed perhaps even that morning. The night before he had lain down on the sofa. But there was no room for two on the sofa, and he had made up his mind that they should lie side by side, and that was why he now dragged, with a great effort, cushions of all shapes and sizes across the whole room from the two sofas and placed them near the curtain. Somehow or other he managed to make up the bed; he then went up to the prince, took him tenderly and rapturously by the arm, raised him up, and led him to the bed; . . .[2]

Even if we disregard the evidence which could be culled from some

2.   Fyodor Dostoevsky, *The Idiot.* Translated by David Magarshack (Baltimore: Penguin Books, 1961), p. 654. For a fuller discussion of the novel, see Lesser, "Saint and Sinner—Dostoevsky's 'Idiot,' " in *Modern Fiction Studies,* vol. 4, no. 3 (Autumn 1958).

of his other works, it seems clear that at the unconscious level Dostoevsky knew everything there is to know about the kind of normal jealousy in which a tender feeling for the male rival plays a part. The unconscious nature of the knowledge must be emphasized. Myshkin was conceived as a Christ-like character, and if anyone had asked Dostoevsky if the Prince had any sexually tinged feeling for another man I feel sure that the idea would have been angrily repudiated. On the other hand, the inclusive nature of the knowledge must be stressed also. At one place or another Dostoevsky shows an awareness of practically all the components of jealousy Freud discusses. The word "intuitive," insofar as it suggests a flashing, partial kind of insight, is quite inadequate to describe his knowledge. It seems almost worthy of being called comprehensive.

In *Madame Bovary*, Flaubert reveals no such unconscious understanding of jealousy in depicting either Emma's relationship with Rodolphe (Part Two) or her relationship with Leon (Part Three). Charles unwittingly helps to set up both of his wife's affairs. He has conscious knowledge of some of her meetings with Rodolphe, and both affairs are so protracted and ill-concealed that, were we dealing with real life, we would have to assume that Charles would be compelled to utilize repression or some other defense mechanism not to become at least fugitively aware of them. But Charles is not shown to have any feeling for either of Emma's lovers. Indeed, it is not granted him to display any feelings of jealousy whatever, nor—if we except one occasion when he is forced to wonder if "something" wasn't wrong—any suspicions. Nor do Rodolphe and Leon have any but the most casual feelings for him.

Since Charles is intended to be an example of bourgeois stupidity, our first inclination might be to attribute his blindness to conscious artistic intent. But a close look at the novel suggests that Flaubert's artistic purposes neither required him to make Charles anywhere nearly as blind as he is nor were well served by his doing so. *Madame Bovary* begins and ends with Charles; his role not only allows but calls for him to be the second most interesting character in the novel. Instead, most of the time he is a "flat" character, not only unexciting to Emma—that *is*, of course, part of the conscious design—but to us. Significantly, he escapes these limitations and comes to life only in those moments when he is vouchsafed a degree of understanding—at the end of the novel when he becomes consciously aware of Emma's infidelities and, after the debacle of the operation, when turning to her for sympathy he is rejected so harshly that he weeps, "feeling vaguely as though some baneful, incomprehensible influence were hovering about him." [3]

In terms of our analysis, "vague feelings" can be equated with unconscious apprehensions—and all we are discussing, it should be remembered, is the possible wisdom of permitting Charles to show more understanding on this level. He could have been granted many more such apprehensions, I submit, and the artistic results would be entirely beneficent: he would have still been plodding and pedestrian, quite obtuse enough to irritate his easily irritated wife, but he would be far more appealing to the reader. Instead of a caricature or figure in a morality play, which is what he now seems for long stretches, he would be a rounded human being. He would arouse our sympathy and compassion, not simply our pity.

Granted such apprehensions, moreover, he could have been permitted to become dimly suspicious of his wife and the innocence of her rides with Rodolphe and, later, her visits to Rouen. Then he could have even been shown to have some covert feelings about the other men Emma was seeing or might be seeing. Jealousy after all, even when conscious, is an affective state, and not incompatible with stupidity. Interestingly, however, not even Leon and Rodolphe, who are pictured as somewhat more intelligent than Charles, are allowed any of the feelings I am suggesting Charles might have been shown to entertain, to the benefit rather than the detriment of *Madame Bovary* as a novel.

The *excessive* stupidity that Chalres exhibits to almost the very end of the novel and the complete lack of feeling among the men romantically involved with Emma point in quite a different direction from "conscious design." They suggest that some powerful hidden forces must have been working on the writer who created these characters, forces that drove him to keep Charles almost completely blind and to keep Rodolphe and Leon selectively blind and anesthetized. The writer in question was not only highly intelligent and talented but bisexual— capable, we might suppose, of creating male characters only a shade less complex than Dostoevsky's. Though the pertinency of the observation may not be immediately apparent, let us keep in mind the fact that he *did* create Emma Bovary.

The whole pattern of Flaubert's life reveals his bisexuality. He never married. He lived with his mother almost his entire life. The one woman to whom he felt romantically attracted, Elisa Schlesinger, was clearly a

3.   Gustave Flaubert, *Madame Bovary*. Translated by Alan Russel (Baltimore: Penguin Books, 1961).

mother surrogate. When Gustave met her during a long seaside holiday in the summer of 1836, he was all of fourteen; she was already twenty-six, married and the mother of an infant. His one protracted sexual relationship with a woman, the affair with Louise Colet, was intermittent and stormy. His fear and dislike of her were almost as strong as his passion, with the result that even in the first and most ardent phase of their relationship, which lasted about two years, he found reasons for seeing her only six times, and then for short periods. In contrast, Flaubert had three idealized, long-continued and highly satisfying relationships with men, and even some of the vicissitudes these relationships underwent hint at his latent homosexuality: for example, he never entirely forgave his adored friend Alfred Le Poittevin for marrying.

Flaubert's relationships with his parents help to explain, if they do not foreshadow, his psychosexual development. His father, Achille-Cleophas Flaubert, was head of the municipal hospital of Rouen—successful, highly regarded, and, the evidence suggests, authoritative: altogether a formidable figure. It may be conjectured that Gustave never worked out his Oedipal hostility, envy and fear of his father—the preliminary to achieving a satisfactory identification with him. Flaubert's arrested sexual development and inability, even after his father's death, to achieve a good relationship with a woman is only one strand of evidence for this failure. It is perhaps equally significant that, when he was twenty-one, despite his peremptory literary ambitions, he bowed to his father's will and agreed to study for the law. He did not contrive his escape until his second year in law school and then not by asserting his independence but by the roundabout means of succumbing to a crippling illness, evidently hysterical in nature. By the time he had recovered, some two years later, his father, and also his sister, had died. Now Gustave felt free to pursue his own choice of career. He settled down with his idealized and beloved mother on an estate his father had bought at Croisset, on the Seine outside Rouen, and, except for travel and visits, never thereafter left her or it. Some of the letters he wrote his mother during his absences contain declarations of love which would be less embarrassing if they were addressed to a wife or a mistress rather than a mother. When his mother died, in April 1872, only eight years before Gustave's death, he wrote Georges Sand: "I have realized during the past fortnight that my poor dear mother was the human being I loved the most." This was not a mere expression of grief, or hyperbole, but the literal truth.

The kind of arrestment evident in Gustave's relations with his parents may easily lead to overt homosexuality or some form of perversion. It is not surprising that Flaubert had a deep fear of marriage and fatherhood, which found expression in his life, his letters and his fiction, that his sexual urge was enfeebled, and that his one attempt to achieve a relatively "normal" relationship with a woman was unsuccessful. In extenuation it might be urged that the woman, Louise Colet, was aggressive and dominating, and perhaps also more than ordinarily passionate and demanding, the embodiment of some of the things that made women frightening. But it is possible that if she had not been somewhat masculine Flaubert would not have been attracted to her, and that if she had not been ardent enough to encourage his timid advances, he would not have possessed her. In any case our sympathies tend to shift to her when we find Flaubert maintaining that "when two persons love, they can go ten years without seeing each other and without suffering any ill effects therefrom."

The relationships with men were less demanding and less threatening. The three men with whom Flaubert had protracted relationships, Alfred Le Poittevin, Louis Bouilhet and Maxime Du Camp, were not only congenial but shared Flaubert's literary interests and his commitment to Art with a capital A. They were respected and trusted; indeed, in retrospect, it would appear that Flaubert overestimated the talent of his friends. His faith in their literary judgment was astonishing. He abandoned the first draft of *The Temptation of Saint Anthony*, which he had hoped would be a "thunderclap" and had worked on for three years, when Louis and Maxime told him it was bad. While the friendships were nourished by a mutuality of interests, it is clear that they were libidinally gratifying also. With the exception of Flaubert's attachment to his mother, the relationships with his male friends may be said to have dominated his affective life.

Flaubert's dread of having to face his latent homosexuality was evidently intense. It must be assumed that a great deal of psychic energy was consumed throughout his life in keeping any indications of it from consciousness. Even if no other forces had been operating upon him during the composition of *Madame Bovary*, it seems probable that this dread would have been powerful enough to stir the defensive operations of the unconscious ego into activity and to prevent Charles from being characterized in a way that would betray his creator's well-kept secret.

As it happens, however, the one unconscious factor was powerfully reinforced by others. The combined strength of these factors, which of course made themselves felt collectively, had a decisive influence, I believe, on the way Charles was delineated.

The first reinforcing factor is a supreme example of the kind of cunning accommodations which are sometimes arrived at in the psyche, and which find expression in neurotic symptoms and dreams as well as in art. Flaubert *did* manage to find an outlet for his bisexual urges in writing *Madame Bovary:* he found it in securely disguised form through his identification with Emma. This identification was not only more hidden and hence less dangerous; it offered infinitely richer opportunities for libidinal gratification. Moreover, the identification was an easier one for Flaubert to slip into. He had an acceptable preconscious reason for identifying with Emma. In essence her situation was his own: he too felt that he was being deprived and thwarted by a stupid society, indifferent to his deepest needs. Behind Emma, moreover, there perhaps lurked another woman. It may be conjectured that Flaubert's closest identification in infancy was with his mother rather than with his father. His bisexuality is warrant for the further assumption that the pattern of using identification with a woman as a means of securing libidinal gratification may also have already been laid down.

There was infinite duplicity in this identification. Flaubert could declare "Madame Bovary, c'est moi!" and anticipate that readers would see no more than that she was a symbol of his own rebellion against bourgeois society. He even had a second prepared position to retreat to. Since Emma was a woman, not even the recognition that she was bisexual would divulge the fact that *he* was—or compel him to recognize it.

Nevertheless, it must be assumed that at some level Flaubert "knew" what kind of forbidden gratifications he was experiencing through his little Emma and that certain concessions had to be made to placate his ego and superego. The first of these may be conceived as a kind of pact arrived at by the warring factions in Flaubert's psyche. His libido was permitted this gratification only on condition that it not be noticed; Flaubert as Charles must not know what Flaubert as Emma was up to—and be surprised, outraged and broken when at long last he finds out. If Emma is the representative of Flaubert's libido or id, Charles is, *inter alia,* the representative of his hoodwinked ego. This way of structuring the situation brings us to the second concession made to secure the libidinal gratification. If Charles had to be punished for his obliging blindness, Emma had to be punished still more severely for her illicit and destructive behavior. From one point of view *Madame Bovary* may be regarded as a cautionary tale, and the person for whom the "danger" signal was primarily intended was Flaubert himself. If Emma had been less drastically punished, or vouchsafed more happiness, his own bisexual impulses might have become harder to control.

There is more evidence than can or need be cited of Emma's bisexuality. If one disregards such incidental indications as her envy of Rodolphe's promiscuity and her reasons for desiring a boy rather than a girl, Emma's masculine tendencies are betrayed by her efforts to dominate all of the men in her life. She succeeds not only with Charles but with Leon. "He had become her mistress rather than she his" (p. 289). Rodolphe alone escapes being mastered by her—and he because he recognizes that she is "tyrannical and interfering" (p. 202) and is sufficiently uninvolved to defend himself adroitly. Through the identification with Emma, Flaubert secured rich vicarious gratification of both his masculine and feminine sexual needs.

The gratification had a curious secondary consequence: it reduced the need to use Charles (and of course Rodolphe and Leon also) for the same purpose. Thus the forces in Flaubert which were mobilized to keep him from endowing Charles with his own psychosexual organization did not have to fight as hard as they otherwise might have. But the effects upon the novel itself of the almost too satisfactory discharge of libido through Emma, are mixed. Her bisexuality contributes to her complexity and almost preternatural vitality. But the full erotic release Flaubert secures through Emma is partly responsible, I believe, for the devitalization and partial desexualization of the men with whom she becomes involved, most especially Charles. If all three men strike us as somewhat pallid, it is in part an indirect result of the liberality with which Flaubert provides Emma with libido and opportunities for gratifying it.

As though it were not enough to want to deprive Charles of his own bisexuality and keep him in blindness about Emma, Flaubert had still another reason for picturing his leading male protagonist as obtuse and futile: he hated him.

This hatred, like the sympathy for Emma, had a conscious or preconscious basis and a deep under-structure. At a scarcely concealed level Charles represents an abhorred aspect of the abhorred bourgeoisie: their dullness, their torpor, their almost animal-like preoccupation with bodily and material things. But Flaubert hated these aspects of the bourgeoisie, there is reason to believe, because they represented the fulfillment of certain of his own tendencies which he feared and fought unremittingly: they represented what he felt he might become if he did not devote himself to art and what he sometimes thought of himself as being even though he *did* devote himself to it—a too passive, dull, stodgy, plodding human being. Usually Flaubert plumed himself upon the slowness with which he worked—it was testimony, he assured himself, to his scrupulousness as an artist—but at other times, most especially during the period when he was writing *Madame Bovary*, he could not down the fear that, on the contrary, his snail-like progress revealed his limitations.[4] Actually, if Flaubert could not write *Bovary*, as he lamented, at anywhere near the speed at which he had written *The Temptation of Saint Anthony*, it was chiefly, I believe, because he was treading on eggs. The fear of divulging his homosexuality not only compelled him to make numerous delicate adjustments, of the kind here discussed, but to screen everything even more carefully than he usually did to make sure that the devices and disguises he was resorting to were achieving their purpose. Whether the fears of being a plodder were justified or not, it must have afforded Flaubert considerable relief to be able to project them onto Charles. He felt no conflict about depicting *him* as sluggish. Indeed, impelled by his dislike and the need to make Charles also a cautionary figure, an image of what he, Flaubert, might become if he yielded to his passive inclinations, he pictured him as totally devoid of drive and ability. There is some irony in the fact that the more stupid and spiritless he was made, the more he was hated by his creator.

At a still deeper level, Charles represented a still earlier enemy. Behind the bungling, unsuccessful, lightly regarded Officer of Health, it is possible to discern a wish-fulfilling reversed portrait of Flaubert's evidently competent, eminently successful and highly regarded father. Looked at closely, all the essential parts of the portrait fall into place. Apart from being decent and well-meaning, Dr. Flaubert was conscientious and hard working. His son concedes this much, and assigns these qualities to Charles. But did Gustave's father really know what he was about during all those interminable hours he spent in the hospital and in the morgue where Gustave and his sister Caroline, for whom Dr. Flaubert had no time, would sometimes spy on him, though they knew that if they were noticed, they would be frowned at and waved away. It may be supposed that, if only because the tasks which preempted nearly all his father's time were resented, his excluded son, struggling with the conflicting emotions of admiration and envy, sometimes doubted his father's competence.

Gustave had a better objective basis for thinking his father unperceptive. Beginning in boyhood Gustave had begun to write plays and stories; his literary ambitions had real substance. Nevertheless, Dr. Flaubert had decreed that his son should study for the law. Nor did he show any more understanding when his son became seriously ill. More than a year and a half after his first attack, Gustave, who had recovered

4.   For some particularly striking expressions of this fear, see Francis Steegmuller, *Flaubert and Madame Bovary* (London: Collins, 1947), pp. 269–270.

sufficiently to do a great deal of additional writing, summoned the courage to speak to his father about pursuing a literary career. Dr. Flaubert agreed to listen to some of his son's work, then fell asleep during the reading! Awakening, he neither apologized, commented on what he may have heard, or offered his son an opportunity to continue the reading. He simply remarked, "If a pen had been *my* only tool, my family would have starved" and took his departure. Thereafter Gustave felt open animosity towards his father and expressed it in letters to his literary friends.

Flaubert's hatred of Charles had many sources, conscious and unconscious. Whereas he satisfied his unacknowledged sexual cravings through Emma, he discharged his no less intense aggressive feelings *upon* Charles. But one would not be justified in leaping to the conclusion that such hostility inevitably has deleterious artistic effects. In *Madame Bovary* itself there is a character who should make us hesitate about accepting so sweeping a generalization: Homais. So far as one can tell, the hatred felt for Homais was much closer to the surface. But I believe that the nature of their roles does far more to explain the quite different ways Flaubert's hostility affected his portrayals of Charles and Homais. A negative quality of Charles is stressed—his stupidity. Flaubert could document it easily by piling blow upon blow—by making Charles unperceptive time after time, by having him invariably say just the wrong thing. In contrast, to bring out Homais' hateful qualities—for example, the disparities between his progressive facade and his actual conduct, in particular the indefatigability, cunning and even unscrupulousness with which he pursued his self-interest—Flaubert was compelled to invent and specify, to show Homais saying and doing a wide variety of things, many of them interesting precisely because they betray his duplicity.

We may have chanced here on a general point of some importance. Many discussions of the creative process seem to take it for granted that certain factors affecting it are desirable or undesirable *in themselves,* that they always have substantially the same effects. In actuality, matters are probably seldom so simple. What is of decisive importance in many if not most instances, the present study would suggest, is rather the way the various conscious, preconscious and unconscious forces playing upon an author interact with one another and intersect with the requirements of a particular work or those parts of it affected by the forces.

As a writer of fiction if not as a man, Dostoevsky was more fortunate than Flaubert. Because of his real-life experience and above all his incredibly rich psychic activity, Dostoevsky knew more than the French novelist about the human heart—knew more, in a sense which must be carefully defined, than all but a handful of the people who have ever lived. A relatively large amount of this extraordinary fund of knowledge was actually available to him. Even the conditions under which he worked, though they cost him great suffering, were advantageous to his art; they virtually precluded his screening his material to see what it might reveal about himself. All of these things set the stage for him to create such characters as Myshkin and Rogozhin and to endow them with his bisexuality, his sado-masochistic tendencies and many other characteristics of which his own psyche was the original source. In addition, as I shall try to show, there were forces in Dostoevsky prodding him to use the kind of material which appears in *The Idiot* and his other great works, material many writers would have shunned if it had been available to them to begin with. The nature of Dostoevsky's psychic activity, structure and needs happened to mesh perfectly with the requirements of his craft.

In a sense Dostoevsky's experience is the ultimate source of the almost unparalleled knowledge of character he displays. He was a more complex and comprehensive person than Flaubert. His internal as well as his external experience was more varied and more intense. But if his psychic structure had been different, much less of his knowledge would have been at his disposal for later use. It must be assumed that throughout Dostoevsky's life, not simply when he was engaged in writing fiction, many questionable ideas gained admission to consciousness, and that some of them were either not securely repressed or not repressed at all. In effect, he accumulated a file about the vagaries of the psyche—or, more accurately, *files,* for the knowledge was stored at all levels—conscious, preconscious and unconscious.

For our purposes the essential point to observe about Dostoevsky's psychic structure is that throughout his life both his instinctual impulses and his superego possessed extraordinary strength; his ego was squeezed between these powerful antagonists. It was never able to reconcile their conflicting claims well enough to achieve a stable balance. There was almost continuous intrapsychic warfare; and the conflicting claims of id and superego could barely be controlled, much less silenced. In disguised if not direct fashion they frequently forced themselves into awareness. One has the feeling that in Dostoevsky the barriers between unconscious, preconscious and conscious were exceptionally permeable. That "flexibility of the repressions" which plays such a vital part in creative achievement, and which some artists go to extraordinary lengths to bring about, imposed itself upon Dostoevsky.

Dostoevsky not only had comparatively easy "access to the unconscious"; in his case the unconscious seems to have been in a more or less constant state of eruption. His notes and letters and reports of his conversations, as well as his fiction, indicate that he was frequently presented with "ideas" which in all probability would never have occurred to a writer like Flaubert. It would be a mistake to assume that all the ideas which hovered on the threshhold of Dostoevsky's mind could be entertained without anxiety. A frequent purpose of his epileptic attacks, I suspect, was one he ascribed to Myshkin: to keep certain ideas from consciousness.

A second consequence of Dostoevsky's psychic organization is that his ego was too busily occupied and perhaps too careless, even demoralized, to subject the material used in his fiction to careful screening to exclude disturbing material or material which might reveal something damaging about Dostoevsky himself. Here also it is easy to exaggerate matters. It is likely both that some screening went on and that the use of certain material involved a heavy cost. But as compared with Flaubert and most other writers Dostoevsky was not fussy. It would seldom have been feasible for him to be so even if the inclination were there. The same kinds of intemperate impulses reveal themselves in practically all the material which presented itself to him for possible use in his fiction, including the variant plans he sometimes developed before proceeding with a particular work. Moreover, Dostoevsky could seldom bring himself to get down to work until his situation was so desperate that he had to produce at frantic speed. The Idiot was written under harrowing conditions.

Dostoevsky's use of his unconscious knowledge was also facilitated by the fact that his imagination was predominantly dramatic and visual. In consequence he did not have to "understand" his material in the customary sense of that word. His knowledge came to him in concrete and often disguised form—as an idea for a story, a particular scene, or an incidental bit of "business" (Myshkin twice absent-mindedly picking up a knife during his first visit to Rogozhin's home). The significance of the material was not intellectually grasped, or at best was grasped but dimly, even as it was being used; Dostoevsky could show characters doing or feeling certain things which he was sure they would do or feel, even though he could not fully explain why this was so. This is a strange sort of knowledge perhaps; yet long before Freud its existence was occasionally noted. In the "Apology" Plato has Socrates declare: "[Poets] are like diviners or soothsayers who also say many fine things, but do not understand the meaning of them."[5]

5.   See Lesser, Fiction and the Unconscious (Boston: Beacon Press, 1957), especially chapters 6 and 9, for a fuller discussion of the way meanings may be transmitted in fiction without being formulated in conceptual terms.

As is obvious, this kind of knowledge is not readily available for general intellectual purposes, for example as a basis for generalizations and abstract thought or as a clue to self-understanding. Certainly it was not available to Dostoevsky for such purposes; he was not a conceptual thinker nor—despite the skill with which he analyzed his characters—possessed of much insight into his own behavior. However, his knowledge, in the form in which it was possessed, was an asset of incalculable value for a writer of fiction.

"Sometimes when my heart is swimming with love," Dostoevsky wrote his brother Mikhail while still a young man, "you can't pull a kind word out of me." Did he know, then, of the extent to which irritability, sullenness and spitefulness are often based on repressed hostility? In a way, yes. He "knew" well enough to make the unprepossessing "hero" of Notes from Underground not only credible but in the end, half against our will, sympathetic. He used the knowledge also in drawing the principals in "The Eternal Husband," Trusotsky and Velchaninov, and a host of other characters. But he did not know what he knew in a way which would have permitted him to state his knowledge in general terms, or to identify repressed hostility as the source of his own frequent ill-humor.

In precisely the same way, he knew a thousand other things—specific things, the way that the discovery of some small detail can make one decide on a course of action which until then had seemed conjectural and unreal; or the way two apparently contradictory ideas can occur to one at the same time. He knew how difficult it is to love your neighbor as yourself, and how invariably even intense love is admixed with hate. He knew how readily impulses to such crimes as calumny, profligacy, rape, pedophilia, murder and even parricide could find a haven not simply in the hearts of "others"—for example, abandoned criminals—but in people like himself, intelligent and capable of generous and idealistic feelings. He knew that the human heart is "roomy," capable of accommodating more loves and more kinds of love than morality would always sanction or common sense find coherent.

In the same way, also, Dostoevsky knew everything he has Myshkin, Rogozhin and Nastasya Filippovna feel or experience. His repressed hostility and ambivalence have been referred to. The whole pattern of his life bears witness to the presence of the sadistic and masochistic tendencies with which he endowed the three principal characters in The Idiot, and his sadism would be even more apparent were it not that, as Freud points out, most of it was directed against his own person; it was one of the factors responsible for his strong sense of guilt. He had had one neurotic, unhappy marriage with a woman with whom, at times at least, he may have been impotent. He had formed warm relationships with both this woman's first husband and the young man in Kuznetzk to whom she became attached after her husband's death. There are still other indications of latent homosexuality, but it is perhaps unnecessary to marshal the evidence; the diagnosis has already been made by so qualified an observer as Freud:

> . . . Such a [bisexual] predisposition must certainly be assumed in Dostoevsky, and it shows itself in a viable form (as latent homosexuality) in the important part played by male friendships in his life, in his strangely tender attitude towards rivals in love and in his remarkable understanding of situations which are explicable only by repressed homosexuality, as many examples from his novels show.[6]

Though Dostoevsky's unusual psychic organization helps to explain both his knowledge of man's perversity and the ease with which he could call upon that knowledge, it does not fully explain his actual use of what he knew. Another writer possessing similar knowledge might have used it sparingly or not at all, if only because of the fears of revealing or having to recognize too much which unconsciously inhibited Flaubert. Some other force was at work in Dostoevsky which *impelled* him to divulge his almost shameless understanding of the underside of the human heart even when delineating a character like Myshkin. Not until we have identified that force can we feel that our inquiry is complete.

The key to Dostoevsky's need to issue report after report on precisely those aspects of human nature which are usually permitted to go unreported, lies, I believe, in what is perhaps the salient characteristic of his personality, his "unappeasable sense of guilt."[7] We know at least some of the sources of his oppressive guilt feelings. The young Dostoevsky had an unusually severe father to contend with, and the evidence suggests that his own rebellious and aggressive feelings were exceptionally intense. If we knew no more than this, we would expect that his superego would have been exacting. The fact that his parricidal impulses would have seemed to have been fulfilled by the seditious serfs who killed his father must have revived and intensified his Oedipal guilt feelings. The onanism Freud discerns behind Dostoevsky's later passion for gambling and the accompanying fantasies may have also contributed to feelings of guilt and unworthiness. In general the demands of his

6.   Freud, "Dostoevsky and Parricide," in *Collected Papers*, vol. 5 (London: Hogarth, 1950).
7.   Avrahm Yarmolinsky, *Dostoevsky, His Life and Art* (New York: Grove Press, 1960), p. 313.

never well-subdued instincts must have been hard to accept; at times he may have thought of himself as depraved. Ironically, even some of the punishments he imposed upon himself to placate his superego—for example, his heavy losses at gambling and, of course, the abdications of responsibility to which the losses led—may have also been a source of later self-reproach. Throughout his life Dostoevsky had to wage a continual and never more than temporarily and partially successful battle against a tormenting superego.

Unconsciously, it may be assumed, Dostoevsky was constantly searching for ways of reducing the pressure of guilt. Freud has commented on one of the mechanisms he used to achieve this end, his tendency to identify with criminals. It was evidently also the need to reduce guilt which drew Dostoevsky to Christianity. What particularly appealed to him was the figure of Christ, who took the sins of mankind upon his shoulders, and the doctrine that the acknowledgment of one's sinfulness is the prerequisite for forgiveness and redemption.

Both Dostoevsky's interest in Christianity and his identification with criminals are illustrations, I believe, of a life-long tendency to rely on a single basic mechanism for reducing guilt—the acknowledgment of one's unworthiness. This, he seems to have felt, was the indispensable first step for securing forgiveness, acceptance and love. It may be conjectured that there was some prototype experience in early childhood which cut an indentation for this belief. Perhaps the young Fyodor confessed some "bad" activity, or was caught in it, and instead of being punished, or after being punished, was forgiven and assured of the continuing love of the strict but loved parent.

It seems certain that in Dostoevsky the connections between confession, forgiveness and guilt reduction were firmly fixed. He was tormented by what might be called *an urge to confess*. On a few occasions of intense emotional excitement he may have yielded to the urge directly and publicly; the evidence on this point is contradictory and uncertain.[8] But disturbed as he was, it is not to be supposed that he frequently satisfied the impulse so openly. The punishment he had endured for his early imprudences and his suspicious belief that many of his colleagues were envious of him would have reinforced the conventional reasons for reticence. But Dostoevsky must have discovered very early in life that he could *vicariously* satisfy the urge, in perfect security, through his writing. In his fiction, indeed, he could even give body to disavowed impulses and confess them as well as his misdeeds—and no one knew better than he, the creator of Ivan, Dmitri and Alyosha as well as Smerdyakov, of

8. Ibid., pp. 298–303.

Myshkin as well as Rogozhin, how inextricably interrelated the two are and how necessary it is to expiate both.

The influence of the urge to confess makes itself felt in many ways in Dostoevsky's fiction, most obviously perhaps in the frequency with which he has his characters avail themselves of it. The formal confessions, moreover, are only a small part of the whole. Much of the introspection in which Dostoevsky's characters engage and many of the interchanges between them are fragments of confession. Those of his characters who resort to crime, lechery, drink, buffoonery or some other form of self-destructive behavior as a way of becoming aware of their own unworthiness are also confessing to themselves.

Taken as a whole, moreover, most of Dostoevsky's stories are confessions, his own confessions; and they are this in a dynamic, not simply a metaphorical, sense. The strongest unconscious force propelling him to write was the urge to confess and thus alleviate feelings of guilt. More, the urge to confess determined the *kind* of fiction Dostoevsky wrote— why, for example, he wrote so frequently of unbridled egoists, criminals, sinners and wastrels, people who, however great-hearted, could not cope with their lusts, their aggressions or their responsibilities. Finally, the urge to confess explains why he wrote with such relentless honesty as he did in The Idiot and felt less inclination to suppress than to proclaim evidence of impulses other writers would not have permitted their characters to experience.

Of course, the writing of fiction provided still other satisfactions and was undertaken for still other reasons. For example, it permitted vicarious gratification of Dostoevsky's turbulent repressed impulses, and this in turn made those impulses somewhat more amenable to control. But basically, I believe, Dostoevsky wrote to relieve feelings of guilt. Through his fiction, transgressions and even impulses to transgress could be expiated by punishment and suffering. Because that which can be shared is less terrible than that which must be experienced in isolation, the clandestine confessions made through his fiction afforded some immediate relief. But more important, they offered the promise of forgiveness. In effect, Dostoevsky was confessing to an anonymous group of people, his readers; their acceptance of a story and favorable reactions to it would seem equivalent to forgiveness and love. In the aggregate, I believe, the prospect of obtaining such satisfactions as these constituted a positive incentive for doing what his peculiar psychic structure permitted him to do—disclose and body forth impulses which usually escape detection.

✦

Since this study has focussed on just a portion of the work of two writers, a question may arise about the extent to which the unconscious influences discerned, normally affect the creative process. Though the differences between Flaubert and Dostoevsky suggest the hazards of generalizing, some conclusions can, I believe, be drawn.

While the particular forces which affected Flaubert are unique, they are probably *representative* of the ways in which the unconscious influences writers generally. The subliminal dread of having to perceive something one would prefer to keep hidden almost invariably discourages the use of unconscious knowledge, though as Flaubert's treatment of Emma indicates, it does not preclude it when something struggling for expression is well enough disguised. Similarly, unconscious reasons for liking or disliking a character will almost certainly affect the way he is drawn, though the exact nature of the influence they exert will depend in part upon their relationship to conscious and preconscious attitudes, and upon the objective requirements of the characterization.

In contrast, most of the unconscious factors which help to explain Dostoevsky's achievement have a limited applicability. Among people who function well enough to be more than occasional writers, few have probably had so weak a psychic organization, poised precariously just this side of psychosis. Thus few have been vouchsafed Dostoevsky's astonishing repertory of unconscious knowledge, much less his ability to draw upon it almost at will for his fiction. Even fewer writers, it is safe to say, have been driven to write by the unconscious need to confess their unworthiness and thus reduce guilt. Only a handful of writers have been preoccupied to the extent Dostoevsky was with the seamier side of man's nature, and there is no reason for supposing that more than a minority of these shared the preoccupation out of the same inner needs which tormented Dostoevsky.

So far as I am aware, the writing of fiction is more conducive to honesty than is any other form of writing or any other activity. The fiction writer can at once confess and conceal: he can displace his own forbidden tendencies upon the characters he creates, yet make them so "real" and autonomous that few will even suspect that they are disguised versions of himself. On the basis of some dim intuitive understanding of their feelings which permits him to show what they would do, he can communicate many things about them he himself could not formulate—and might disavow if he were to hear them formulated by someone else. Thus he of all people can tell the truth—disclose rather than hide the terrible desires which haunt the fringes of his consciousness. Still, the writer of fiction is a human being, subject to the same fears and anxieties which have given birth to repression and other mechanisms for keeping unwelcome and dangerous information hidden. We can stand only so much of the truth. Let the admission of some fraction of it endanger the balance of forces in our psyche or, in however roundabout a way, threaten to reveal something about ourselves we prefer to keep hidden, and energies are mobilized to keep the dangerous tidings from consciousness. It was fortunate for literature and for humanity that when he practiced his craft Dostoevsky was not only relatively immune to this mechanism but subject to unconscious pressures which impelled him to tell as much of the truth as he knew or could divine.

⚙ *L'Avventura:* A Closer Look

EXCEPT in a few notable books, such as *From Caligari to Hitler* by Siegfried Kracauer and *Movies* by Martha Wolfenstein and Nathan Leites, and, more recently, in the criticism of Norman Holland, the knowledge of the unconscious now at our disposal has been largely ignored in the criticism of movies. The neglect is scarcely surprising. Despite all the rather tiresome (because in most instances merely opinionated) talk about whether such knowledge *should* be used in literary criticism, it is honored there more in the breach than in the observance—and when used is often applied either gingerly or rashly, with a second-hand, inexact, and incomplete knowledge of the concepts upon which it is supposed to be based. Movie critics have less incentive than their colleagues who discuss books to acquire the formidable body of background knowledge needed for making profitable use of what is known about the unconscious. They may feel that their readers prefer superficial commentary, and except where certain kinds of films are concerned (and perhaps then only if the critics have a relatively sophisticated audience or unusual gifts for simplification) this feeling is probably correct. Critics for dailies, and even weeklies, may also be deterred, and are certainly handicapped, by the need for working under short deadlines. The most valuable insights about what a work of art is communicating at the unconscious level are often slow in presenting themselves.

However understandable, the indiscriminate neglect of depth psychology in movie criticism is regrettable. As I have suggested in my book *Fiction and the Unconscious,* novels and short stories probably register

Reprinted from *The Yale Review,* vol. 54, no. 1, Autumn 1964. Copyright © 1964 by Yale University.

on our minds to an unappreciated extent in terms of sense impressions, chiefly visual ones. But movies are cast in these terms from the very beginning; they are "written" in the very language of our dreams and fantasies. Theoretically, movies are in a better position than any other genre to bypass the conscious intelligence and communicate with the unconscious with little or no mediation. Perhaps the chief reason this is not better appreciated is that until recently few makers of movies were aware of the potentialities of their own medium. They concentrated on superficial subjects which could be conveyed through conventional symbols and which evoked ready-made responses, created or reinforced by popular literature. More sadly, even in dealing with promising material, directors were usually overexplicit and heavy-handed, perhaps because they assumed that the understanding of images requires more intelligence than in fact it does, perhaps simply because they lacked visual imagination. But the possibilities of the medium have always been there and they have occasionally been realized—most often, perhaps, until recently, in movies with no trace of "artiness," such as comedies and melodramas. A Hitchcock thriller, *Vertigo*, will serve as an example. Though it seemed to be concerned with a purely external thing, a man's fear of heights, at the latent level it explained his fear, and showed how he was defeated by the clever exploitation of more hidden and encompassing personality weaknesses.

Vertigo, however, had an exciting, clear-flowing story to tell, and thus lent itself with at least apparent ease to customary ways of using the medium. Today a number of directors are emerging who recognize that movies can be utilized for more complex narrative purposes: to tell stories where the action is disjunctive, negative in character, or so elliptical that there may seem to be no story; to project the inner feelings of characters, complex interrelationships, even the moods, unverbalized and perhaps not even verbalizable, which may engulf, say, a couple or even a large group. And these new directors, of whom Michelangelo Antonioni and Ingmar Bergman are the supreme exemplars, accomplish these things not by finding unobtrusive ways of working in an unusual number of verbal cues but by making fuller and more imaginative use of the screen's natural visual idiom.

Besides using more and fresher symbols, Antonioni and Bergman frequently employ overdetermined ones, so that, like novelists for example, they can suggest additional implications of the story they are telling. To the extent that they do this they must resort to symbols which cannot be too easily penetrated, for the more hidden level or levels of meaning are nearly always ones that would arouse anxiety or revulsion in viewers if consciously perceived. Occasionally, moreover, again like their colleagues who depend upon words, they will tell a story which is not intelligible or perhaps even interesting on the basis of its manifest level of meaning, a story which is not likely to be affecting, much less enjoyable, unless it is apprehended unconsciously.

It is when one deals with films of these two kinds that one most keenly regrets the neglect of depth psychology in movie criticism. It must be assumed that these films are intuitively understood by most of the large number of people all over the world who evidently enjoy them; the enjoyment of films of the second kind in particular is inexplicable unless one assumes that they are unconsciously understood. But precisely because they are understood in this fashion, it seems unlikely that many viewers can *account* for their response to the films; to do so, in the face of strong internal resistance, they would have to formulate what has been grasped only subliminally and nonverbally.

It may be surmised that one of the most powerful factors impelling these viewers to read movie criticism is the hope of finding commentary which will help them to understand their own reactions. Unfortunately, most reviewers share the helplessness of their readers and are unable to satisfy these desires. What is worse, and less apparent, is that—more or less inevitably—they often mislead their readers. *Something* must be said, and if a critic lacks the skill to explicate below-the-surface meanings and is not content to be vague, he is likely to stumble into misinterpretations. Nor does the harm which results from the lack of psychological knowledge always end there. Because of a natural tendency to bring one's judgment of a work of art into line with one's intellectual formulations about it, the misinterpretations may sometimes lead to inaccurate appraisals. Unable to decode the meaning of a picture, a critic may conclude that it has none and write a review which fails to do justice to his own immediate, and more correct, reactions.

These tendencies are in evidence, it seems to me, in some of the press and magazine commentary on Michelangelo Antonioni's cinema masterpiece *L'Avventura*. For example, Bosley Crowther of the *New York Times* shows respect for Antonioni's artistry, but declares that in watching *L'Avventura* he felt he was trying to follow a picture of "which several reels have got lost." Even in a piece written long after his original review he refers to the picture's "deliberately garbled story-line." As I shall try to show, the story-line is, on the contrary, tight and faithfully adhered to. A review by Edith Oliver in the *New Yorker* may be an example of the second, and more regrettable, kind of critical failing. She dismisses *L'Avventura* as tedious as well as incomprehensible. Still, she refers to evidence "that Mr. Antonioni has something in mind," and at another point writes, "One reason I am so angry and harsh is that there are also indications, here and there, that some original ideas—Mr. Antonioni's own ideas—have gone to waste." Evidently Miss Oliver felt baffled when she tried to explain *L'Avventura*, but such comments, I like to think, may be vestigial remnants of an intuitive initial recognition of the picture's stature.

The idea for *L'Avventura* may have come as a phrase: *"There is a search. But one has forgotten for whom one is searching."* The idea, even in its more impersonal forms, stirs reverberations. You go into a room to find something and realize you have forgotten what you were looking for. Then you remember, but perhaps feel some vague sense of dissatisfaction: "Was that really it?" This sense of bafflement is likely to be keener when you plan a day, a month, a career. The goals and purposes of life, which in youth may have seemed self-evident, in adulthood seem impossible to define; it goes without saying that the route to one's destination, whatever it may be, is unmarked also. This is one of the themes of Kafka's *The Castle*.

In the erotic life of man the situation seems, if anything, more difficult. How can you possibly find her whom you seek? Her image is blurred. At one time it may seem impossible to find her because there are so many women among whom to choose. At other times it may seem impossible because there are so few. Either way, the essential difficulty remains the same: how can you recognize your long-sought beloved when her image and her qualities are so indefinite and indistinct? How can you know love itself and distinguish it from its innumerable partial embodiments and counterfeits? After a time the hope of success may all but disappear. Because of need, the search may continue, but be pursued with a growing sense of futility and disillusionment.

L'Avventura is, among other things, the story of one such compulsive, interminable quest for someone whom the hero does not really expect ever to find. But *L'Avventura* is not all story—it is part poem and part essay as well—nor is this all it has to say. The movie makes a sweeping, it could almost be said an encompassing, statement about the erotic life of modern man. It is doomed from the start, the movie asseverates: doomed because the quest for the beloved is hopeless and because its hopelessness breeds disenchantment, cynicism, and self-hatred; doomed because sexual fulfillment is so often unsatisfactory and guilt-ridden; doomed because sex is used, wrongly, as solace for frustrations and defeats, as an anodyne for the soul-sickness which afflicts us. because of our own compromises, weaknesses, and corruption, and as an outlet for angry, destructive feelings which besmirch it; doomed, finally, because despite all this the quest goes on and must go on, though joyless, sterile, and, after a time, devoid of any prospect of success. Eternal restlessness and frustration are the inescapable conditions of our erotic life.

From first to last *L'Avventura* is a story of baffled search. It is important to note that Anna and Claudia, to say nothing of the movie's minor characters, are searching for something, just as Sandro is. Anna's father is aware that his daughter is desperately looking for something, but warns her that she will not find it with or through Sandro. She is herself half aware of this. Her sulkiness is only partly explained by the need to choose between father and lover. One senses that to a far greater degree it is a product of her own doubts—about her lover, their relationship, and something in herself.

At the beginning Claudia is left to one side, unexplained and almost unnoticed, but in retrospect it is easy to see that she, too, is searching, and that her search is no less desperate than Anna's. At the beginning, in fact, she is in the unenviable position of searching *through* her friend. She has no lover herself, and no unattached male has been invited on the cruise as a possible partner for her. Nevertheless, she accompanies Anna. It is not an accident that time after time—beginning of course with the lovemaking of Anna and Sandro very early in the picture—she is forced to witness "primal scene" material. She is the observer—the outsider, the third party, the child watching the parents—of the weary, paid-for lovemaking between the Princess and her paramour, of the hostility that is the only link between Giulia and Corrado, the only married couple on the yachting party, and, later, of the exultant, vengeful lovemaking between Giulia and the young Italian "artist." Toward the end there is the more poignant confirming scene where she finds what she has been unconsciously searching for, her father-lover entwined in the limbs of the wanton he found at the Princess' party. Here she can feel her grief more fully, more poignantly and, as it were, more justifiably, for she has at once re-created and reversed the prototype situation: she is still the outsider, but now in part a betrayed outsider, the mother from whom the envious daughter has stolen the father. It is chiefly through Claudia, whether as jealous daughter or, as in the last scene, part daughter, part wronged mother, that we are reminded that love almost invariably involves competitiveness and a sense of taking from someone else, one of the reasons it is tainted by feelings of guilt. Claudia has reason to know—not only because she has apparently failed to work out her jealousy of her mother but also because, even though Anna is evidently dead, she has the feeling of having stolen Sandro from her. At some level his infidelity is not only an expected and familiar pain but a warranted punishment, one reason she is able to forgive him.

It is upon Sandro's search, however, more than Anna's or even Claudia's, that *L'Avventura* chiefly focuses. Gabriele Ferzetti is able to suggest that his restlessness long antedated his relationship with Anna, confirming the doubts her father's warnings have already implanted in us. While we are not fully prepared for Anna's physical disappearance, we are prepared for the fact that Sandro's search will not end with her.

The failure to explain what happened to Anna is undoubtedly one source of the complaint that *L'Avventura* does not tell a coherent story. At first glance the criticism may seem justified, for Anna's disappearance is one of the most dramatic external incidents in the movie. But *L'Avventura* is nowhere concerned with external events for their own sake; certainly it is not a mystery story in which our main concern should be, "what happened to Anna?" It is a psychological story of the quest for love and the beloved.

Once this is remembered—and Antonioni never forgets it—it seems clear that this incident is treated with the same sureness as everything else. An explanation of Anna's disappearance would be not only superfluous but distracting. The discovery of her body, for example, would call for additional reactions from everyone and in all probability would raise further questions. The movie confines itself to what is relevant: Anna disappears. She vanishes from Sandro's life and, very quickly, from his consciousness also, as in one way or another she was bound to. And she disappears while herself searching for something—or perhaps fleeing from something, which is another aspect of the same thing.

Except as a reproach, she soon disappears from Claudia's consciousness also. From the beginning Claudia has envied Anna and wanted her lover, who, we sense, is attractive in part because he is her lover. The scene toward the beginning when she is compelled to wait outside, with feelings we can divine, while Sandro and Anna make love is only one of the things that whisper this to us. We sense it also from the readiness with which she borrows her friend's clothing, both before and after her disappearance, from the scene in which she dons a brunette wig, and from her immediate sensitivity to Sandro's desire for her. Though she makes no overt gesture of enticement, it is significant that the first physical contact between her and Sandro occurs as a result of her stumbling as she tries to pass him. Speedily enough she reaches the point where she confesses that she no longer cries for her lost friend but fears that she may be alive.

The more difficult and audacious thing *L'Avventura* achieves is to make Sandro's quick acceptance of Anna's disappearance so understandable that we do not refuse to identify with him. Here we have little to go on except the longing for Claudia which quickly manifests itself (and this would arouse revulsion if we were not in part prepared for it) and what Gabriele Ferzetti has been able to suggest about Sandro's character and inner feelings. In part because we do not have to be given an explanation but simply reminded of one, this is sufficient: we intuitively realize that Sandro has no real desire to find Anna. Before her disappearance, we sense, the relationship was played out. Anna had already been exposed as a surrogate, one of a long succession of women who had to be possessed and then renounced because none was the one for whom Sandro was searching. This is another reason why psychologically it is better that Anna's fate should be left in doubt: the search for her is at bottom a pseudosearch. It is engaged in to save face and to relieve guilt rather than to find Anna.

Such sorrow as Anna's disappearance does arouse in Sandro, it may be surmised, is due to what it does to recall the disappearance of the original love object, the mother. At the very deepest level the failure to account for Anna's disappearance rings true psychologically because it recapitulates that earlier experience, which cannot be explained in terms of the love object's being alive or dead. She has "disappeared" because she has been thrust into the unconscious and can no longer be sought for *in propria persona:* she is taboo.

What we sense about Sandro's real feeling for Anna, and all the nameless women who have preceded her in his life, helps us to work our way to the core of Antonioni's picture. It can almost be regarded as a dramatization of a text from Freud:

> . . . when the original object of an instinctual desire becomes lost in consequence of repression, it is often replaced by an endless series of substitute-objects, none of which ever give full satisfaction. This may explain the lack of stability in object-choice, the "craving for stimulus," which is so often a feature of the love of adults ("The Most Prevalent Form of Degradation in Erotic Life").

We know in advance, and Claudia knows, that Sandro's feelings for her will be subject to the same vicissitudes responsible for his easy acceptance of the loss of Anna. Claudia is a surrogate also, as we are reminded by Sandro's infidelity with the prostitute he finds at the party. It is a virtue of *L'Avventura* that even though the relationship between Sandro and Claudia survives this, no assurances are given that it will endure indefinitely; the picture ends on an uncertain note. Indeed, far from trying to dissipate the melancholy impressions conveyed by the first part of the picture, the latter part deepens them. The relationship of Sandro and Claudia seldom escapes the burden of guilt which has encumbered it from the start. He is never able to feel any happiness, and some of the things which occur after the search for Anna becomes no more than an excuse for him and Claudia to travel together help to explain why this is so.

In one of the towns to which their search brings them Sandro leaves Claudia and goes for a walk. He chances upon a drawing in which a young man, evidently an aspiring architect, has faithfully reproduced the beauty of a detail of a nearby building. The drawing is at Sandro's mercy; the young man who has made it has walked some distance away to chat with a friend. Sandro lets his key ring dangle ever closer to a bottle of ink near the drawing; in the end he cannot resist the impulse to ruin the drawing by knocking over the bottle.

He rushes back to his hotel full of inarticulate grief about his act and the cluster of feelings responsible for it. We know that the impulse to sully the young man's work was born of the angry realization that he has sullied his own. Precipitately, brutally, impersonally, he tries to compel Claudia, who is well aware that at the moment he is scarcely aware of her, to have sexual relations with him. He seeks to use her, and sex, to console himself for the dreams he has forsaken. Antonioni is in effect asking a rhetorical question: what chance does sex have to give us happiness or even pleasure when it is misused in this fashion? Taken as a whole, moreover, his picture tells us that sex is likely to be so misused, particularly in our time.

But there is nothing condemnatory about Antonioni's attitude. He is not indicting sex, or his characters, or, like *La Dolce Vita,* with which *L'Avventura* has been mistakenly linked, an age or social system. Tears are a purge also, and the Sandro who weeps at the end of *L'Avventura* feels genuine sorrow—sorrow for the suffering he has caused his beloved and sorrow for his own unhappiness, for the restlessness and richly rewarded mediocrity to which he perceives himself to be doomed.

☸ The *Odyssey:*
The Hidden Dreams

THE *Iliad,* as every critic and teacher triumphantly notes, is not about the Trojan War but about the wrath of Achilles. It is less often noted that the *Odyssey* is not about the wanderings of Odysseus, which last about as long as the Trojan War, some ten years, but about his return home: the very last stage of his travels and the homecoming itself. The poem begins with Zeus's assenting to Athene's appeal that Odysseus be permitted to return. It ends with his return, his reunion with his family and faithful servants, his vengeance upon his enemies, and the establishment of a peace which we are assured will be enduring.

Even from the point of view of the duration of the action, the *Odyssey* invites comparison with the *Iliad,* which concentrates on fifty days of a ten-year war. Following the discussion with Zeus, Athene visits Ithaca to prod Telemachus. One specific measure she suggests is that he visit Nestor and Menelaus to seek news of his father. The time devoted to this mission is uncertain but surely not long. Moreover, Telemachus's return journey overlaps the part of the story in which Odysseus holds the center of the stage. The time covered by this part can be estimated with reasonable precision. The *Odyssey* ends on the thirty-fourth day after Zeus sends instructions to Calypso to release Odysseus and we first meet that redoubtable but now unhappy man face to face.

The *Odyssey* is no less sure in its subject and its focus than the *Iliad.* Coleridge regarded its plot as one of the three greatest in the entire realm of fiction. The structure, as well as the content of the work, shows that its subject is the efforts of its hero to get back to his home and the homecoming itself. But, surprisingly, few people have asked why a narra-

Reprinted from *The Minnesota Review,* vol. 7, no. 4, 1967.

tive poem with that subject should have had such a profound appeal to the society for which it was composed and why it has continued to appeal to countless generations of readers in all parts of the world.

One reason, of course, is that the answer seems obvious. The *Odyssey* yields innumerable delights and satisfactions, and most of them, including many of those directly related to the central theme, are visible to the naked eye.

It is self-evident that the attainment of any goal for which one has to struggle is likely to provide satisfaction—to the person who has had to struggle and anyone who identifies with him. It is self-evident too that there are few goals the attainment of which provides such rich pleasure as the one to which Odysseus has clung, with only understandable periods of forgetfulness, for ten long years. It is sweet to rejoin one's loved ones and to regain one's power and authority. Man being the kind of creature he is, it is sweet also for him to defeat and take vengeance upon his enemies and to attain a position which permits him to reward his friends.

The radiant surface of the *Odyssey* also affords rich satisfactions. As Mark Van Doren declares, the world Homer creates in the poem "is above all a bright world, open under space; and itself is full of space. Reality shines in it like mica. . . ." The women in this world, whether mortals or goddesses, are lovely to behold. Most of the men, surely all those whom Homer thinks of, in Van Doren's phrase, as "natural kings," are handsome, stately and assured. They are also courageous, equitable, hospitable and generous. Their houses are splendid, and the ceremonies of social intercourse invariably gracious. Food is described as if it had just been discovered. There are luxuriant gardens—for example, Calypso's, which before the god Hermes delivers Zeus's message he must pause to admire; at times the whole world seems a garden. Even objects are described with love. Ugliness is not absent: it prevails in Ithaca and there are reminders of it from time to time even in the conduct and thinking of the gods. But it is subordinated. The world conjured up by Homer is perhaps the loveliest compliment ever paid to a civilization and mankind. It is easy to understand the satisfactions it gave the chieftains at whose great houses it was recited or who were present as retainers or guests. To believe that they might be descended from such men as Odysseus, Menelaus and Nestor dignified their lives. The values the poem commemorates confirmed those its hearers tried to live by. Nor are our values and our conception of what is admirable in human beings so different from those of the ancient Greeks that we do not share these satisfactions to some extent. We cannot easily reject so flattering an image of what we would like to be ourselves.

We are so well pleased with the world of the *Odyssey* that we are content to dwell in it without raising questions. Indeed, we are so beguiled that we do not note how much that world differs from the one we know. No one would invoke the word "realistic" to describe Homer's art or confuse his world with those delineated by most nineteenth- and twentieth-century novelists, but we do tend, I believe, to minimize the extent to which it deviates from the everyday world.

In part this blindness is due to Homer's greatness as a poet. In equal part, however, it is due to his matchless skill as a storyteller. Things that, less adroitly done, a twentieth-century reader would reject as farfetched, beyond the pale of adult fiction, Homer makes entirely credible. Consider, for example, how quickly he makes us accept both the existence of gods and their intervention in the affairs of men. He is equally successful in making even stranger events seem both natural and understandable. Dante frequently—and even such a poet as Yeats occasionally—depends upon symbols which only the erudite can fully comprehend without the help of explanations and footnotes. Unconsciously if not consciously the most outlandish happenings in the *Odyssey* yield their meaning at once to the average reader; that is why, as we read, they do not seem outlandish.

Homer's skill in ordering his episodes also helps to make the *Odyssey* credible. By beginning with Telemachus, for example, he eases us into his work in what is probably the most effective possible way to achieve that willing suspension of disbelief upon which he can place more and more dependence as we become increasingly entranced. He starts his story with the part of it most likely to deceive us into believing that it is going to be perfectly straightforward and realistic. Little occurs in the first four books which is likely to give rise to questions. The only god extensively involved in the action is Athene, and most of the time she seems no more than an exceptionally prescient, alert, and energetic friend of the family. Her mortal disguises are easy to accept. The things she accomplishes for Telemachus are never sufficiently spectacular to mark her as a supernatural being and arouse our scepticism.

In subsequent books there are larger and larger infusions of unrealistic elements. But the transitions are so gradual, the episodes so fascinating and so well told that as we read we are not likely to stop and notice the changed nature of the scenery.

Rhys Carpenter demonstrates that the *Odyssey* is a skillful blend of reality-oriented fiction and saga, "folk tale, fairy lore and fancy," or, to use the words other writers employ for the same kind of material, myths and legends. Once we escape the magic web the poem weaves about us as we read, we cannot fail to see that this is so. At latest by Book IX, when

Odysseus begins to recount his early adventures, we take our leave of the world in which we have our daytime being. (Even then we may not notice. The fact that Odysseus himself tells us what has happened to him vouches for its authenticity. The fact that he is telling what happened to him before we meet him sets his adventures back in time—not just a few years but an indeterminate and, it seems, much longer period.) We now enter a world of gigantic, cannibalistic, anarchic monsters, some of them one-eyed; of straits so perilous that no group of mariners can pass through them unscathed. To be sure, all of these creatures and perils have rich psychic meaning. Scylla and Charybdis, for example, are probably concrete representations of at least equally intolerable and more numerous fears of a still partly unexplored world. They also symbolize certain recurring elements of the human predicament—how often throughout history the phrase "Scylla and Charybdis," or some equivalent, has had to be invoked. Scylla, before whom men are helpless, must also incarnate the infant's talion fears of the "gigantic" mother, whose body, especially in moments of rage, it may conceive of itself as eating.

But I do not want to get too far away from the point that we are still under the spell of Homer's magic if we retain the illusion that the *Odyssey* is a straightforward, realistic story. When we look closely, we see that even parts of it that at first glance may seem firmly placed in the world we know are not so in fact. The entire Phaeacian episode will serve as an example. Here there are no gross indications that we have moved into a different world; but is not everything that happens to Odysseus in Scherie, even Euryalus's insult, which gives him a chance to demonstrate his mettle, too patently a fulfillment of everything a sorely pressed, shipwrecked and exhausted adventurer would long for? And is not the life of the Phaeacians itself too easy, happy and free of conflict to be entirely credible? Borrowing a distinction Eric Auerbach makes between the legendary and the historical, we may say that things now begin to run far too smoothly for Odysseus; his life and his hosts' lives are far too frictionless to bear the stamp of reality in the world we know. Even if we do not notice any of this, we should be able to recall that there are unmistakable fairy-tale aspects about Odysseus's trip home. We have already been told in passing that the ships of the Phaeacians are magical. They require "no steersmen, nor steering-oars. . . . Our ships know by instinct what their crews are thinking and propose to do."[1] Almost as soon as Odysseus boards the ship which is to carry him home, he falls into a profound sleep which is not broken either as he is whisked across the

1.   The *Odyssey*, translated by E. V. Rieu (Penguin Books, 1961), p. 137. Subsequent quotations are also from this translation.

water, faster even than "the wheeling falcon, the fastest thing that flies" (p. 204) or even when he and the rich treasures the Phaeacians have given him are landed on his native Ithaca. The ship is clearly a close relative of the magic carpets of Oriental fairy tales. Its appearance here, incidentally, suggests that even Odysseus, prototype of the determined, indomitable hero, and we his no less intrepid companions, have passive inclinations also, and that these too cry for satisfaction.

It is necessary to insist on these fabulous aspects of the *Odyssey* because unless we take account of them we are likely to be misled into thinking that it is simply a singularly successful adventure story whose life is entirely on the surface. Indeed, even so eminent a critic as Auerbach, who knows very well to what an extent Homer utilizes legendary material, falls into this trap. "This 'real' world into which we are lured," he writes, "exists for itself, contains nothing but itself; the Homeric poems conceal nothing, they contain no teaching and no secret second meaning." But of course legends, myths and fairy stories are nearly always exceptionally rich in sub-surface meaning. Almost invariably at a secret level and sometimes quite openly they are concerned with dreams and desires too foreign to our conscious ideals, too narcissistic, or too unrealistic to be acknowledged. Often too the means by which the unavowed desires are attained are too ruthless or too far-fetched to be acceptable to the governing part of the self.

2

One hesitates to identify the first of these hidden references because it is certain to arouse the cry of "reductionism." It links the *Odyssey* with many kinds of adult fiction held in low esteem and even with an immense body of children's fiction. Still, neither the cry nor the fear which gives rise to it is justified. If the *Odyssey* is like some second-rate fiction in one or two respects, it is quite unlike it in many others. Nor is there anything shameful about the fact that the *Odyssey* covertly satisfies some of the same desires which are dealt with in less reputable fiction, even fiction addressed to children. Freud has taught us that in some respects we never outgrow our childhood: the desires of that period are never relinquished but persist in the unconscious. Though new demands arise as we grow up, we never cease to seek at least vicarious gratification of those early desires. We simply ask that the make-believe nature of the gratification not be too noticeable, and of course our ideas of what constitutes plausibility are more exacting than a child's.

Moreover, the first of the hidden desires to be discussed, one which permeates the entire story, is not peculiar to childhood. It is a desire we cling to with part of our minds even when we are allegedly grown-up and objectively well aware that it is untenable. This desire we will not forsake is to be invulnerable—to be impervious to the blows of fate or a mortal enemy or in any event not to be killed or seriously injured by them. I suspect that the desire interferes with our efforts to think rationally about such matters as the dangers of atomic war, cigarette smoking, or driving an automobile; when we are compelled to, we concede that the dangers exist, but emotionally we cannot bring ourselves to believe that we are subject to them. It is when the conscious ego is relaxed, as it is when we read fiction or compose our own fantasies and dreams, that the wish to be invulnerable comes into its own. It discloses itself in what must be one of the most common of all dreams, one in which the dreamer is a spectator-participant in some terrible catastrophe, perhaps an atomic attack, in which everyone or nearly everyone but the dreamer is killed. Psychoanalytic experience, based on reports of countless dreams, indicates that in the unconscious we cannot conceive of our own destruction. It is not to be wondered at that we are susceptible to fiction which panders to our wish to be invulnerable and to other narcissistic needs. "His Majesty the Ego," Freud declared in an early paper, "[is] the hero of all day-dreams and all novels." Most obviously he is the hero of the novels Freud was discussing, the widely read stories of unpretentious writers.

How well the *Odyssey* embodies and satisfies the age-old dream of immunity from serious hurt will be immediately apparent. There were evidently more than 500 men in Odysseus's party. He is the only one who survives. Most of the adventures he relates in Scherie involve loss of life. Many of his men are killed by the Cicones after the sacking of Ismarus. Six more are eaten by Polyphemus. The occupants of all the other ships but Odysseus's are killed by the savage and cannibalistic Laestrygonians. Elpenor meets an accidental death when the band leaves Aeaea. Six more men fall victim to Scylla. All the rest, except Odysseus, are killed when Zeus wrecks their boat at the behest of the Sun-god, whose cattle Odysseus's forewarned but hungry men have eaten. In the trials to which Odysseus's party was subjected mortal men were outmatched. The actuarial odds against any of them surviving were prohibitively high.

It is an eloquent tribute to Homer's artistry that despite all this we neither think of the *Odyssey* as unbelievable nor mistake it for an ordinary adventure story. By the skill with which he gradually dulls our scepticism and, equally, by the skill with which he depicts and motivates his hero, he makes his survival credible.

The very fact that Odysseus is strongly motivated makes a qualitative difference: it alone distinguishes him from the vaguely defined heroes of a million ordinary adventure stories. The typical hero of one of our century's "Westerns" is weakly and almost impersonally motivated: he is either a drifter with some vague sympathy for the underdog or, more usually, a lawman (in other genres, detective or spy) just doing his job. Odysseus is obsessed by a motive whose force we not only understand but feel: the desire to get home. We are sure he will extend himself to the utmost to survive and achieve his goal.

Beyond this he has qualities which make it seem possible that, against the odds, he will achieve it. He is strong, intelligent, intrepid, resourceful, and decisive. It is a combination of these qualities that enables him to outwit Polyphemus and save himself and his still undevoured companions. It is caution born of intelligence as well as experience which keeps him from following his captains into the cove when they reach the land of the Laestrygonians; and all that we have heard and seen of him tells us that it is computer-quick and correct thinking, not cowardice, which leads him to slash the hawser of his boat and order his men to their oars when he sees what is befalling his comrades in the cove. When he is shipwrecked, strength, courage, and the will to live sustain him as he swims for two days and nights in heavy seas. The veil Ino gives him helps to buoy his hopes, as Zeus's decrees have buoyed ours earlier, but he and we know that if he is to survive it must be through his own exertions. What Charles H. Taylor, Jr., says of the help Athene gives Odysseus is true in general of the help he receives from the gods: "When she comes to his assistance, she reinforces his strengths, but only after he has proven himself capable of survival without her aid."

While the qualities of Odysseus which have been noted help to account for his survival, they are perhaps not the ones which do most to explain his appeal for us. We claim him—the whole Western world since the time the *Odyssey* was first recited and our own twentieth-century American society in particular—we claim him also for the qualities which get him into trouble. It was curiosity and adventurousness, not unmixed with acquisitiveness, which led Odysseus to await the giant owner of the cave in the land of the Cyclopes, despite his own forebodings and the entreaties of his men; and it was pride and egoism, feelings we condemn but fully understand, which led him to taunt his outwitted enemy and identify himself to him. To this roster of qualities we must add sometimes excessive self-reliance, assertiveness and, let us not balk at the word, aggressiveness. Perhaps only the last two qualities, the ones about which we are ambivalent and may therefore be slow to identify, require documentation, though I cannot resist noting the most marvelous example of his self-reliance. This is surely his refusal, even when shipwrecked, to follow the instructions of the goddess Ino, who has befriended him; he insists on assessing his situation himself. " 'No,' he decided; 'I will not leave the boat at once. . . . Instead, I shall do what I myself think best' " (p. 97).

Odysseus's assertiveness and aggressiveness are even evident in his relations with gods, though perhaps less obviously than in his relations with his men, his enemies, the Phaeacians, and, upon his return, with some of his servants and even with his own son. As he swims along the coast of Scherie looking for a safe place to land, he comes to the mouth of a river. He prays to the god of the river, ending with the request: " 'Take pity on me, royal River. I claim a suppliant's rights' " (p. 100). "Claim" is the revelatory word. In many of his colloquies with Athene also Odysseus is claimant as well as suppliant; indeed, he does not hesitate to mix reproaches with his appeals for help.

We recognize the mixture of qualities Odysseus displays without hesitation: it is ourselves. More accurately, he is a magnified and improved version of ourselves, what we would be if many of our appetencies were not undeveloped or denied a suitable outlet. Odysseus is the archetypal Western man, the man who has already gone far in conquering and appropriating the material universe and who, if he does not first destroy himself, is surely destined to complete the conquest. He is the precursor of Robinson Crusoe and many other fictional heroes, but greater in stature than any of them. There is little danger of mistaking such a hero for an ordinary one simply because he happens to exemplify our dream of invulnerability.

3

Under its lovely surface, moreover, the *Odyssey* also deals with a related cluster of more significant dreams. So far as I am aware, there is no other story which tries to gratify so many of the longings which, however mature we become, we can never bring ourselves to give up completely.

Most of these hidden gratifications accrue during the last half of the story. One reason we do not notice them is that the rich pleasure this part of the story gives us seems to have such obvious sources. With Odysseus we are experiencing the joy of being reunited with our wife, son, father and servants and finding that they have never ceased to love us, long for our return and defend our interests. Homer wrings the last drop of pleasure out of these satisfactions of homecoming. The main device used is to disguise Odysseus so that we are aware that he is in the presence of Eumaeus, Telemachus, Eurycleia, the Suitors, and Penelope long before they are. The pleasure—in the scene with Eurycleia, the titillating anxiety—is doubled by anticipation, by being postponed and stretched out.

But this pleasure is a cover for others. Indeed, if we were not now seeking to gratify still dearer longings, we might not be able to accept the surface happenings. If we allow for the fact that those happenings invite comparison with the world we know, whereas many of the earlier adventures of Odysseus approach more nearly to pure make-believe, it might be claimed that what befalls him after he returns to Ithaca is more incredible than his getting home. Given the kind of physical and intellectual qualities with which Odysseus is endowed, plus resoluteness and a great deal of luck, one man out of a very large group might conceivably survive the perils which destroy his comrades and find his way home. But consider what he would find when he arrived there after an absence of nineteen years. Many of his loved ones would be dead. Of those who survived a number would be so ravaged by time as not to be immediately recognizable: nor would he be readily recognized even by those who knew him best. (This facet of reality is acknowledged but only to be played with: in the poem Odysseus's altered appearance is brought about by reversible magic, not the inescapable corrosion of time.) The wife who had borne the homecomer a child would by now be middle-aged, perhaps on the threshold of old age. In all probability she would have long since remarried and perhaps had children by another man. The property of the returning hero would long before have passed into the not unwilling hands of his wife, his son or others. So too with his power: many would have been impatient to seize it. What might be equally wounding to the long-absent man is that he would find himself forgotten. Though his loved ones and some of his friends, servants and subjects would think of him from time to time, even they would long since have accepted and adjusted to his absence and his death. He would find that he had been long buried in the shifting and infinite sands of time and that everyone he met was preoccupied with his own claims on life, his own affairs.

These reality considerations should not be pressed too far. Our memory and our unconscious live in the same eternal present in which Homer's characters have their entire being. Though our bodies age, we may still remember, still desire, someone we loved a score of years before. To a degree, moreover, subjective factors can nullify the work of time. The return of Odysseus, who was perhaps recognized by Penelope long before he was acknowledged, might have rejuvenated her, and his long-nurtured desire for her would have made her seem more youthful as well as more beautiful than in fact she was. Nor should it be suggested either that reality considerations are entirely ignored in the *Odyssey*. The need for Athene's help in making some of the characters more youthful looking is referred to at a number of points. When Odysseus talks to his mother in the Halls of Hades, he expresses fear that his wife may have remarried and that someone may have succeeded him as king. Even when sleeping, Penelope is not always able to forget the passage of time. After her husband is back in Ithaca in disguise she dreams at least twice of him being in her bed and "looking exactly as he looked when he sailed away . . ." (p. 306).

But it is astonishing how few and insignificant these concessions to reality are and how successful the *Odyssey* is in eliminating—or denying—whatever is painful. The Battle in the Hall, perhaps the poorest scene in the entire poem, seems so patently rigged that adult readers may become consciously aware of its lack of realism—and perversely sympathize with the Suitors. It is they who seem outnumbered; and the indiscriminate slaughter, which takes the life of decent as well as villainous men, is hard for a modern reader to accept. It should be noted too that much of the reality-oriented material which dots the poem, the last part of it in particular, is so used as to keep disagreeable matters at bay. The purpose of the allusions to Clytemnestra's infidelity, for example, is to highlight Penelope's fidelity: it is this which Homer wants us to focus upon and believe in. When all allowances are made, the homecoming part of the *Odyssey* must be regarded as a wish-fulfilling reversal of what we fear would really happen if we were away a very long time. It offers us a succession of gilded dreams—but the dreams are so enticing that only the one which is least important and least well handled, the dream of vengeance upon rivals and enemies, is likely to be recognized as a dream.

The most significant dreams describe the reunion of Odysseus with those closest to him: wife, son, and father. The reunion with Penelope is the climax of the tale, and Homer handles it with a skill which befits its importance. It could not be enjoyed, by Odysseus or by us, if the Suitors were not first defeated and gotten out of the way, but it is delayed not only by this, but by Odysseus's disguise and Penelope's refusal to accept the stranger who has prevailed over the Suitors as her husband even when she is told who he is. The reunion is brought about only when Odysseus more nearly resembles the man she remembers, and then by a perfect test, one which only the man who had shared her marriage bed could pass and a wife who was a match for him could devise. The consummation of their reunion is described with a naturalness, a combination of candor and tact, an ease, which perhaps only the writer who is both gifted and the first to attempt such a scene can hope to achieve.

Yet there is much that we have to ignore to accept this idyllic reunion at face value. Putting to one side the physical impact of time, we must believe in the indefinite persistence of love. We must believe not only that Penelope has been constant to a man she is no longer convinced is living, but also, what is perhaps less credible, that she has accepted her lonely, starved life without resentment and has not been scarred by it, is free of anger and discontent, and has no dreams of fulfillment with others. Yet, even when there are good reasons for it, the departure of a husband from a wife who loves him may half-seem like a desertion; and what can justify an absence of nineteen years. George Devereux argues persuasively that Penelope was "far from unambivalently happy either over Odysseus's long absence or his long delayed return" and attributes her tardiness in recognizing him to her ambivalence and her need to defend herself against the temptation of accepting a plausible imposter as her husband. Penelope's curious defense of Helen's infidelity in Book XXIII, he suggests, stems from the need to justify some of her own vagrant thoughts. There is another passage in the *Odyssey* which more clearly suggests that the surface picture of Penelope may be somewhat prettied up. Athene has come to the great house of Menelaus to urge Telemachus to return home. She finds him lying in bed awake, full of anxiety about his father's situation—and his own. After expressing the fear that, under pressure from her father and brothers, Penelope may marry Eurymachus, the most generous of the Suitors, Athene continues:

> There is also the danger that she might carry off some of your own things from the house without your permission. You know what a woman's disposition is. She likes to bring riches to the house of the man who is marrying her, while, as for her former husband and the children she has borne him, she never gives him a thought once he is dead, nor enquires after them. (p. 230)

This may seem a strange place in the poem for a passage with a "return of the repressed" ring; but, if we stop to realize that here, as elsewhere, the thoughts of the mortal character, Telemachus, are perhaps being projected upon a god and that if the character were transposed to a later and darker work, he might be playing the part of Hamlet, the strangeness disappears.

In Odysseus's reunions and relations with his father and son there are also many things that we are likely to ignore as we read. In obeisance to the demands of reality Telemachus has grown up physically. But he is a fledgling, not quite a man in his own right. He is frequently referred to as the son of Odysseus, and while this is natural enough in view of the fact that in the early part of the poem he is visiting comrades of his father, the whole nature of their response to him shows that they think of him as a youth rather than a full-grown man, as the Suitors frequently do also. What is more significant, he thinks of himself as still a youth. Though he is dissatisfied with his situation, he does not dream of taking over his father's possessions and authority; perhaps as a protection against such dangerous desires, he believes that he is incapable of accomplishing either of these things. Like many a son of an illustrious father, Telemachus clearly finds it difficult to take the last fateful step into adulthood. In desisting from his fourth attempt to string the great bow when he sees his father nod, Telemachus is yielding to the requirements of the immediate situation. But though the speech which follows is dictated by the need to explain his action, I believe it also expresses his real feelings: submerged grievance against his father for compelling him to give up this opportunity and self-reproach for his own subservience and weakness. These he knows to be chronic and inner. They help explain his failure to challenge the Suitors. They are in evidence again a little later when Odysseus uncharacteristically asks his son to suggest strategy for keeping the news of the massacre of the Suitors secret for a time and Telemachus promptly tosses the problem back to his father.

Just as Telemachus is eliminated as a possible claimant of Odysseus's authority by being shown to be too young to assume it, Laertes is eliminated by being shown to be too old. There is no indication that he was king before his son. Still, in a patriarchal society the father of a king, if still vigorous, might well be called upon to assume the responsibilities of a long-absent son, most especially if the date of his return was uncertain. But we must believe that Laertes was already old at the time of his son's departure for Troy, and he has been further aged by the death of his wife and the absence of his son, whom he, like everyone else, assumes to be dead. By handling the ages and temperament of the three related male characters as he does, Homer protects Odysseus from competition and hostility from above and from below. He annuls two of the most painful of all conflicts, conflicts a man in the prime of life like Odysseus may have to experience simultaneously: the conflicts between son and father and between father and son.

At the same time Homer is protecting the entrancing dream being spun at the latent level. If Laertes or Telemachus had aspired, even unconsciously, to succeed Odysseus, he—or they—would feel some *disappointment,* however fugitive and slight, when the long-absent hero returns alive. This would irreparably disrupt the dream, just as any consciously noted indication of ambivalence on the part of Penelope would disrupt it. It is Odysseus's dream which is the secret material of the poem, and it is right that in that dream everything should be arranged to give him pleasure. Those he loves must be unreservedly happy that he has returned; and this requires that their aims be identical with his. The Suitors of course are not subordinated to the desires of Odysseus, but the pleasure of the dream is enhanced by his triumph over them. In the homecoming part of the poem, as in the voyage homeward, His Majesty the Ego—Odysseus and the reader identified with him—is the dreamer. The dark, conflict-ridden worlds conjured up by Aeschylus in *Agamemnon,* Sophocles in *Oedipus the King,* and Shakespeare in *Hamlet* are still many eras away.

There is another dream which underlies those already discussed and unites many facets of them, a dream which is less tenable but more indispensable to mankind than all the rest: it is the dream of survival after death, of having one's interests safeguarded and, more important, of being remembered and loved even when one is no longer living—and of being able to witness all this in person. This dream, the crudest form of the dream we call immortality, incarnates our stubborn refusal, sublime perhaps but pathetic also, to believe that even after we have died we are really dead or at any rate will stay dead.

This is the hardest dream to document, for nothing is more impalpable than time, most especially time as it is dealt with in the *Odyssey.* But there is now a wealth of evidence that in the unconscious "going away" signifies death; and even in the everyday world given accepted form by law an absence far shorter than Odysseus's involves a presumption of death. Odysseus is in the position of children who daydream of running away (and sometimes even act out the fantasy) so that, returning, they can find out how much they were missed and were, and are, loved; and of the far larger number of people, mostly grownups, who dream of cheating death by not really being dead when they are thought dead or of returning from death to their old haunts. In a curious way the latter, probably more usual, form of the dream is represented in the poem: before Odysseus is permitted to return home, he is compelled to visit the world of the dead.

In a larger sense, triumph over death is the subject of the entire poem. The return of Odysseus from seeming death, after surviving a series of trials which enabled death to snatch up all his comrades, is a defeat of death itself, man's implacable and insatiable enemy. Rhys Carpenter cites persuasive evidence suggesting that the Odyssey is a relatively sophisticated version of the old and widespread folk tale of the Bearson and that in antiquity Odysseus was widely regarded as being descended from a bear or a man who was part bear. Odysseus would then be simply another incarnation of the legendary figure of the Bearson. According to Carpenter, "the real theme" of the Bearson folk tale is "death in the midst of life, and some hope of life even after the crushing calamity of death. . . ." If this thesis is correct, the idea of besting death, of resurrection, which is discernible below the surface of the Odyssey, was already present in some of the raw material out of which the poem was fashioned.

The very ambiguity of Odysseus's situation in the hidden story being told, it is worth noting, makes his victory over death far more attractive than the vision of death embedded in Greek religion, at any rate the religion of the chieftains to whom Homer was addressing himself. As W. K. C. Guthrie points out, for the Greeks death "was the separation of the life of man, his psyche, from the body," and their image of happiness was too much bound up with the pleasures of the body for them to look upon death, or even old age, as anything but "a grievous evil. . . . It was not extinction, but meant dragging on an existence deprived of all that made life worth living. Hence the Homeric conception of the dead as strengthless, miserable wraiths. . . ." But Odysseus was not a wraith, either a wraith consigned to the Halls of the Dead or one vouchsafed no more than a brief, comfortless glimpse of his homeland. He was someone thought of as dead who was in fact in the prime of life, and he was being permitted to return to the sunlit world the Greeks had the good sense to value.

For good measure, he returns to a world which is almost untouched by time, a world in which there have been only such changes as are utilized sooner or later to increase the pleasure of his homecoming. His wife has been faithful to him and is still beautiful, just as he himself is still in the full vigor of manhood. His son has grown up but displays not the slightest tendency toward insubordination. His mother is dead, but she had died of grief for him. His father has never ceased to lament his absence and is bowed by it. Not only the members of his family who are still living but even some of his servants have done their best to protect his interests; their own claims upon life have been gladly deferred. He is still loved, respected and admired by all those he cares most about.

Underneath the surface, itself lovely and life-affirming, of this immortal poem lies one of the most enticing and comprehensive dream fabrics ever spun. The dreams comprising it satisfy hopes which few men in any age can bear to do without. At the deepest level the *Odyssey* offers a wish-fulfilling triumph over the things which do most to make life onerous: death and inexorable disfigurement by time; the need, because we know our own heart, to distrust even those we most deeply love; and the competitiveness and ambivalence which mar, and sometimes engulf, the relationship which, because it begins wholly in giving, unqualified by need, is perhaps the most nearly perfect one available to man: the relationship of parent and child—specifically, in this archetypal tale of the patriarchal era, the relationship of father and son.

⚙ "Sailing to Byzantium":
Another Voyage, Another
Reading

*Art . . . shrinks . . . from every ab-
stract thing, from all that is of the brain only, from all that is not a fountain
jetting from the entire hopes, memories, and sensations of the body. Its
morality is personal, knows little of any general law. . . .* Yeats[1]

1

"Sailing to Byzantium" seems to occupy a special place among the several poems by Yeats dealing with the bleakness of old age. In this poem,
it appears to be widely believed, Yeats triumphantly confronts and liq-
uidates his fears of aging and death. He does so by virtue of the fact that
he—or, more accurately, the "I" of the poem—is a poet and a student of
poetry: he discovers that engrossment in poetry is the only, but a sufficient, recompense for the privations of old age.

It would be interesting to discover, if that were feasible, how much
influence a single essay, Elder Oldson's widely known "'Sailing to Byzantium': Prolegomena to a Poetics of the Lyric," has played in the acceptance of this viewpoint.[2] What makes the question worth raising is
that, so far as I can ascertain, the essay has not been challenged in any
head-on way in the more than twenty years it has been in print, though

1. From *The Cutting of an Agate,* reprinted in *Essays and Introductions* (New
York, 1961), pp. 292–293.
2. The essay originally appeared in the *University of Kansas City Review* (Spring
1942). It was reprinted in *The Permanence of Yeats,* edited by James Hall and Martin Steinmann (New York, 1950), which was reissued as a Collier paperback in
1961, and more recently, in Wilber Scott, *Five Approaches to Literary Criticism*
(New York, 1962; hardcover edition, 1963).

surely the poem with which it deals can be read in more than one way. It seems absurd to suppose that a single essay could impose itself on an entire generation of critics, most especially since for a time it may not have commanded much attention, and one casts about for other factors which would help to explain the fact that so few interpretations have appeared which contravene Olson's. Certainly the difficulty of the poem itself is one such factor: the depths one senses under the poem's shimmering surface are intimidating. One should make allowance also for the fact that even in our age of criticism essays that focus on a single work are relatively rare. This helps to explain, for example, why R. P. Blackmur, Cleanth Brooks, John Crowe Ransom and Kenneth Burke, all of whom touched on "Sailing to Byzantium" before Olson (Ransom more than once), dealt with the poem so glancingly; their essays were basically concerned with more general subjects.[3]

Still, it would be my guess that the Olson essay has exerted considerable influence. As it happens—I do not for a moment suggest that Olson had any ulterior rhetorical aim in working out his analysis—the interpretation the essay advances must be seductive in its appeal to many of those who would be drawn to it: people who love literature and have made sacrifices to create or study it. The hope that something we write or say may survive us seems frequently to serve as a mild but helpful defense against the dread of annihilation. At first glance the idea that we ourselves may survive in some form and continue to "sing," if not create, may be still more alluring. Moreover, the dazzling brilliance with which Olson sets forth his ideas gives them authority. Olson's mind has the kind of precision and systematic quality we attribute, perhaps mistakenly, to computers. In reading him, one can almost hear wheels spinning, erroneous possibilities being methodically eliminated, the way being inexorably cleared for the only answer that fits all the premises. Olson's essay is formidable as well as brilliant, and I believe it has had the effect of compounding the difficulty the poem presents and of discouraging alternative readings. It takes an intrepid and perhaps foolish person to cross pens with Olson. Nevertheless, I wish to do just that—in part because I feel he has misinterpreted "Sailing to Byzantium" and has unquestionably misread it at one or two points; and to an even greater ex-

---

3. Actually the Burke essay to which I refer, "On Motivation in Yeats," and the second of Ransom's essays appeared somewhat later than Olson's (in the winter 1942 *Southern Review, 7*) but evidently before Burke or Ransom had read Olson. When Burke did read him, it seems only fair to add, though disagreeing with some aspects of Olson's theory of poetics, he expressed admiration for his interpretation of "Sailing to Byzantium." See *A Grammar of Motives* (New York, 1945), pp. 465–484.

tent because I think it important to try to ascertain how a critic so obviously gifted as Olson could fall into such errors. If I am not mistaken, much of the blame should be attributed to the critical approach he employs. One tendency of that approach seems to me so undesirable that I believe it should be identified and guarded against in literary criticism generally: I refer to the tendency to pay as little attention as possible to the emotional content of literature and to our emotional responses to it.

2

The gist of Olson's interpretation of "Sailing to Byzantium" may be gleaned from two early paragraphs. So that his way of seeing the poem will be fresh in the minds of readers I quote these in full:

> In "Sailing to Byzantium" an old man faces the problem of old age, of death, and of regeneration, and gives his decision. Old age, he tells us, excludes a man from the sensual joys of youth; the world appears to belong completely to the young, it is no place for the old; indeed, an old man is scarcely a man at all—he is an empty artifice, an effigy merely, of a man; he is a tattered coat upon a stick. This would be very bad, except that the young also are excluded from something; rapt in their sensuality, they are ignorant utterly of the world of the spirit. Hence if old age frees a man from sensual passion, he may rejoice in the liberation of the soul; he is admitted into the realm of the spirit; and his rejoicing will increase according as he realizes the magnificence of the soul. But the soul can best earn its own greatness from the great works of art; hence he turns to those great works, but in turning to them, he finds that these are by no means mere effigies, or monuments, but things which have souls also; these live in the noblest element of God's fire, free from all corruption; hence he prays for death, for release from his mortal body; and since the insouled monuments exhibit the possibility of the soul's existence in some other matter than flesh, he wishes reincarnation, not now in a mortal body, but in the immortal and changeless embodiment of art.
>
> There are thus the following terms, one might say, from which the poem suspends: the condition of the young, who are spiritually passive although sensually active; the condition of the merely old, who are spiritually and physically impotent; the condition of the old, who, although physically impotent, are capable of spiritual activity; the condition of art considered as inanimate—i.e., the condition of

things which are merely monuments: and finally the condition of art considered as animate—as of such things as artificial birds which have a human soul. The second term, impotent and unspiritual old age, is a privative, a repugnant state which causes the progression through the other various alternative terms, until its contrary is encountered. The first and third terms are clearly contraries of each other; taken together as animate nature they are further contrary to the fourth term, inanimate art. None of these terms represents a wholly desirable mode of existence; but the fifth term, which represents such a mode, amalgamates the positive elements and eliminates the negative elements of both nature and art, and effects thus a resolution of the whole, for now the soul is present, as it would not be in art, nor is it passive, as it would be in the young and sensual mortal body, nor is it lodged in a "dying animal," as it would be in the body of the aged man; the soul is now free to act in its own supremacy and in full cognizance of its own excellence, and its embodiment is now incorruptible and secure from all the ills of flesh.

What do I feel is erroneous here? Exaggerating somewhat, I would answer: the interpretation as a whole, the entire chain of reasoning on which the conclusion depends. I cannot understand how any sensitive reader of the poem can fail to feel that the conclusion, at any rate, *is* mistaken—this though he may have no more than a dim notion of how such a feeling could be justified.[4] In general, however, I imagine that this hypothetical reader would verbalize his reaction in some such way as this: Olson's interpretation assumes that "Sailing to Byzantium" is a happy poem in which, at the end, all the old man's problems are neatly worked out.[5] But it seems to be a sad poem—even a desperate one—and not a happy one.

In fact, the poem is a cry of agony. There is no resolution; or, more accurately, there is a negative resolution: the "I" of the poem sees what must be achieved to make his situation bearable and finds he cannot

4. With T. S. Eliot, who declared ". . . genuine poetry can communicate before it is understood," I believe that the general meaning of a poem can be intuited before one begins to reflect upon it, much less analyze it. These immediate divinations of what a poem is saying are of course not sacrosanct and may be erroneous. But in my judgment—assuming that they are the responses of readers who are intelligent, sensitive and sophisticated—they are less likely to be erroneous than later conceptualizations which fail to take them into account.
5. In a later essay Olson describes the effect of the poem as "a kind of noble joy or exaltation." See "An Outline of Poetic Theory," in *Critiques and Essays in Criticism, 1920–1948*, ed. R. W. Stallman (New York, 1949), reprinted in *Critics and Criticism, Ancient and Modern*, ed. R. S. Crane (Chicago, 1952).

achieve it. The final stanza, which Olson takes to be a happy resolution of all the "terms" previously introduced, is scarcely that at even the most superficial level. (Perhaps poems should not be analyzed in terms of terms.) To be sure, the scene it depicts may possess a momentary prettiness to *bystanders,* including readers who are "outside" the poem. But is it not clearly a bitter, tinselly travesty of what the "I" of the poem—or Yeats or any creative person—values and would want of an afterlife? When we look more closely, moreover, we see that neither the poem as a whole nor the final stanza is about an afterlife. The old man is telling us how he would choose to be reincarnated, if that possibility were open to him, in order to make us feel his present despair. The idea of retaining any semblance of his human form, as the sages have, is rejected, perhaps out of the fear that it would stir painful memories of mortality. Beyond this, the old man rejects the idea of living again in any shape or form. In electing to be reincarnated as an inanimate object, a mechanical bird, he is saying, "Aging and facing death are so intolerable I would go to any lengths not to have to endure them again."[6]

3

Let us look at the poem stanza by stanza. The first stanza presents few problems. It demonstrates what it forthrightly declares, that the particular part of the world in which the "I" of the poem lives is no place for old men, since all its inhabitants, "fish, flesh or fowl," are preoccupied with the quest for sensual gratification, a pursuit for which the old have presumably limited capacities and opportunities, a pursuit, too, which may stir painful memories in the old of earlier, happier days. This gratification is of such preemptive importance that people devote themselves to it to the exclusion of art, though art objects are unaging whereas living things and sexual gratification are both ephemeral. Not even the old are exempt from this obsessive concern with sex, despite their limited opportunities for securing satisfaction. Olson mistakenly assumes that only the young are "caught in that sensual music," but the poem is here much clearer than poetry often is. If Yeats had wanted to say that the young "neglect monuments of unaging intellect," it seems reasonable to suppose that he would have used the pronoun "they." Instead, he says "all." But if

6.   I am aware that in a 1937 radio broadcast Yeats said that he used the bird "as a symbol of the intellectual joy of eternity, as contrasted with the instinctive joy of human life," a statement which of course tends to support Olson's interpretation. But the statement came many years after the completion of the poem. Even if it had been made during the heat of composition, I would say that it is no more than another example of the fact that writers are often unaware of what they are saying.

there is the slightest degree of ambiguity, it is dissipated by stanza III: even in Byzantium the old man prays to the sages to "consume [his] heart away" and describes himself as "sick with desire." Long before this, however, the reader knows that if the old man were exempting himself from the universal concern with sensuality, there would be no poem. Still, there is a difference between the situation of young and old, as the first six lines of the second stanza proceed to make clear. It is unseemly for the old to remain under the sway of lust. An aged man is but "a paltry thing" unless, in direct proportion as his body grows old, thus presumably reducing the need for sexual gratification, he is able to devote himself increasingly to things of the spirit and intellect, such as art. This involves effort: the only way one can exult in art—take pleasure in it or create it—is by studying existing art objects. These six lines are programmatic.[7] The "I" of the poem sees what he must do to live with dignity, and in the concluding lines of the stanza—with wings as swift as meditation or the thoughts of love—he does it: he journeys to Byzantium.

It is of course a metaphorical journey to a metaphorical destination. As Olson declares: "Byzantium is not a place upon a map, but a term in the poem; a term signifying a stage of comtemplation wherein the soul studies itself and so learns both what it is and in what consists true and eternal joy." Still, the "I" "goes" there. By stanza III he is in a different place, or stage—the "this" implied by the "that" at the very beginning of the poem. Olson's analysis tends to ignore the speed with which the poem moves—at points, even to forget that it moves at all; it assumes that everything takes place in a single moment of intuition.[8] In fact, while

7. Though Margaret Rudd's interpretation of the poem as a whole is quite different from mine, she has written in somewhat similar terms of the first two stanzas: "They are almost, and poignantly, a lecture or reminder to himself that he must grow old gracefully. . . ." *Divided Image: A Study of William Blake and W. B. Yeats* (London, 1953), p. 169.
8. Olson is analyzing "Sailing to Byzantium," it is to be remembered, as a preliminary to developing a poetics of the lyric. He argues, correctly I believe, that a problem (rather than plot or character) orders the poem. But in an excess of zeal to distinguish a lyric from a tragedy he further contends that "there is here no plot, no ordered tissue of incidents, for, first of all, the whole poem is of a moment—the moment in which the old man confronts the monuments and addresses them—whereas a tissue of incidents, a plot, must extend over a span of time." This seems to me arbitrary in the extreme; except perhaps for the "that" at the beginning of the poem, for which there are more satisfactory alternative explanations, there is no evidence that stanzas I and II are, as it were, flashbacks and that the "action" of the poem is crowded into the old man's prayer. It would have little poignancy if that were so. In general, this way of looking at the poem greatly understates the amount of movement and drama it contains.

the poem deals with a problem, it has a submerged narrative structure: there is an illusion of movement which permits the fundamental conflict to be worked out sequentially. The "I" voyages to Byzantium. Now, in the opening lines of the third stanza, he beseeches the sages of the less worldly place to be singing masters of his soul.

As he prays, however—and this is another shift Olson's analysis disregards—he becomes aware of the futility of his request. Though his capacity to secure sexual gratification has diminished and he knows he should be less concerned with it, he finds that he is still "sick with desire." Nor can he free himself of thoughts of his impending death. The twin obsessions of "that country" are with him still, so urgently that he cannot even have a sense of human and personal identity. Even death seems preferable to his present misery and he abandons the plea for instruction and prays for death—this though he recognizes that there is nothing after death. He is content—he *wants*—to be gathered "into the artifice of eternity."[9] This one phrase, I believe, reveals the erroneousness of Olson's interpretation. It stands out even in a poem replete with inspired phrases. It is impossible to suppose that Yeats was oblivious of either the phrase or its plain meaning. Yet Olson not only fails to discuss the phrase, but ignores it in a more serious way: he assumes that the "I" of the poem has an ingenuous kind of faith in the soul's immortality.

The final stanza clinches matters. Far from representing a happy resolution of everything, with all negatives extirpated, all positives realized, and the "I" of the poem reincarnated complete with soul, the last stanza summarizes and gives added intensity to what has already been said or suggested. It too is a kind of prayer, though it is couched in the form of a declaration. Aging and having to face death are so unendurable, Yeats or his persona is saying, that I pray that I may never have to face them again. Once I am dead I hope that I shall never live again, whether as a human being or any other kind of creature subject to time's inexorable will, to decay and death. I will sing, but as a bird made of perdurable gold, not as a living creature. I will sing of time, but myself be immune to its influence.

9.   This may seem an abrupt shift, but we sense that it is less abrupt than it appears. The very way the old man expressed himself betrays the ambivalence involved in the decision to renounce the world and devote himself chiefly to art. He perceives the program he develops to be desirable, rather than actually embracing and desiring it. As Richard Ellman declares, "Searching for the monuments of unaging intellect is as much a *pis aller* as a goal. . . ." *Yeats: The Man and the Masks* (New York, 1948), p. 256.

4

It is perhaps necessary to say a little more about what seem to me some of the mistaken or unwarranted aspects of Olson's analysis of "Sailing to Byzantium," but I have no desire to attempt a full-scale refutation.

The first question I shall raise about Olson's discussion of stanza I will, I fear, seem trivial. After noting that "the use of 'that' implies a possible 'this'," he adds, "that is, there is a country for the old as for the young." The subjunctive "may be" would have seemed more natural as well as more accurate. It might have paved the way for sharing the "I's" discovery, at Byzantium, that in fact there is no happy country for the old.

The failure to note that in "that country" *all*, not merely the young, are absorbed in sensuality and neglect art is, of course, a more serious error; it persists and ramifies. In the paragraphs quoted, Olson refers to the old as "physically impotent." In the second following paragraph, he declares that "stanza I presents a rejection of passion, stanza II an acceptance of intellection." Still later he asserts that "old men can no longer participate" in the sensual delight which occupies the young. If matters were that simple, and if the disjunction between young and old were that complete, there would be no problem in this area—and no poem. Nor would there be the tension which not only persists through the second stanza but mounts, reaching its climax only at the very end of stanza III. The old man's situation is agonizing in large part because he is still subject to sensual desire but incapable of either gratifying it readily as the young do or of sublimating it as he would like to.

Olson's misreading of "young" for "all" blinds him to the distinction underlying the entire argument (to use his word) of the poem; or perhaps the failure to have the distinction in mind led to the misreading. There is still another possibility, to which we shall return: Olson may be too intent on finding sharp and neat antitheses. What is certain is that this is a strange error for a critic as committed as Olson is to paying close attention to the terms of a work of art. The error leads to a misinterpretation of the first stanza and, to an extent, of the entire poem. The first stanza draws a different distinction between young and old than Olson supposes: it depicts old men as subject to the same desires as animals and the young, but denied opportunities for gratifying them and thus suffering not only from frustration but, it is implied, from envy also.

The difference between Olson's reading of stanza II and my own has perhaps been adequately covered, but there is much more to be said about stanza III. The stanza begins with the "I" invoking certain sages in

Byzantium. They are evidently immortal spirits, for they stand in God's holy fire and move "in the circular motion which alone is possible to eternal things" (Olson). Otherwise their identity seems to be unspecified. Olson, however, interpolating, equates them with art objects—not, however, the passive, inanimate art objects of the first two stanzas, which are referred to as "monuments," but "insouled monuments." It is the discovery that the works of art have souls, he further argues, which leads to the old man's realization that the body may be dispensed with and that he will then be secure from corruption and all the ills of the flesh—and hence to his plea for death. There is no warranty for any of these assumptions. So far as I am aware, Olson is alone among critics who have discussed the sages in regarding them as insouled embodiments of works of art, and one critic, Harry Modean Campbell, has explicitly challenged the interpretation.[10] Earlier versions of the poem suggest that the saints are saints in the usual sense of that word. Olson's other assumptions depend almost entirely upon this shaky initial one. No convincing further evidence is introduced. For example, the belief that the soul can exist apart from the body and is immune to the ills of the body is not of itself a sufficient explanation for a longing for death. And while the poem makes one feel that it is painful to be old and face death, it nowhere implies that "no song is possible to the soul while even a remnant of passion remains." On the contrary, no attentive reader can fail to sense that "Sailing to Byzantium" itself was born under, and even of, just such "impossible" conditions.

Earlier, in discussing stanza II, Olson declares: ". . . if the soul can wax and grow strong as the body wanes, then every step in the dissolution of the body—'every tatter in its mortal dress'—is cause for a further augmentation of joy." Of course, even in exhorting himself, the old man of the poem does not put it that way but the other way around, and the difference in emphasis is all important. Immersion in art is introduced as a compensation for the deprivations of aging; no claim is entered for the proposition that, for poets at least, old age is a happier time than youth.[11] Now, in discussing stanza III, Olson makes the somewhat inconsistent declaration that joy is not possible "until the body be dissolved." He

10.   ". . . the appeal is no more to the works of art or to the artists than the prayer of the Roman Catholic is to the statues of the saints, or the sculptors of the statues, before which he kneels." "Yeats' 'Sailing to Byzantium,' " Modern Language Notes, 70 (December 1955).
11.   At a later point, Olson himself declares that "finding a suitable compensation for the losses suffered in old age" is the problem ordering the poem, but he seems oblivious to the difference between this way of stating matters and the way he states them in the passage just discussed.

maintains that the old man reaches the suspect and repugnant conclusion that it is better to be dead than to be alive. To the extent that this is so—and it is true that the old man prays for death—it is a confession of defeat, not a whoop of victory; and it is not clear that the act of praying, like everything which follows, is also an indirect form of commentary upon the old man's present predicament, a way of saying, "Even when I seek refuge in the realm of art, I cannot forget sexual tension and my aging body."

What is hardest for me to understand, however, is Olson's belief that the old man's problems are happily resolved, that the final stanza represents the realization of all his hopes. To be sure, the belief follows logically from everything else Olson says. Nor have I any grounds for hoping that his emotional responses to the poem would suggest other possibilities and stir up doubts; not only Olson's mode of analysis but specific things he says about the reader later in the essay suggest that he feels such reactions have no value for criticism. Still, Olson is a poet himself as well as a critic and a scholar. If only because of this, I should think that even a cool, analytical reading of the final stanza might have led to a reconsideration of his interpretation. In a note to "Sailing to Byzantium" in the Collected Poems, Yeats refers to reading somewhere of artificial birds that sang in the Emperor's palace at Byzantium. Olson, in a footnote to his essay, identifies the Emperor as Theophilus and says that "the birds conform to the description of certain automata constructed for him." Might not the word "automata" have given Olson pause? An artificial bird which sings a set song, or songs, is an expressive image of the printed page, or phonograph record, through which the poet may hope to survive and communicate after death, but it is hard to understand how Olson could believe that the old man of the poem, or any poet, would be happy to spend eternity in such a form, one which mocks the joy he experiences as a creator of poems.

It is difficult also to link the idea of soul with such a creature. And it seems more fanciful still to attribute freedom to it, to argue that, encaged in such a form, the soul is "free to act in its own supremacy and in full cognizance of its own excellence." There is no evidence that the bird enjoys any freedom. It is "set [my italics] upon a tree to sing . . ." and presumably limited to the mechanical repetition of that which is born to the living poet in mystery, then fashioned with a sedulousness fueled by love. Again, there is no evidence that the bird's song is of any particular importance, much less that it is ". . . a song of spiritual joy in praise of eternal things." Olson declares that "what is past and passing and to come" represents the divisions of eternity, but so far as I know there is no evidence for this.[12] In literature, certainly, eternity is often conceived as a perpetual present, without temporal divisions. To return to the poem, the rest of the description tends to minimize the importance of the bird's song: it is of just sufficient interest "to keep a drowsy Emperor awake" and, possibly, to bemuse a semi-captive audience of courtiers.[13]

"Sailing to Byzantium," Ernest Schanzer declares, like Keats's "Ode to a Nightingale," ". . . can be regarded as [a poem] of escape, escape from a world of flux where the poet is faced with physical decay and pain to a world of changelessness into which human suffering cannot enter."[14] But, as Schanzer proceeds to point out, the escape involves a heavy cost. It leads to the loss of ". . . qualities that only belong to the world of flux: happiness, plaintiveness, ecstasy." And as Schanzer declares, "Yeats knew this as well as Keats." The evidence for this is in the poem. Though Olson is blind to the attraction the world of youth and lovemaking has for the old man, the tension between that attraction and the realization that he must try and find another center for his own life is the basic subject matter of the poem.[15]

Schanzer and some other Yeats scholars believe that Yeats had Hans Christian Andersen's story "The Emperor's Nightingale" (sometimes simply called "The Nightingale") in the back of his mind when he wrote "Sailing to Byzantium." If so, it would seem even less likely that the concluding stanza is meant to be a happy ending, an exalted kind of wish fulfillment, for the mechanical bird is invidiously compared to the living nightingale in that story. But there is no need to move so far from what

12.   Olson is evidently thinking of the tale of Er which Socrates recounts at the end of *The Republic*, where Lachesis, Clotho and Atropos sing, respectively, of the past, present and future. But it is by no means clear that these represent the divisions of eternity even in this tale.

13.   William Empson goes much farther than I do here in disparaging the golden bird. "Then, as to symbolism, the more you think of birds as able to take messages up to Heaven, intensely spontaneous in their lyrics, and so forth, the more a clockwork bird with a built-in tweet-tweet is bound to seem pathetically ludicrous." "Mr. Wilson on the Byzantium Poems," *A Review of English Literature*, 1 (July 1960).

14.   " 'Sailing to Byzantium,' Keats and Anderson," *English Studies*, 41 (December 1960).

15.   It is worth adding that the symbols of sensuality used in the first stanza probably possessed more attraction for Yeats himself and for his Irish readers than they do for later readers in other lands. As A. Norman Jeffares declares, Yeats ". . . would remember that in Celtic legendry the salmon is used as a symbol of strength; the hero Cuchulain is renowned for his 'Salmon leap,' and his energy is compared to the flight of a bird." "The Byzantium Poems of W. B. Yeats," *The Review of English Studies*, 22 (January 1946), p. 47.

the poem itself communicates. A fairy-tale quality of momentary attractiveness the last stanza undoubtedly possesses; but as soon as one thinks of the golden bird as the eternal incarnation of a once-living poet, all the luster vanishes.

Any interpretation must be judged, I believe—a belief I imagine Olson shares—by how well it fits and illuminates the work with which it deals. Still, it is interesting and comforting to note that there is considerable external evidence, much more than I can cite, which tends to corroborate the general correctness of the interpretation offered here, especially its correctness as compared with more optimistic interpretations, such as the one advanced by Olson. "Sailing to Byzantium" is placed at the very beginning of the volume of poems called *The Tower*. Shortly after it appeared, in 1928, Yeats wrote Olivia Shakespear, "Re-reading *The Tower*, I was astonished at its bitterness and long to live out of Ireland that I may find some new vintage. Yet the bitterness gave the book its power and it is the best book I have written."[16]

John Unterecker, Hugh Kenner, and other Yeats scholars believe that in planning all of his books Yeats was careful to select poems that belonged together and commented on one another. "The Tower," the poem immediately following "Sailing to Byzantium," is very clearly a more discursive treatment of the same material. In this poem, too, here more in his own person, Yeats is "making [his] soul," but it is more unmistakable that he is doing this because he sees that it is necessary and not because he finds it desirable. And he is explicitly doing one of the very things Olson denies that the old man does in "Sailing to Byzantium"—raging against old age:

> Did all old men and women, rich and poor,
> Who trod upon these rocks or passed this door,
> Whether in public or in secret rage
> As I do now against old age?

Lust as well as rage are confessed in the often quoted lines from "The Spur," written a good decade after "Sailing to Byzantium":

> You think it horrible that lust and rage
> Should dance attention on my old age;
> They were not such a plague when I was young:
> What else have I to spur me into song?

16. Quoted in John Unterecker, *A Reader's Guide to Yeats* (New York, 1959), p. 170.

Frequently, too, Yeats proclaims his regard for the body, nowhere more beautifully than in another superb poem in *The Tower*, "Among School Children," where he rejects the subordination of body to soul:

Labor is blossoming or dancing where
The body is not bruised to pleasure soul . . .

5

What remains is to try to understand how so intelligent and knowledge-able a critic as Olson could stumble into as many errors as I believe he has. Inevitably such an endeavor must be speculative, though it is less speculative than it may appear, for certain tendencies make themselves felt in Olson's sketch of a poetics as well as in his exegesis of "Sailing to Byzantium." The endeavor may seem presumptuous also, most especially if my interpretation seems mistaken. These are unavoidable risks. I am more concerned, particularly since I have a tendency to express myself vehemently, about the possibility that I will seem to be attacking Olson personally or basing my conjectures on some knowledge of him as an individual. This is not the case. My quarrel with Olson is bitter but impersonal. He is a representative of an approach to literature which, as I indicated years ago, I feel we are justified in distrusting on a priori grounds and towards which I feel a deep and growing antipathy. The approach is responsible, I believe, for a great deal of shallow, sterile, and sometimes erroneous criticism. The source of my antipathy, however, lies deeper: it stems from the conviction that the approach is inappropriate to the object to which it is applied—imaginative literature. It tends to divert those who use it, and sometimes their students and readers also, from the foul rag-and-bone shop of the heart, which is I think both subject and source of the greatest literary works, to a world of tidy, antiseptic abstractions; it conveys a false impression of literature itself. The approach may have particularly harmful effects on people who are timorous, anxious and fastidious, who have unrecognized fears or even feelings of repugnance for much of what literature has to say—and we all know people of this sort, people who have been attracted to the field of literary study because they think of it as offering a refuge from life rather than a distillation of it.

Though Olson clearly regards himself, and is generally regarded as a neo-Aristotelean, it is both more useful in understanding his approach and more accurate, I believe, to view him as a formalist. What is certain is that he places primary—in his theory, it could even be said, almost exclusive—emphasis upon form.

His predilection for confining himself to form to the greatest extent feasible reveals itself very early in his essay. Though he declares that a poetics of the lyric should be arrived at inductively, before he begins his analysis of "Sailing to Byzantium," which is to be a first step in the development of such a poetics, he lays down restrictions which leave practically no room for inductive activity. He begins, reasonably and innocently enough, by establishing one condition: a poetics may consider only those questions which might be raised about a lyric *qua* work of art. But Olson defines this condition in such a way that it excludes practically every significant question that might be raised about a poem: no question can be considered if it falls, even in part, in the purview of some other "science." Thus it would be unjustifiable, for instance, though Olson does not use this example, to consider a lyric as a communication—though this among other things it assuredly is—and differentiate it from other forms of communication in terms of its properties and effects, explaining, for example, why it is so much more efficacious than most other forms in engaging the emotions as well as the mind. The consideration of effects is explicitly proscribed: ". . . a question relevant to [a poem] as productive of, say, social consciousness, falls under politics." *Any* question which is related to subject matter is presumably excluded, since it is difficult to think of a theme of poetry which is not to some extent of concern to some other field. In fact, I believe, form is excluded also, for of course it is not peculiar to poetry either. But it must be salvaged somehow or Olson would have nothing to work with. How is this accomplished? Quite easily. Olson simply equates "purely poetic principle" and "formal principle." Once this has been posited, everything Olson wants to follow follows as a matter of course. There is only one thing an analysis need or should consider: "the poetic structure of a particular work in the sense of inquiring what form has been imposed upon the medium of words."

This is not ground clearing; it is demolition. In his zeal to eliminate from consideration all those aspects of poetry he prefers to disregard, Olson has left himself practically nothing to work with. Indeed, both when he develops his poetics and when he analyzes "Sailing to Byzantium," he is compelled to restore some of what he has razed. After all, the argument which he regards as the principle of the poem is to some degree a tissue of what is being said as well as of the way statements are arranged. But the restoration is minimal. Olson does want to disregard content to the greatest extent possible and focus upon form; and he is nothing if not conscientious in his search for evidence of organization. He finds antitheses, symmetries and analogies everywhere:

. . . there are . . . two major divisions which divide the poem precisely in half, the first two stanzas presenting art as inanimate, the second two, as animate: . . .

Within these two halves of the poem, further divisions may be found, coincident with the stanzaic divisions. Stanza I presents a rejection of passion, stanza II an acceptance of intellection; then, turning on the realization that art is insouled, stanza III presents a rejection of the corruptible embodiment, and stanza IV, an acceptance of the incorruptible. There is an alternation, thus, of negative and affirmative; out of passion into intellection, out of corruption into permanence, in clear balance, the proportion being I:II:III:IV. . . .

Here and elsewhere in Olson's essay we find signs of a curious contradiction. It appears that he is over-intellectual in his approach to poetry. Yet at points he also seems to be guilty of over-simplification and forcing. There are certainly parallels, contrasts, and analogies in "Sailing to Byzantium." But, they are not as inclusive, as mathematical in their relationship, or perhaps as numerous, as Olson indicates. For example, as we have seen, there is nowhere in the poem the kind of unequivocal rejection of passion or acceptance of intellection Olson finds.

How is it possible for a critic as well qualified as Olson to make such mistakes and fail to perceive some of the meanings and qualities which account for the depth and complexity of "Sailing to Byzantium"? The proximate cause, I believe, is the critical approach he employs. The attempt to analyze literature entirely in formal terms is *likely* to lead to error; there is no theoretical or practical justification for such an approach. Moreover, powerful emotional needs underlie the choice of the approach, and these needs, too, are likely to cause trouble, most especially since they are usually unconscious so that the critic is unable to safeguard himself against their influence. Finally, the critic is tempted into error by the kind of "product" characteristic of the approach, the abstraction, or creation, of a formal scheme which is held to unify a work of art and yet is distinguishable from it—which in fact comes to possess a separate existence.

The attempt to analyze a literary work in purely formal terms is likely to lead to error because there is no such thing as "form" in any objective sense. The only thing the critic has before him is a work of art as an entity, an entity in which whatever is being communicated is already structured and expressed in a certain way. This is not to say that "form" and "content" are not potentially useful *analytic* terms, but certain cautions are in order when one employs them. I have already written about this in my book *Fiction and the Unconscious,* and while I was there discussing narrative art what is said is equally applicable to poetry:

> Those who use the terms have to remember that content and form are no more than hypostatized constructions, and that there is a certain arbitrariness in assigning any given attributes to one or the other; it is impossible to say categorically where one ends and the other begins. Secondly, it is necessary to respect *both* content and form. If one is going to attribute the effect of fiction entirely to one or the other, it is hardly worth employing the terms in the first place; one would do better to discuss a work as an entity.[17]

Since form and content are abstracted from a common matrix, it seems obvious that each may shed light upon the other. It is equally obvious that it is an abuse of the analytic possibilities inherent in the terms to exalt one at the expense of the other. Indeed, the connections between form and content are so close that one cannot proceed very far with the analysis of either if one forgets that they are not autonomous. For example, if a critic "tries to ignore the substance of literature and . . . discuss it in rigidly formal terms, [the] ultimate rationale of the formal effects he takes note of will elude him: he may observe their inner consistency, but will not be able to account for their appropriateness" (pp. 72–73).

Though one cannot neglect either content or form with impunity, at the risk of seeming partisan I must add that it seems to me even more dangerous to ignore content than to ignore form. This feeling is based on the belief that a poet or novelist is usually impelled to write by something he wishes to say. In the creation of literature, I suspect, form usually functions as means rather than end. Formal characteristics are selected or developed in order to present the material struggling for expression with maximum impact—this whether the thinking involved is conscious or unconscious. Thus while form is no less important than content in the finished work of art, content, I suspect, is the more fertile starting point for critical analysis. As has been suggested, a profound understanding of content is almost indispensable for a dynamic exploration of form, for understanding *why* the various formal characteristics function well or fail to. And for most critics I believe that insights into content are also more likely to have heuristic value than are insights into form. The realization that, on one level, Marvell's "The Garden" deals with a regressive wish may at once call attention to and explain the curious constructions of the fifth stanza, which make the "I" of the poem a

17. Boston, 1957; New York, 1962, p. 72.

passive recipient of boons; noticing the constructions is perhaps less likely to make one aware of the hidden theme.

Since formal analysis is by its very nature not too likely to direct one's attention to hidden themes, it is doubly unfortunate that the most potent emotional force determining the selection of that approach in probably fear of the kinds of things great literature has to say, especially at the latent level. To some extent this fear is universal. As the slow acceptance of the Freud-Jones explanation of Hamlet's delay perhaps suggests, many students of literature do not wish to be reminded that not only people of the commoner sort but even people of intelligence, ability, and generosity of spirit, *people like themselves,* may be swayed, even overwhelmed, by terrible, dark, anarchistic impulses. People attracted to formal analysis may be repelled by the intimation that literature is often centrally concerned with such material. Attention to form provides an excuse—or if one prefers, a justification—for focussing upon less dangerous matters.

Literature not only deals with unsavory and threatening material; it is unruly and insubordinate, hard to pin down—at times, as I have tried to show in my analysis of "My Kinsman, Major Molineux," guilty of a kind of duplicity. "Sailing to Byzantium" exhibits all these unregenerate tendencies. If I am correct in my understanding of the poem, the old man in it confesses to all sorts of bodily needs and fears it would be better for him not to have. He does not succeed in emancipating himself from them even when he attempts to devote himself mainly to art. Worse still, even in describing the world from which he fears he must flee, he cannot resist suggesting its attractiveness. As and even after the old man comes to the realization that he must find a different life pattern from the young, he says and does things which show he has a great deal in common with the young. Why can't he be consistent? There is certainly something undependable, even slippery, about an old man like this—and doubtless about the poet who created him.

The abstract of the form of the poem Olson arrives at is certainly tidier than this, and it is also more stable and definitely fixed. The young are sensual, but "old age . . . excludes a man from the sensual joys of youth." Indeed, the old are "physically impotent." Everything is neatly placed in some labelled compartment. The abstract has other virtues. It makes the poem as a whole, and the last two stanzas in particular, quite ethereal. Moreover, everything moves briskly along. Once the old man sets his course there is no backsliding. And in the end, of course, his problems are neatly and happily resolved.

It is apparent that the abstract is not as threatening as the poem; indeed, it is not threatening at all—the poem has been domesticated.

Though it is less apparent, it is also true that the very development of such an abstract provides reassurance against fear. It puts the critic in control of the work of art instead of leaving him passively subject to it.

An abstract is not without utility. At least for inattentive readers, an abstract may bring out the structure of a literary work more clearly than the work itself does. However, the development of an abstract involves certain dangers. These arise in large part from the fact that the abstract comes to acquire an independent existence, a fate which more broadly based interpretations somehow avoid. Since the abstract is the critic's contribution, and not even critics are free of narcissism, some of his energy and love may be deflected from the work of art itself to the abstract. Once that shift has occurred, the critic must be forgiven if he feels an impulse to make the abstract, which is his art object, as attractive as possible. This may, however, lead him to overemphasize the literary work's symmetry and formal excellence.

The danger is compounded by pressures from other sources. As I have tried to show in *Fiction and the Unconscious*, one of the chief functions of form is to reduce anxiety—not simply the anxiety aroused by the content of a particular work but the free-floating anxiety arising from our own unacceptable longings. "Our admiration of form is an indirect way of protesting our innocence of destructive impulses, our commitment to life and love" (p.130). The development of a formal analysis is of course a very conspicuous way of exhibiting such admiration, a spacious gesture. The intuitive feeling that formal analysis will quiet fears, which leads some people to adopt the approach, is fully justified. But, as is apparent, this feeling too may tempt the critic to exaggerate the extent to which the expressive content has been controlled and ordered by form.

On occasion these tendencies may lead a critic to see beauties which do not exist or to force matters a bit so that a symmetry will emerge in full perfection. The same tendencies may cause him to slight, or disregard, recalcitrant aspects of a literary work, such as indications of ambivalence or ambiguities, since these resist manipulation and intolerably complicate that task of demonstrating that every detail of a work is part of a flawless composition. When there is much such tidying up and selective blindness, the formal abstract becomes a Procrustean bed; one senses that the literary work has been made to fit the contours of the abstract, whereas ideally the abstract should follow the outlines of the literary work, even if these are irregular.

Many of the things already said about Olson's exegesis of "Sailing to Byzantium" illustrate, I believe, this tendency to bend a work to the critic's will. I cannot resist adding one more example, one which is trivial in a way but perhaps all the more revelatory because of that. In his essay Olson shows an awareness of the fact that line two of the poem refers to "birds in the trees." Yet at one point he cannot refrain from saying: ". . . in stanza I a mortal bird of nature amid natural trees sings a brief song of sensual joy in praise of mortal things . . . ; in stanza IV an immortal and artificial bird set in an artificial tree sings an eternal song of spiritual joy in praise of eternal things. . . ." The desire for a neater antithesis than the poem happens to provide is here almost pathetically betrayed.

In somewhat less evident ways the same kind of forcing evinces itself throughout the entire essay. In fact most of Olson's "terms" represent gross and sometimes inaccurate simplifications of the material they seek to summarize. It is this which permits the old man's problem to be worked out with such ease and unqualified success. Evidently Olson finds no indication of ambivalence anywhere in the poem. But it is present, I believe, in a more pervasive and dynamic way than has been indicated. We have seen that it evinces itself in the way the attraction of "that country" becomes visible in stanza I, as it were against the old man's will. But in the light of what we know of his emotional situation, is it not clear that the *disparagement* of sensuality in that stanza and the next one also reveals his ambivalence: he is trying to defend himself against the attraction of the world from which he sees he must begin to wean himself. What is explicit in stanza III is already covertly present in stanzas I and II. Olson's failure to see how much appeal the scene depicted in stanza I has for the old man is quite curious. Film makers, even quasi-illiterate ones, know that the sight of "The young/in one another's arms" is almost certain to arouse desire and envy in the hearts of spectators. Olson undoubtedly knows this too, but it may be a kind of knowledge he seeks to deny, and disregards, when he analyzes poetry.

Olson has been betrayed, I believe, by the approach he has employed and by the unknown emotional factors playing upon him. Under the guise of reconstructing the argument of "Sailing to Byzantium," he has in fact developed a detailed outline of a somewhat different poem. It cannot be denied that the poem sketched is superior to Yeats' poem in various respects—in its symmetry, for example, in the smoothness of its flow and the exactness with which the shifts in thought correspond to the stanzaic breaks, and in the faultless perfection with which all elements are dovetailed and worked out. If Olson's essay had been available to Yeats before he began to write, doubtless he would have tried to turn out a poem which measured up to it.

The poem he did write is admittedly somewhat rougher-hewn, and its materials are less firmly subdued. However, it faces the problems of its old man in all their complexity and, though it sometimes resorts to indirection, is scrupulously honest in its treatment of them. The poem does not shun ambivalent feelings and, in large part because of this, possesses tension and a much more intricate dialectic than Olson perceives. It is also highly dramatic. Moreover, the poignancy of the poem may actually be enhanced by the occasional evidence of tension between form and material. For example, the apparent disjunctiveness of the thought at various points may suggest not simply the richness of the poem's subject matter, but also the intensity of the old man's emotions and the sense of urgency he feels about coming to terms with his problem. Overall, "Sailing to Byzantium" may not be inferior to the smoother poem which might be composed on the basis of Olson's abstract.

Olson's essay seems saddening to me not only, or primarily, because I feel that in some respects it misinterprets "Sailing to Byzantium"—though that is melancholy enough in view of the greatness of the poem and the qualifications of the critic—but also because the kind of criticism it espouses and exemplifies, though suitable perhaps for a carefully reasoned philosophical treatise, is so out of keeping with poetry. To a greater extent than any other literary genre, even fiction, lyric poetry expresses and conveys emotion. To a greater extent than any other genre also, it is a product of what Frederick Clarke Prescott, in his unjustifiably neglected work *The Poetic Mind,* calls "the primitive imagination."[18] The primitive imagination is roughly equivalent to what Freud calls primary process thinking, the language which is supreme in the unconscious and dominates our fantasies and dreams. To be sure, secondary process thinking, the ordinary processes of conscious thought, are usually called into play also, though at times, if we may credit Coleridge, Housman, and many other witnesses, to an astonishingly small extent. The primitive imagination is always importantly involved, even—perhaps especially—in poems which, like "Sailing to Byzantium," are written over a number of years. A critical approach which ignores this fact is bound to prove inadequate.

Necessarily the writing of criticism, unlike the writing and reading of imaginative literature, is predominantly a cerebral kind of activity. I would like to suggest that despite this the critic cannot afford to neglect the emotions—either the emotions in the work with which he is dealing or his own emotional responses to that work. Those responses are among the best data at his disposal when he turns to the critical task of conceptualizing his understanding of the work. They suggest valuable questions about it, provide guide lines, serve as reality checks.

Ideally, the critic should also seek to become aware, insofar as that is

18.   New York, 1922; Ithaca, New York, 1959.

possible, of the emotional factors which actuate him as critic, which influence his predilection for a particular approach, his interest in a particular work, and his particular slant on that work. Though the value of this kind of self-awareness may not be immediately apparent, I believe it is very great. It is generally recognized that the emotions are unreliable guides, upon which the mind must keep a wary eye. But when the mind seeks to insulate itself from feeling it becomes an unreliable guide also. The danger of taking wrong turns swells when the mind ignores the emotions which affect its own activity, most especially irrational tendencies, biases, and fears. It is when the mind is blind to these that it is most likely to be swayed by them.

❖ Oedipus the King:
The Two Dramas,
the Two Conflicts

THE word "two" has an almost mag-
ical relevance in any modern scrutiny of *Oedipus the King*. In a sense it is
motive for writing, for when the drama was first presented it won only
the *second* prize, and this was an injustice that any close reader of our
century must feel an urge to rectify. Though Sophocles' play has its peers
among the tragedies of Shakespeare, it has never been surpassed by any
subsequent work in insight, concision, cunning of construction, or pro-
fundity and range of meaning. It is *primus inter pares*.

The word "two" must also be used repeatedly in any attempt to write
about *Oedipus the King*. Though Sophocles scrupulously observes the
unities of time and place and only one action is dramatized, there is an
important sense in which it may be said that *Oedipus the King* is not one
play but two. Formally, the play is constructed like a box containing a
smaller box, though this metaphor, like anything which has been said
about the play or can be said about it, seems inadequate. The boxes are
permeable; the background drama arises out of the foreground one: it is
composed of what is repressed and wins its way to the light despite and
against resistance. At the same time the drama with which the play begins, ends and is chiefly occupied, the foreground drama, is in a sense
the continuation and completion of the background drama; each of the
plays is born of the other. Because of this, and because Oedipus is the
protagonist in both dramas, there is some overlapping and there are intricate relationships and parallels, substantive as well as formal, between
the two parts of the play. Coleridge regarded *Oedipus the King* as one of

Reprinted from *College English*, December 1967.

the three great plots in all fiction. During the many centuries in which men have been writing plays, no more sophisticated formal structure has been devised.

A parallel tribute must be paid to the play's subject matter. Like *Hamlet*, *Oedipus the King* is a drama of internal conflict;[1] both the foreground and background dramas revolve around such conflicts. In each drama one conflict is central but traces of another may be discerned, and in each case the second conflict, the minor one, echoes the major conflict of the other drama: though each of the dramas deals with two conflicts, there are only two conflicts in all. If not universal, these conflicts are almost certainly the most widespread, and the most critical, with which western man has had to struggle through the centuries and must struggle today. *Oedipus the King* is not simply a superbly constructed and written play; it is the archetypal tragedy; and Oedipus, who never rationally "resolves" either of the conflicts though he is belatedly forced into what may look like a resolution of one of them, is the archetypal tragic hero—the ancestor of us all.

The word "two" has significance also for most of the speeches and developments which comprise the play: nearly every detail of the play has at least two different meanings, one for one or more of the characters and another meaning for others, or one for all the characters concerned and another for the audience. In a veiled way Teiresias tries to tell Oedipus why he does not wish to speak, but Oedipus assumes that he is balking for a completely different reason. When Teiresias finally blurts out the truth, Oedipus again misunderstands—or understands nothing whatever. Conversely, words sometimes have a more significant meaning for the person who hears them than for the person who speaks them: when Jocasta tries to reassure Oedipus, some of the things she says penetrate the film which has kept him from understanding what Teiresias told him. This doubleness of meaning of so much in the play is the source of the famous reversals on which Aristotle rightly set so much store: the "good news" the Messenger from Corinth brings is in the larger context of the play the beginning of the end for Oedipus; the reassurances to which the news leads spin a major part of that web of objective evidence from which Oedipus cannot escape no matter how desperately he struggles. Throughout the play we nearly always unconsciously see and understand more than the characters do at any given point, and Sophocles sometimes communicates with the audience over the heads

1.   Freud must have half-perceived this. He noted that the drama proceeded like an analysis without pursuing the observation. It was of course what I call the background drama that most interested him.

of his characters in a way which more obviously prepares us for the reversals; when Jocasta tells Oedipus that the one servant who escaped the massacre of the king's party asked to be sent as far from the city as possible once he saw the situation at the palace, the alert spectator or reader immediately infers the reason for his request whereas Jocasta and Oedipus disregard the possibility that it has any significance.

Finally, Sophocles makes even time do double duty: it marches simultaneously forward and backward. Each scene, each encounter, carries the action relentlessly forward; but it does this by carrying us progressively back in time. We go back finally to Oedipus' infancy, to his birth, and even beyond this to King Laius' fear of his unborn son. The action that fear precipitated is in one sense the beginning of *Oedipus the King*; in another sense, it seems part of a drama which goes on without end, a drama of which *Oedipus the King* is only a segment.

2

Though ours is reputedly an age of psychology, most literary critics, even those who write *about* Freud, make little or no use of his findings in their examination of literature. They seem blind—sometimes, one feels, they are determinedly blind—to indications of internal conflict and resistance and unconscious motivations, even when the evidence for these is copious and fairly obvious. Hence though it is disappointing, it is not surprising that, so far as I have been able to discover, only one nonanalytically oriented critic of *Oedipus the King*, Lillian Feder, shows an awareness of the fact that Oedipus is in conflict about discovering the truth, a perception which is indispensable, I believe, for explaining much of the ambiguity in the play and penetrating to a deeper and fuller understanding of it. Unfortunately, though Miss Feder's essay is searching and stimulating she does not exploit her insight to the full; she notes only a few instances of Oedipus' aberrant behavior and is not able to explain these satisfactorily in dynamic terms. Miss Feder expresses regret that a number of recent studies of the tragedy by classicists "lead only to traditional and rather narrow conclusions."[2] The fact is that *Oedipus the King* is only one example of an important group of works which are unlikely to yield their deepest secrets to critics who neglect depth psychology. The criticism which utilizes the findings of psychoanalysis has long been on the defensive. Let me make one modest affirmative claim for it: it has decisive advantages over alternative approaches in the explication

2. " 'The Unwary Egotist': A Study of the *Oedipus Tyrannus*," *Centennial Review*, 5, 1961. The quotation is from p. 261.

of works in which unconscious motives and conflicts, and behavior reflecting these, are of central importance.

To analyze the foreground drama in *Oedipus the King*, which involves grasping its meaning and nature consciously, we must somehow get "outside" the play, and in particular Sophocles' manipulation of time, and put all the events of the play in their correct chronological sequence. This is not easy, for the purpose of the manipulation, which is adroit and successful, is to regulate the disclosures of information so that they will have maximum dramatic impact and hold us enthralled. Still, the job must be done. By some deliberate effort of will we must either try to reread the play in relatively disengaged fashion or coolly rearrange its events in our mind.

The foreground drama is chiefly about seeing. Thebes is suffering from a grievous plague, and Oedipus, a responsible king, has anticipated the wishes of his subjects and sent his brother-in-law Creon, co-ruler with himself and Jocasta, to the temple of Apollo to find out what can be done to end it. Creon returns and relays what he has learned. The failure to discover and punish the murderer of the previous king, Laius, is the pollution responsible for the plague. The murderer must be found and driven from Thebes or put to death. Now Oedipus assumes responsibility for discovering the unknown murderer.

But how can such an enterprise be a source of conflict and dramatic tension? One possibility, of course, would be to have the inquiry opposed by some person or persons, and an unwary reader might suppose that this explanation holds for *Oedipus the King*: both Teiresias and the Herdsman are opposed to the inquiry and try to withhold information, and at one point Jocasta implores Oedipus to abandon the inquiry. But she quickly sees the uselessness of her attempt and gives up, and in quite different ways the resistance of both Teiresias and the Herdsman is soon overcome. If the source of the resistance to discovering the unknown murderer were external, the tension it leads to would be felt only intermittently and briefly. No observant reader can fail to feel that it is continuous and mounting. Moreover, it continues to increase even when the reader, with Jocasta, becomes consciously aware of the truth; indeed, it is most intolerable between that point and the point when Oedipus himself finally perceives it.

The explanation is simple: the source of the resistance is not external—it is in Oedipus himself. From first to last he fights his own inquiry. He has undertaken it in his public capacity as king, out of a sense of what he *should* do, of what is expected of him. As a man, as Oedipus, he has no stomach for the inquiry from the start and resists it at every step.

Still, there is one important shift. Towards the end of the scene with Jocasta, shortly before the arrival of the Messenger from Corinth, Oedipus finally realizes—consciously realizes—that *he* may be the murderer of Laius; at a deeper level he may no longer have much doubt about the matter. To the extent that he may be said to continue the inquiry at all, he now changes and perverts its original purpose. His conscious intent, which has been to discover the murderer of Laius, shifts to disentangling himself from the thickening web of evidence indicating that he is the murderer: he asks Jocasta to send for the Herdsman in the hope that he will confirm the single discrepancy between his original account of what happened at the three crossroads and Oedipus' revivified memory of what took place there. Oedipus is taking a risk, but the need to free himself from the anxiety which envelops him is so urgent that it overrides all other considerations; and he is still able to keep the possibility that the Herdsman may confirm his guilt from the forefront of his mind.

Strictly speaking, Oedipus is no longer prosecuting the inquiry: he is desperately trying to prove his own innocence. He no longer has even a nominal interest in serving his subjects and discovering the truth. Nevertheless, the inquiry continues. To some extent during the talk with Jocasta and, more markedly with the arrival of the Messenger, it acquires a momentum and, it appears, a will of its own. Oedipus' unconscious resistance continues also, but the basis of the resistance undergoes a significant shift. Up to the fateful exchange with Jocasta the chief purpose of the resistance was to keep the idea that he might be the murderer of Laius from reaching awareness. At the very time that he becomes able to face this fear, at least momentarily, he becomes increasingly preoccupied at the unconscious level with more terrifying fears—fears centering around his identity, the two prophecies, the emerging but still amorphous notion that he may be guilty of parricide and incest. Once the Messenger arrives, these fears become the focus of his resistance. He tries to keep from consciousness any information or any implication of information which threatens to give them shape or validity. From first to last the crucial question in the foreground drama is not whether sought information can be uncovered, but whether Oedipus can be brought to accept information, much of it information he already knows. The primary movement is not from ignorance to knowledge but from denial to confrontation.

Once all the events in *Oedipus the King*, those recounted as well as those dramatized, have been arranged in chronological sequence in our minds, the reasons for Oedipus' resistance seem obvious enough. Shortly before he arrived at Thebes, we know, he had killed, he believes,

every member of a party of five men which included one older man of
authority who might well have been a king; once at Thebes, he married
the widow of the former king, a woman far older than himself. Shortly
before these events he had been told by the oracle at Delphi that he was
destined to murder his own father and lie with his own mother. Granted
that he discerns no connection between the prophecy and the events—
and he of course wards off the very possibility of there being any—he
has understandable reasons for feeling guilty and frightened.

Once we have all this information firmly in mind, we may notice that
there are indications of fear and conflict in Oedipus even before the inquiry begins. Perhaps the plague stirred feelings of guilt and unworthiness which had long slept under the nurtured feelings of competence
and pride. Oedipus may have even felt that in some obscure way the
plague was aimed at him. Though he acts before his countrymen directly
ask him to, it appears that he was slow to act; the plague has clearly
gripped Thebes for some time. When his help is besought, he first tells
the Chorus that he has already dispatched Creon to the temple of Apollo
and that he is overdue, and then adds a nervous, gratuitous comment, as
we shall see him do on subsequent occasions also:

> But when he comes, then, may I prove a villain,
> if I shall not do all the God commands.
>
> (76–77)[3]

It is a curious addition. Even as early as this, we may fugitively wonder
why he should even entertain the possibility of disregarding the God's
commands.

Once Oedipus is told the exact nature of the task the God has laid
upon him, his ambivalence is constantly and, for the psychologically
oriented reader, sometimes conspicuously in evidence. It is not simply
that he is fainthearted about the inquiry and irresolute, even resistant, in
his quest of the truth. His repressed fears and guilt feelings reveal themselves in many other ways. Sophocles seems to know everything there is
to know about unconscious psychological processes. In a way it is naive
to be surprised: the unconscious has been a part of man and a prime
mover of his actions since the beginning of time. Still, only a few writers
have been vouchsafed so comprehensive and specific a knowledge of it
as Sophocles. He shows a faultless familiarity with innumerable
mechanisms which were not to be isolated, named, and conceptually
analyzed until Freud achieved that breakthrough. In knowledge of the
unconscious, as in other areas, Sophocles has few peers.

3.   This and all subsequent references are to the superb David Grene translation
of the play.

3

When Creon tells Oedipus the God's command, which is to punish King Laius' murderers, Oedipus responds with a speech which is not far from a whimpering complaint:

> Where are they in the world? Where would a trace
> of this old crime be found? It would be hard to guess where.

(108–109)

The speaker is Oedipus, who had the courage, resoluteness and intelligence to confront the Sphinx, though the cost of failure was death, and who a little before that had not hesitated to become involved, over a trifle, in a struggle with five men. Still, it is early in the play; we might fail to note how far short Oedipus' response falls from what might be expected of him. But Creon's reply gives us a second chance to achieve perspective: it is part reproof, part pep talk. Creon finds himself in the curious position of having to inspirit his king:

> The clue is in this land;
> that which is sought is found;
> the unheeded thing escapes:
> so said the God.

(110–111)

As though this were not enough, a little later on we find Oedipus giving himself a pep talk. After a series of questions about the murder of Laius and the reasons it was not investigated, he accepts the duty of conducting an inquiry in words that have a firm ring (132–135), then weakens the force of what he has said by an addition which suggests that he is still having to convince himself to do something we thought he had already decided to do.

> For when I drive pollution from the land
> I will not serve a distant friend's advantage,
> but act in my own interest. Whoever
> he was that killed the king may readily
> wish to dispatch me with his murderous hand;
> so helping the dead king I help myself.

(136–141)

None of these indications of the faintheartedness of Oedipus is obtrusive. They are woven into the warp and woof of the play with a skill which renders them akin to nature's protective adaptations. But they feed that unconscious understanding which eventually—as it seems in a flash—leads us to realize consciously that Oedipus himself is the murderer of the previous king, and they help to explain our acceptance of that revelation and the curious intellectual satisfaction it gives us.

In the same fashion Sophocles gradually makes us subliminally aware of the guilt and fear which explain Oedipus' ambivalence. The indications of these feelings, too, are usually inconspicuous or indirect. Typically they take the form of remarks which on casual reading seem entirely natural. For example, when Creon first mentions Laius to Oedipus, he remarks:

I know of him by hearsay. I have not seen him.

(105)

Even though we do not pause over this, we may sense that the second comment is gratuitous and defensive. The words with which Oedipus begins his proclamation to the Chorus, ". . . what I say to you, I say / as one that is a stranger to the story / as stranger to the deed" (219–220), have a more pronounced defensive ring.[4]

Later in the same speech, after soliciting the help of the Chorus in tracking down the unknown murderer and pronouncing a curse upon anyone who withholds information and the murderer himself, he adds a comment which, even on first reading, may strike us as curious and superfluous:

If with my knowledge he lives at my hearth
I pray that I myself may feel my curse.

(253–254)

In this early part of the play Sophocles makes still more frequent use of a form of evidence which is likely to pass completely unheeded unless one is already observing a person with close attention, even suspicion. He has Oedipus betray his guilt repeatedly by slips of the tongue.

The first of these occurs in the opening scene with Creon. He tells Oedipus that one man survived the slaughter of Laius and his party and that, though too frightened to give a clear account of what happened, he provided one piece of information which may prove helpful:

This man said that the robbers they encountered
were many and the hands that did the murder
were many; it was no man's single power.

(122–123)

---

4. The "irony" of these words has been commented upon innumerable times, but so far as I am aware their significance in terms of Oedipus' psychology has gone unremarked.

The idea of plurality, of "many," is heavy in that speech, yet Oedipus replies:

> How could a robber dare a deed like this
> were he not helped with money from the city,
> money and treachery?
>
> (124–125)

Is this a meaningless slip, perhaps simply stemming from carelessness on Sophocles' part or his translator's? Hardly. Sophocles has Oedipus make the same slip a half dozen additional times.

Even police who have never heard of Freud are unlikely to disregard discrepancies of this kind. Moreover, the slips occur in connection with a matter of pivotal importance, and Sophocles emphasizes its importance by an irony. Later, in the scene with Jocasta when Oedipus begins to realize consciously that he may be the murderer he seeks, the one thing that sustains him is the hope that the Herdsman will stick to his story that a band of men killed Laius.

Following the opening scene with Creon, in the proclamation to the Chorus from which I have already quoted, Oedipus absentmindedly refers to the murderer of Laius in the singular five times. Indeed, it is not until relatively late in the speech that he mentions as a possibility what he has already been told as a fact—that the murderers were "many"; and even after this he again lapses into the singular.

Later, the Chorus tells Oedipus what Creon has already told him:

> It was said
> that he was killed by certain wayfarers.
>
> (292)

Once again Oedipus disregards what he has just been told:

> I heard that, too, but no one saw the killer.

This slip and the one it echoes, made after Creon gave him the same information, are the most significant. It might be argued that in the long speech to the Chorus, the references to the murderer in the singular were dictated by convenience—this though Freud has demonstrated that factors of this sort play no more than a facilitating role in parapraxes. In the slips directly following those in which the murderers have been referred to in the plural the argument is not even admissible: it would be more convenient, and more natural, for Oedipus to stick to the same number. To a greater extent than the other slips, moreover, these do double duty. They of course reveal Oedipus' secret fear that *he* is the murderer. In addition, they—or more accurately the conflict responsible for them—keep him from recognizing what he does later recognize in the reassuring presence of Jocasta, the possible value of these accounts in establishing his innocence. He throws away two ready-made public opportunities to eliminate himself as a suspect.

4

The fears Oedipus is struggling so desperately to repress rise to a peak during the scene with Teiresias. He has reason to be afraid of the prophet, "in whom alone of mankind truth is native," and whom the Chorus also describes as "[seeing] most often what the Lord Apollo sees." Might not these very words have stirred faint memories in Oedipus of what Apollo's oracle had told him? Oedipus has summoned Teiresias not on his own initiative but at the suggestion of Creon. His fear may help to explain the fact that he does refer to the murderers in the plural in speaking to Teiresias; indeed, it may be partly responsible for the self-control evident throughout his initial speech. Later his fear is to reveal itself in far more obvious and ugly ways.

His sense of duty dominates him at the start of the interview, and for a time he continues to urge Teiresias to divulge whatever he may know. But this victory of conscious purpose is achieved at a heavy cost. Oedipus is able to keep pursuing the truth only by blinding himself to what Teiresias is broadly hinting—that he, Oedipus, would be hurt by what would be disclosed if he were to speak. In one way or another the irreconcilable conflict between wanting to uncover the truth and wanting to keep it hidden prevents Oedipus from functioning competently throughout the inquiry. A little later in this scene he becomes so obtuse that he becomes incapable of grasping things which are openly said. Sophocles knew the effect emotional conflict has upon understanding as he seemed to know everything else.

Once Oedipus gives up the attempt to persuade Teiresias to speak, it becomes clear that *unconsciously* he has understood the blind prophet's hints all too well: he accuses Teiresias of being "complotter" of the murder of Laius, charges that he planned the crime, and expresses regret at his inability to claim that Teiresias executed it single-handedly. There is of course no scintilla of evidence to support these charges. The only possible explanation for them is that the prophet's hints have so alarmed Oedipus that his guilt feelings have become literally intolerable: he must project them upon someone else. Teiresias, who clearly knows more than he says, is a natural person for him to select. Later we shall see that the choice is influenced by a deeper lying factor also.

Ironically, Oedipus' baseless charges achieve what his reasonable appeals could not: they induce the prophet to speak out. Now he accuses Oedipus directly of the murder of Laius: ". . . you are the land's pollution." In the exchange which follows we see one effect of anxiety upon understanding—the mechanism of repression at work—in almost diagrammatic fashion. Oedipus owes his election as king to his intellectual power no less than to his intrepidity. But now, shortly after Teiresias has spoken, he is forced to confess that he cannot recall, and did not really understand, the plain words of the prophet:

> I did not grasp it,
> not so to call it known. Say it again.
>
> (361)

Now Teiresias is even more explicit:

> I say you are the murderer of the king
> whose murderer you seek.

Oedipus' reply shows clearly that unconsciously he had understood the first accusation also:

> Not *twice* you shall
> say calumnies like this and stay unpunished.
> (italics added)

Angry himself, Teiresias threatens to say more and, when Oedipus refuses to mollify him, hints at the incestuous nature of the king's marriage. In the angry exchange which follows he suggests that blindness and ruin lie ahead for Oedipus. By this point Oedipus is frantic. Projection explodes into a related but more comprehensive form of irrationality: a paranoid outburst. He charges that the whole inquiry is a plot by which Creon and Teiresias hope to depose him and gain power—Creon the throne, Teiresias a place at his side. There is, of course, no evidence whatever for this charge either. Indeed, there is some counterevidence: Oedipus himself refers to Creon as "friend from the first and loyal." The charge is wholly a product of forces in Oedipus himself—most obviously of his rage and unendurable fear. It is fed also by his ambivalence toward the inquiry. It reflects a wish to give up the inquiry and regret that he ever undertook it; it is a way of saying, "They tricked me into this."

In the last part of this scene Teiresias amplifies his accusations sufficiently so that we should be able to foretell all the revelations to come. But, consciously at least, we are no more ready to acknowledge the truth at this point in our immersion in the play than is the Chorus—to say nothing of Oedipus himself. The main reason, I believe, is that we are in league with him. If it seems strange that we should be, that may be because this attempt to identify the disavowed sources of his behavior has made him seem a less sympathetic character than in fact he is. In more ways than can be specified, his predicament is our own. Each of us has tried, perhaps many times, to look into his heart and past, only to encounter almost insurmountable resistance; how many men have succeeded more than momentarily and partially in penetrating the amnesic veil which forms over their infancy and early childhood. So with the conflict between Oedipus' public and private roles—we have all experienced it, even if we have not waged the struggle for such momentous stakes. We ourselves know what it is to be trapped into pursuing a given course out of some sense of what is expected of us while all our instincts pull us in a different direction.

5

The short second scene with Creon furnishes confirmatory evidence of the irrational nature of Oedipus' charges. Though he has learned nothing new, he now says that it is "proved" that Creon murdered Laius and is plotting with Teiresias to seize the crown. His own hostility to the man he accuses of hostility to him is openly avowed; he tells Creon that he will be satisfied with nothing less than his death. Some other secret springs of his behavior come into the open—his desire to remain king and the need he feels, even as he pursues the inquiry, to safeguard his own interests. He tells Creon bluntly, "I'll not be proved a murderer."

Neither the baselessness of his charges against Creon nor his general intemperance is lost upon the Chorus, which here and elsewhere represents public opinion. In effect, the Chorus judges between the two men and entreats the king not to "cast [Creon] away dishonoured on an obscure conjecture." Oedipus' reply reveals the essentially irrational nature of his accusations:

> I would have you know that this request of yours
> really requests my death or banishment.

(658–659)

At first glance this reply may seem so wild as to be incomprehensible. Theoretically there are innumerable people, in and out of Thebes, who might have murdered Laius. There may seem to be no justification for Oedipus' feeling that he will be found guilty if he does not succeed in pinning responsibility for the crime on the particular scapegoats he has selected. But the unconscious has its own logic which on occasion is swifter and more unerring than that of the conscious mind. While it is not necessary that Creon and Teiresias be proven to be murderers, it is necessary that they—the prophet, in particular—be discredited as witnesses. In addition to easing Oedipus' sense of guilt, his accusation serves this defensive function.

6

With Teiresias and Creon, Oedipus has been on guard. We can almost see him relax when his brother-in-law leaves and he is left with the Chorus and Jocasta. There is relatively little fear of competitiveness in his attitude toward the Chorus, which has been respectful and considerate even when it sided against him, and the refusal of the Chorus to be too specific in telling Jocasta about his quarrel with Creon in Oedipus' own words softens his anger. And he clearly loves Jocasta. She is the one person in whom he feels he can confide.

Jocasta for her part begins to comfort her troubled lord. She sees that he is frightened; she later uses this word to describe his state in speaking to the Chorus. What she says at that point supports the reader's feeling that she also understands that the accusations and predictions of Teiresias are responsible for his fright. Now, to reassure him and to lessen his fear of Teiresias and prophecy in general, she tells him the story of the prophecy made to her previous husband shortly before she bore him a son, of the way they treated that son and of the way Laius met his death—a way which she thinks is completely at variance with the way it was predicted he would meet it.

It is of course yet another "irony," in a play replete with them, that instead of reassuring Oedipus her story has the opposite effect. A single detail—the fact that Laius was killed "at a place where three roads meet"—rivets itself upon Oedipus' attention and intensifies his fear. He carefully questions Jocasta and each additional fact she gives him about the murder of Laius further increases his fear. For the first time he faces the fact that *he* may be the slayer of Laius. To explain that fear, he gives Jocasta a succinct account of the essential facts of his life before his encounter with the Sphinx. We shall save most of that account for later consideration, for in telescoped fashion it seems to me to describe a drama which deserves separate attention. But the climax of the account must be looked at now. It is a confession: a confession that shortly before Oedipus arrived in Thebes he had become involved in a fight with five men and, he believes, killed them all. Nor does he blink at the fact that his memory of the party he fought with and the outcome of the fight squares in nearly every way with the description of King Laius' party and the way the members of it met their death.

Dramatically, the turn of events in this great scene is ironic. Psychologically, it is entirely realistic. It is natural that Jocasta should want to reassure her troubled husband—and equally natural, *in view of what we already know or expect,* that the attempt should backfire. It is also natural that Oedipus should be able to divulge hidden facts about his past and achieve some degree of insight while talking to a woman he loves, after going to bizarre lengths to avoid seeing anything while talking to Teiresias and Creon, whom he fears and hates. It is far easier to look into one's self and acknowledge one's weaknesses and misdeeds when one is in the presence of someone from whom one expects love and sympathy. The understanding Sophocles displays here conforms not only with what we ourselves know and find to be true in our daily experience; it tallies with much that has been subsequently learned about the transference situation in psychoanalysis and other forms of therapy and with the way insight usually occurs there.

At the same time the power of unconscious resistance is not forgotten, either in this scene or anywhere else in the play; what is perhaps most amazing is how much Oedipus still fails to perceive. By this point he has compelled himself to face many terrible aspects of his past and knows almost everything he is ever to know about the murder of Laius and his retainers. He knows that the prophecy made to Laius shortly before the birth of his son matches the one the oracle at Delphi made to him. He knows that he may *not* be the son of Polybus and Merope, and we might suppose that he would be very much aware of this. He has just told Jocasta of the failure of both of his attempts to discover if they were his real parents, and we recall that the one taunt vented by Teiresias that he could not cope with by denial or projection was a reference to his parents. "What parents?" he cried. "Stop! Who are they of all the world?" (437)

Oedipus now knows too that the murder of Laius and his party almost certainly occurred at the place where he committed his murders and occurred at about the same time. He knows that the composition of Laius' party tallied exactly with that of the party with which he became embroiled. He must recall too that the leader of the party, the man in the carriage, looked like Laius as Jocasta has described him; if time and circumstances did not permit Oedipus to note his victim's resemblance to himself, he must at any rate have seen that his hair was "grizzled . . . nearly white." Finally, Oedipus knows that when the one survivor of Laius' party returned and found Oedipus king, he asked to be sent as far as possible from the city.

This request provides almost certain evidence that Oedipus is the

murderer of Laius; later we will find it has a still more horrendous significance. But Oedipus appears to glide over this item of information as he
does most others. Though he begins to see, and this is a significant
breakthrough, all that he sees, in the sense of being willing to acknowledge, is that he *may be* the murderer of Laius and his party, and because
of this and his marriage to the former king's widow, the pollution of the
land. On the basis of a single discrepancy between the reports stemming
from the Herdsman's account and his own memories, a discrepancy
which with a little thought could be understood, he clings to the hope
that his fight was with a different party of five.[5] He remains completely
blind to the possibility of any kinship between himself and Laius. We
might suppose that he would be struck by the way the prophecy made to
Jocasta and Laius dovetails with the one made to him. In fact, he keeps
his attention fixed on some of the facts Jocasta throws out about the
murder of Laius and hardly seems to take in the point those facts are intended to illustrate or to hear the rest of the account of which they are a
part.

In contrast, by the end of this scene, the reader, I suspect, is unconsciously prepared for all the revelations to come. Even before Oedipus
tells his story, it seems clear that he is the murderer of Laius. His fright
and the request of the one survivor of Laius' party seem to admit of no
alternative explanation. When Oedipus does tell his story, we sense the
ominous way in which it meshes with Jocasta's revelations and all that we
have learned before.

Jocasta is in a position intermediate between the reader and
Oedipus. When towards the very end of the scene, he tells her that he
awaits the arrival of the Herdsman with hope, she voices questions
which have a skeptical, even despondent quality. At least momentarily, it

5.   The account the Herdsman has given of the death of Laius, which is of course
false, provides an excellent illustration of the economy, subtlety and sophistication of Sophocles' art. The purpose of the falsification was to let Oedipus know, in
case he sought to find out if any member of Laius' party had returned, that the
Herdsman would protect Oedipus' secret—this so that Oedipus would have no
motive for killing him. As matters work out, Oedipus learns of the account when
he is so upset and guilt-ridden that, far from wondering if it is not a deliberate
falsification and then asking himself why the survivor would want to lie, he is incapable of taking in its plain sense; he overlooks the emphasis on plurality. Later
his hopes are so exclusively fastened on this aspect of the account that he again
fails to consider whether the account might not be untrue and, if so, why the
Herdsman would have wanted to lie. The final irony is that when Oedipus finally
talks to the Herdsman he does not even ask him whether one man or many killed
Laius and his attendants. The question of whether he killed Laius has been
supplanted by a more terrible one—whether he is guilty of parricide and incest.

appears, she consciously suspects that Oedipus is the murderer of her former husband. To be sure, when Oedipus reminds her that the Herdsman spoke of Laius having been killed by a band of men, she too clutches at this straw. The further remarks she makes, however, suggest that she does this to strengthen her defences against more intolerable fears about the identity of Oedipus and the prophecy made years before to Laius and herself. If these fears prove justified, calamity looms ahead for her also, and though the fears are assuming shape in her mind and are closer to the fringe of consciousness than they are in Oedipus, she is struggling almost as desperately as he to repress them and to keep from seeing the overall pattern which the reader is now ready to perceive.

7

Oedipus' reply to Jocasta's questions about his reasons for wanting to talk to the Herdsman inadvertently reveals that he has forgotten the original purpose of the inquiry. But with the arrival of the Messenger matters are taken out of his hands. From this point on everything follows what appears a foreordained course.

The Messenger's news and revelations are a source of profound and bitter irony. Though he believes he is a bearer of good news and is originally accepted in this light, his presence on the scene and the information he volunteers bring about the discoveries which draw the play to a climax. The irony is heightened by the skillful way Sophocles uses another facet of his knowledge of the way emotional factors affect understanding.

The Messenger enters just as Jocasta uses the word "frightened" to describe her lord. In fact, both she and Oedipus are frantic with fear. That is why they react to the Messenger's news with hysterical relief and elation. Their almost willful misinterpretation of the significance of Polybus' death sets the stage for the ironic reversal, though in this scene, as in the previous scene with Jocasta, it stems immediately from an attempt to reassure Oedipus.

Actually the Messenger has brought no news which is unequivocally good. We know, even if he does not, that the prospect that Oedipus is to be elected king in Corinth is meaningless unless he can clear himself from the web of guilt forming round him in Thebes. In construing the news of Polybus' death as good both Jocasta and Oedipus are simply deceiving themselves. Grateful for any opportunity for escaping from their fear, they shift their attention to the question of whether correct prophecy is possible, then answer the question in the negative by falling back on the assumption that Oedipus is the son of Polybus. Of course, the deception is not deliberate. However unjustifiably, Oedipus has thought of Polybus and Merope as his parents most of his life, and, until the talk Jocasta has just had with her husband, she had no reason to doubt that they were. But now there are cogent reasons for doubt, and as we know both Oedipus and Jocasta should have these fresh in mind. As a result of the information they have just exchanged, moreover, they both know that the prophecy made to Laius and Jocasta before the birth of their son matches the prophecy made to Oedipus at Delphi. Both also know that Oedipus may be the murderer of Laius. Examined closely, all this information fits together. It is precisely because Oedipus and Jocasta secretly fear that he is the son of Laius that they resort to wishful thinking and accept as certain something they know to be doubtful—the assumption that he is the son of Polybus.

Their irrational elation provides the basis not only for the irony but for the stunning impact of both this scene and the next one. The revelation that Oedipus is not the son of Polybus and Merope and the later revelation that he is the son of Laius and Jocasta would have less force if they had been openly faced as possibilities instead of being denied.

Once the Messenger has told Oedipus that Polybus and Merope are not his parents, the pace of the play perceptibly quickens. Under Oedipus' questioning enough comes out about his origins to make it all but certain that it was he whose ankles Laius had pierced and then given to a servant to abandon "upon a pathless hillside." All the essential facts for understanding Oedipus' predicament are now either known or easy to infer. There can be no doubt that the two prophecies have been fulfilled. Jocasta perceives this and begs Oedipus to drop the inquiry. In contrast, he refers to the Messenger's revelations as "clues" and sticks to his intention of examining the Herdsman, who has been sent for because he is the only survivor of Laius' party but is also the man who years before gave the infant child of Laius and Jocasta to the Messenger. Jocasta rushes off—as we surmise and are shortly to be told, to self-inflicted death.

Oedipus attributes Jocasta's plea to the fear the further questioning will reveal that he is baseborn. Since neither she nor anyone else has said anything about such a possibility, at first glance the accusation may seem random and incomprehensible. In fact, the motive Oedipus ascribes to Jocasta explains why he feels compelled to see the Herdsman: he wants to find that he *is* baseborn, and thus not guilty at any rate of parricide and incest.[6]

The fact that he clutches at such a straw, however, betrays the des-

6. As we shall see, the idea that such a motive may impel one to abandon an inquiry into one's origins may have a still earlier determinant.

perateness of his situation. He is ignoring not only everything he has learned but the real significance of Jocasta's fright and appeal to him, though it is not difficult to discern. If anyone would know the parentage of the fettered infant handed over to the Herdsman years before, the reader realizes, it is Jocasta herself.

8

Oedipus has insisted on questioning the Herdsman because he is desperate. He persists in questioning him for the same reason. He persists even though more and more evidence emerges which shows the futility of persisting. He ignores the probable significance of the Herdsman's reluctance to speak and his attempts to hush the Messenger, just as he has previously ignored, misinterpreted, or refused to understand whatever he did not wish to understand. Even after the Herdsman has told him that the child he gave to the Messenger was Laius' and was given to him by Jocasta, Oedipus continues to ask questions, some of them clearly gratuitous or irrelevant. As Morton Kaplan observes, he behaves like a patient in analysis resisting an insight which is dangling in the air, crying to be voiced;[7] he strives to escape the truth or at any rate to defer the moment when he must face and accept it. It comes out in spite of his exertions.

Like so much else in *Oedipus the King* which has evidently been missed by many of those who have written about it, this is stated in the play itself.[8] After Oedipus rushes to his self-inflicted punishment, the Chorus declares:

Time who sees all has found you out
against your will . . .

(1213–1214)

The fact that the truth comes out despite Oedipus' resistance is worth stressing because it should dispel the common misconception that his self-blinding is punishment for his *hubris* in seeing. In fact, he punishes himself, among other reasons, for having been *unwilling* to see, for refusing to look into himself and find out who and what he was.

7. "Dream at Thebes," *Literature and Psychology*, 11, 1 (Winter 1961). I wish to acknowledge my indebtedness to this ground-breaking essay.
8. Among those who have written about the play without recognizing that Oedipus resists his own inquiry, I must in candor include myself. While my discussion of the play in *Fiction and the Unconscious* indicates I had become aware of at least one bit of evidence of Oedipus' ambivalence, something inhibited me from pursuing this and examining the whole pattern of his behavior.

Oedipus has grown to manhood, dealt with problems of the external world in ways which have won him renown, and achieved a position of authority and power—all without making a single sustained attempt to know his own past or to understand his own nature and the reasons for his actions, past and present. In this respect also—in somewhat magnified fashion—he typifies western man.

9

Earlier in his life Oedipus had experienced an even more crucial conflict between unconscious desires and conscious intentions: a conflict over whether to master or act out what today—such is the waywardness of language—it is most convenient to call his "Oedipal" impulses. We of course now "know," conceptually, that this conflict is intimately related to the conflict—a variant of which Oedipus experiences in the foreground drama—between the conscious desire to bring the truth to light and unconscious tendencies to keep unwelcome aspects of it hidden. As we grow up and discover that sexual feeling for the mother and hatred of the father are abhorred—hence "bad" and dangerous, involving the risk of dread punishment at the hands of the father and the loss of both parents' love—we become reluctant to acknowledge that we harbor, or ever harbored, such feelings. That reluctance is a prime motive for repression; and repression involves not only a "forgetting" of the Oedipal (and other forbidden) impulses of infancy, and thus the loss of the most significant part of our early affective experience, but also a resistance against recapturing that experience if we should seek to and a tendency, which becomes progressively stronger, to deny later manifestations of Oedipal (and other disavowed) tendencies access to consciousness and to thrust them out of awareness quickly if they do break through. By extension, our fears of our erotic and aggressive impulses may come to have a still more calamitous consequence: since so many of them are suspect if not guilt-ridden, we may be gradually overcome by a diffuse and powerful tendency not to look inside ourselves at all, since that way danger lies, but to concentrate our attention on the external world—and even in exploring that world to focus on matters not likely to remind us of our own unacceptable drives.

Intuitively, men must have always known of this intimate connection between forbidden impulses and repression; otherwise *Oedipus the King* could not have been written, or understood and enjoyed. The play twice stresses the connection. In what I have referred to as the foreground drama, precisely what Oedipus resists seeing is the past and present fulfillment of his Oedipal desires. The connection is emphasized in the background drama also.

In form this "drama" is of course a narrative: the brief, elliptical account Oedipus gives Jocasta of his early life. But Sophocles is instinctively dramatic; he makes it easy for us to flesh out this account into scenes comprising a coherent drama. Moreover, he is so unerring in his choice of details that we can even reconstruct the motives for each of Oedipus' actions.

This drama, too, begins with a conflict about seeing. At a dinner, a drunken man accuses Oedipus, already a young man if not a full-grown adult, of being a bastard and not, as he had assumed, the son of Polybus and Merope. Oedipus goes to them and reports the incident, thus at least inferentially asking them to tell him if the charge is true. They angrily deplore the drunken man's words but, it appears, do not flatly deny them; and Oedipus evidently does not press them for a yes-or-no response.

He is probably held back in part, as any young man might be, by timidity about prying intimate information from parents. But he is deterred also, it may be surmised, by a far more unusual and powerful fear, one which is the polar opposite of the wish which years later impels him to question the Herdsman—the fear of discovering that he is of lowly origin. During latency and early adolescence, we now know, most children become more aware of their parents' limitations and become dissatisfied with them or even ashamed of them. These feelings may lead them to imagine that their "real" parents are more exalted personages than the ones they live with—and may even impel them to establish relationships with people who can easily be recognized as idealized replacements of mother or father.[9] Oedipus is in precisely the opposite situation of these fugitives from ordinary parents; as he himself puts it, "I was held greatest of the citizens/in Corinth. . . ." He must feel that he has everything to lose and nothing to gain from the discovery that Polybus and Merope are not his real parents.

Nevertheless, the story rankles, he is still troubled, and he makes one further attempt to discover the truth: he secretly goes to the oracle of Apollo at Delphi. But the oracle not only refuses to satisfy Oedipus' curiosity about his past but prophesies horrors in his future:

> that I was fated to lie with my mother,
> and show to daylight an accursed breed

9.   This cluster of feelings, and the fantasies and acts they give rise to, is referred to in psychoanalytic literature as "the family romance." For a more complete discussion, see Freud, "Family Romances," *Collected Papers*, vol. 5 (London, 1950).

which men would not endure, and I was doomed
to be murderer of the father that begot me.[10]

(791–793)

Though Oedipus does not realize it, he now faces a crisis on which
his entire life depends. All the terrible acts he is later to commit and all
the consequences which flow from those acts stem from his failure to
face his situation resolutely and deal with it wisely. But he cannot face it;
he is overcome by panic and flees:

When I heard this I fled, and in the days
that followed I would measure from the stars
the whereabouts of Corinth—yes, I fled
to somewhere where I should not see fulfilled
the infamies told in that dreadful oracle.

(794–798)

Though this is a terse description, it is not too terse: it covers all that
Oedipus knows and believes about his behavior and the reasons for his
behavior. It is essential, however, that at this point we interpolate and
achieve an understanding of what Oedipus should have done and of the
reasons he acted as he did.

What he should have done, as Morton Kaplan has pointed out, is re-

10. It is hard to resist the speculation that in the real world known to Sophocles,
and perhaps also in the archaic period from which the Oedipus myth stems, such
predictions as this were sometimes based on the capacity of someone associated
with the oracle to gauge the character of inquirers. The chapter on "The Procedure of the Oracle" in H. W. Parke's and D. E. W. Wormell's monumental work,
The Delphic Oracle (Oxford, 1956), shows how this might come about. Because
the Pythia only prophesied no more than nine days a year, the priests might have
had ample time to perceive, for example, the rebelliousness, fractiousness, uncertain self-control and instability of any real-life prototype of Oedipus who may have
presented himself. And the priests had abundant opportunity to interpret, and
even influence, the Pythia's prophecies: ". . . the confused and disjointed remarks
of a hypnotized woman must have needed considerable exercise of imagination
to reduce them to the form of a response. In this must have lain the chief temptation for the priests. Where must they draw the line and confess that they were
merely reading their own thoughts into the Pythia's gabble? No doubt in this matter individual priests on particular occasions took a very different course. In a special emergency when it seemed expedient that one particular answer must be
given, the priest may have consciously or half-consciously substituted his own
predetermined reply as the authentic utterance of the prophetess. Perhaps some
of the priests may have found means to implant suggestions in the Pythia's mind
which would emerge as though they were spontaneous utterances when she was
under a trance. At any rate, the history of Delphi shows sufficient traces of a consistent policy to convince one that human intelligence at some point could play a
deciding part in the process" (pp. 39–40).

turn to Corinth and *insist* that Polybus and Merope tell him if they are his parents and, if they are not, provide as much information as they can about his birth and lineage. It is now essential that he have this knowledge to escape the dire prophecies of the oracle. He has a right to demand that he be told the truth—and every reason to suppose his demand would be met.

At first glance it might seem that here again the failure is in the area of seeing, that Oedipus' desire to learn the truth succumbs to the unconscious forces which inhibit him from discovering it. But he flees because he is in a state of panic, and nothing he might discover by pursuing the inquiry seems capable of arousing such terrible dread as he feels. Moreover, it is the prophecy which has terrified him. He is now afraid, not of what he may see, but of what he may do—lie with his mother and murder his father. His panic fear *is* proportionate to the intensity of his unconfessed desire to commit these acts. It is the other side of the desire—the dread of the dimly perceived but frightening punishment he expects to follow if he yields to the desire. The conflict about seeing has been supplanted by a still more urgent one: a conflict about whether to control his Oedipal impulses or surrender to an almost irresistible urge to satisfy them. It is inauspicious that the unconscious impulses and the fear they arouse are so overpowering that Oedipus acts without thought. Under such circumstances the ego has little chance to defend itself successfully against forbidden impulses. To a greater extent than in the foreground drama, it appears that Oedipus' desire to do the right thing is outmatched from the beginning by the forces arrayed against it.

If we have any doubts about this, they are quickly dissipated. Oedipus runs into his fate, not away from it. Before following his actions, however, we should look more closely still at the factors which impel him to make the calamitous decision he does.

10

Oedipus' fears are not only intense; they are specific. Polybus is the primary target of his still unsubdued competitive and hostile feelings; Merope, the still unrelinquished primary object of his sexual desire. What tells us this is some words already quoted:

> When I heard this I fled, and in the days
> that followed *I would measure from the stars
> the whereabouts of Corinth.*   (italics added)

The fact that Polybus and Merope were the original objects of Oedipus' "Oedipal" impulses should occasion no surprise. He lived with them, they were his parents—so far as he knew, his real parents—during the Oedipal and post-Oedipal periods. Naturally his Oedipal feelings were directed toward them.

The fact has some important implications. In the first place, it must affect our judgement of Oedipus' conduct, not only in the background drama but throughout the play. Oedipus' decision—if that is even the word—to flee from Delphi after hearing the oracle's prophecy was of course "wrong" in the sense of being undesirable and unfortunate. But we could call it wrong in the moral sense only if we assumed, what is patently false, that Oedipus was capable of seeing the alternative possibilities open to him and deciding upon his course calmly and rationally. The distinction suggests the inadequacy of a purely moral approach to tragedy. Oedipus flees and acts as he does at many points throughout the play because he is under the sway of irrational tendencies in himself of which he has no understanding. Under such conditions, the idea of responsibility, as that term is usually understood, has little relevance. This does not mean, however, that his acts are without consequences. Nor does the fact that Oedipus acts irrationally disqualify him as a tragic hero. On the contrary, Aristotle appears to have had him in mind in framing the requirements of the hero. Oedipus is not only "highly renowned and prosperous" but a middling good man, and his downfall is brought about, not by vice or depravity, but by a frailty or weakness. That weakness is precisely his incapacity to look within himself, much less master the impulses he would find there if he did. To an unappreciated extent all his disastrous acts flow from this weakness, rather than being a result of "fate."[11] *Oedipus the King* is a drama of character, in the same sense that *Hamlet, Othello* and *Lear* are. Fate enters only as a kind of editor, underscoring here and there to make some of Oedipus' deeds still more horrible than they first seem.

The fact that Polybus and Merope are the original objects of

11. Interestingly, though no previous commentator to my knowledge has explicitly identified this as Oedipus' weakness, a good many have recognized that what happens to Oedipus is related to his character. George Devereux maintains that Greek drama in general is set in motion by "man's character structure and latent conflicts" and that this is "simply obscured by the Greeks' habit of personifying character structure as 'Fate'. . . ." "Why Oedipus Killed Laius," *International Journal of Psycho-Analysis*, 34, 2. Reprinted in Hendrik M. Ruitenbeek, ed., *Psychoanalysis and Literature* (New York, 1964). However, most of the critics who have sensed that there is a relationship between Oedipus' character and life have either ventured no explanation of *how* they are related or have offered explanations which seem to me to be questionable or clearly wide of the mark. Bernard Knox, for example, attributes Oedipus' destruction to his greatness and his "relentless pursuit of the truth." *Oedipus at Thebes* (New Haven and London, 1957), pp. 50-51.

Oedipus' parricidal and incestuous impulses also means that the acts of
Oedipus which culminate this part of the tragedy, his murder of Laius
and marriage to Jocasta, are far more complex and significant than has
been recognized. Biologically, of course, Laius and Jocasta are the parents of Oedipus, and Sophocles could have found no better way of both
vicariously satisfying the Oedipal impulses of his audience and showing
the dread consequences of satisfying them than by having his hero kill
his actual father and wed and beget children by his actual mother. But
psychologically Laius and Jocasta are surrogates for the parents—
surrogates who happen to be the actual parents; Sophocles has it both
ways. Because Oedipus' climactic acts in the background drama have this
double significance, he invites identification for a wider range of reasons
than has been recognized. As Freud perceived, all men have psychic af-
finities with Oedipus. His fate moves us "because it might have been our
own . . . we were all destined to direct our first sexual impulses toward
our mothers and our first impulses of hatred and violence toward our
fathers."[12] As Freud also proceeds to point out, in slaying Laius and wed-
ding Jocasta, Oedipus provides vicarious wish fulfillment of desires
which are still extant in us, however firmly they may be repressed and
subdued. Though Freud stopped here, there is still more to be said. In
extreme form, Oedipus also exemplifies the actual *behavior* of an ines-
timable but undoubtedly large number of men—the countless
thousands in every generation who never successfully resolve their Oedipal tendencies and achieve that successful indentification with the father
which is a prelude to full maturity. He is the first literary representative of
the innumerable men who go through life, as he did, acting out their
unresolved Oedipal tendencies. Such men may unconsciously seek
father figures on whom they can vent their hatred, their competitiveness
and their sullen insubordination. Similarly, their selection of sexual
partners is always influenced and often governed by the fixation on the
mother.

11

Oedipus' behavior throughout the drama reveals the strength of his unresolved Oedipal strivings. He could flee Corinth and the couple he unjustifiably thought of as his parents, but he could not flee from his own
character and destiny.

Soon after hearing the oracle pronounce his fate, he encounters a

12.   "The Interpretation of Dreams" in *The Basic Writings of Sigmund Freud* (New
York, 1938), p. 308.

party of five men, including a herald and one man being carried in a carriage. It seems reasonable to suppose that only kings, princes, and a few other people of position and power traveled in this fashion. Oedipus could not have failed to realize that this was a party of someone of importance; and very possibly, therefore, of someone considerably older than himself. It seems reasonable to suppose also that most solitary travelers deferred to such parties, giving a little ground so that they could pass unimpeded. But Oedipus would not give way. An attempt had to be made to thrust him aside by force. To some extent his behavior might be attributed to the fact that Oedipus has been brought up as a prince and was not used to yielding to anyone save, necessarily, Polybus. But other forces must have been working upon him also. Consider: under ordinary circumstances the prudent course would have been to step aside—he was one man against five. And Oedipus was traveling under circumstances which were anything but ordinary. He was fleeing, presumably, to escape the fate predicted for him and did not know who "of all the world" his parents were. The only way he could be sure of escaping his fate was by avoiding potentially murderous conflict with anyone old enough to be his father and sexual union with any woman old enough to be his mother. Yet Oedipus now "permits" himself to become embroiled in mortal combat with a party which, he must have known, included at least two men who might have been old enough to have sired him: the Herdsman and the man in the carriage.

Oedipus' behavior was ill-advised to the point of seeming perverse. But it will be immediately understandable to anyone aware of the difficulty men who have not worked through their hostility to the father are likely to have with authority figures from teachers and bosses to kings and presidents—and even institutions. It was precisely the fact that Oedipus was, in effect, being asked to yield to someone who possessed power and authority—and was in this sense a father—which roused his combativeness.

Thus the last person in the world who should do so, Oedipus, becomes involved over a trifle in a to-the-death struggle with five antagonists. He continues his journey only when, he believes, he has killed them all.

Oedipus' next encounter is with the Sphinx, and there is no evidence that, in the more intellectual mortal struggle he now has with her, guilt either diminished his self-confidence or interfered with his mental agility. Routing the Sphinx may have further bolstered his confidence—made him feel a child of "beneficient Fortune"—for with the same rashness with which he risked or even invited a head-on struggle with Laius' party he not only assents to becoming king of Thebes but accepts the widow of the former king as his wife. There was no chance that the disparity between her age and his could have passed unnoticed.

12

The foreground drama also contains evidence of both the intensity and diffuseness of Oedipus' unresolved Oedipal feelings, in particular his parricidal impulses. Though here the Oedipal feelings are subordinated to the conflict about seeing and developed somewhat sketchily, in hidden ways they significantly influence Oedipus' behavior. He is the hero of the entire drama, and he is the same man who fought with and, he believes, killed five men rather than give way to them. The hostility and irascibility which were mobilized then live in him still.

It is possible that Sophocles meant this to be evident in the scene in which Oedipus tells Jocasta of that early murderous encounter, particularly at its climax:

> I became angry
> and struck the coachman who was pushing me.
> When the old man saw this he watched his moment,
> and as I passed he struck me from his carriage,
> full on the head with his two pointed goad.
> But he was paid in full and presently
> my stick had struck him backwards from the car
> and he rolled out of it. And then I killed them
> all.

(806–813)

Certainly there is no evidence of contrition here. Relating the experience may rekindle Oedipus' wrath against those who expected him to docilely yield the right of way. As he talks he may re-enact the killings, and this may be indicated by his voice and gestures.[13]

The rage is displayed anew and dramatized in the scenes with Teiresias and Creon. We have glanced at the immediate determinants of the paranoid accusations Oedipus makes against them. Oedipus has some reason to seek to discredit Teiresias, who says many things which fill him with fear and clearly knows more than he says. Yet if Oedipus had been capable of calm reflection, his fear would have been easy to control. Whatever Teiresias knew he had long kept secret; and when

13.   I am indebted to a brilliant student production of the play at the University of Massachusetts in 1962 for this suggestion. The young man who played Oedipus delivered the lines in the way here described, and once one had seen and heard him, no other way of interpreting them would seem satisfactory.

summoned, his wish—his offense—was that he wanted to remain silent. The basis of Oedipus' fear and suspicion of Creon seems more tenuous still. Indeed, the only justification he can find for his feelings and charges is the fact that Creon anticipated the Chorus in suggesting that the blind prophet be consulted. No suggestion could have been more obvious or more guileless.

Even when allowance is made for Oedipus' fright and need to prove his innocence, it seems clear that his behavior toward Teiresias and Creon cannot be entirely explained on the basis of the immediate situation. One is impelled to ask whether his hostility toward them did not have earlier determinants also. Might not their very position in the community have made them the target, from the time of Oedipus' arrival in Thebes, of the unextirpated negative feelings toward the father which asserted themselves so violently just before his arrival. Like the unknown head of the party met at the crossroad, both Creon and Teiresias had attributes which would have led Oedipus to look upon them as fathers. As Jocasta's brother, Creon was a member of the royal family, with some of the aura of a king. As a quasi-religious figure, Teiresias enjoyed a kind of respect Oedipus may have felt he could not aspire to and a status which was not affected by the vicissitudes of politics.

While there is no evidence of earlier friction with Creon, the whole pattern of Oedipus' behavior suggests that it would not have been easy for him to share authority with any man. There are tangible indications that Oedipus had negative feelings toward Teiresias long before the action of the play begins. Unlike the paranoid accusations in Oedipus' bitter tirade (380–403), the denunciations of the prophet—as, for example, a "juggling trick devising quack"—do not seem improvised. Indeed, the taunt that Teiresias was unable to do what Oedipus could and did do, solve the riddle of the Sphinx, suggests that Oedipus may have regarded the prophet as a rival from almost the time of his arrival in Thebes. It appears that Oedipus was irritated by the twice-offered suggestion that he solicit the help of Teiresias. If so, one of the reasons, it may be conjectured, is that the suggestion stirred feelings of competitiveness long present in dormant form.

The way Oedipus speaks to Teiresias and Creon suggests another source of his tendency to regard them as fathers and then feel envious and hostile toward them. Both men have personal qualities which are not native to Oedipus and which he cannot assume for long. When we look closely, we see that even the presently used title, *Oedipus the King*, has overtones of irony. Though Oedipus is king and thus in a sense father of his people and though he has children of his own, throughout this play—in contradistinction to *Oedipus at Colonus*—he is a son figure, not a father figure. He lacks the inner assurance, composure and poise to sustain the role of king more than briefly. He very quickly ceases to speak to Teiresias as king to subject—to command him or beseech him to serve the common good. Instead he talks to him as a feared and hated rival, as he later talks to Creon also; indeed, in the exchange with his co-ruler he lapses more obviously into a childish and pettish tone. Though from his youth he has longed for authority and power, even when he has them he does not possess them.

Of course, all of the past determinants of Oedipus' behavior operate in dynamic fusion with the factors playing upon him in the drama we witness. It is because Sophocles makes us feel this that we accept the frenzied lengths to which Oedipus is driven. His envy of what must seem the secure position of Creon and Teiresias grows more intense as his own position becomes more precarious. Similarly, his envy of certain personal qualities of Teiresias and Creon which proclaim their maturity is exacerbated as his own hold on those qualities becomes more uncertain. Whereas Oedipus is maddened by fear during the scene with Teiresias, the prophet, though old and physically helpless, is unintimidated by his threats. Similarly, even when Creon's life is threatened, he retains his poise and self-control and reasons with Oedipus calmly and well. Oedipus must sense that he appears and is weak in comparison with the men he is attacking. The feeling fans his jealousy and brings his hatred to a boil.

Only the feared or actual presence of other people keeps that hatred from following the same trajectory it took in the fateful meetings at the three crossroads. Death would be the only suitable penalty for the treason and participation in the murder of Laius of which Oedipus accuses Teiresias. Only a realization of the esteem in which the prophet is held, it may be surmised, deters Oedipus from proposing it. He does propose the death penalty, almost offhandedly, for Creon:

> Creon
> What do you want to do then? Banish me?
> Oedipus
> No, certainly; kill you, not banish you.
>
> (622–623)

As James Schroeter has pointed out, murderous onslaughts upon father surrogates occur before our eyes in the dramatized portion of Oedipus the King.[14]

14. "The Four Fathers: Symbolism in Oedipus Rex," Criticism, 3 (Summer, 1961). Reprinted in Albert Cook, Oedipus Rex: A Mirror for Greek Drama (Belmont, Cal., 1963). This is a stimulating essay, which makes many valuable and valid observations. The premise of Schroeter's interpretation is that all four of Oedipus' an-

13

The punishments Oedipus inflicts upon himself express many things. Schroeter maintains that the first punishment, exile, is "a voluntary deprivation of the highest good—citizenship—conferred by the political community" and thus "a fitting expiation of the parricide"; and that the second punishment—blinding—is "a deprivation of the highest good conferred by the gods" and thus appropriate for "the more private . . . yet more hideous crime of incest." However, it is doubtful that acts done at such a moment would fall into quite so neat a pattern as this.[15]

tagonists in what I have called the foreground drama—Teiresias, Creon, the Messenger, and the Herdsman—are father figures. Schroeter justifies grouping the four men on the basis of two considerations: (1) their age; and (2) the fact that they have all functioned in some conserving or protecting capacity toward Oedipus. But surely the relevant consideration for a psychological interpretation of the play (Schroeter also offers an anthropological and a poetic interpretation) is not what various characters have done for Oedipus but *how he views them.* He actively dominates the course of events from the time he learns that he may not be the son of Polybus and Merope until late in the play. If Oedipus' feeling toward other characters is used as the basis for classifying them, it is clear that the Messenger and the Herdsman cannot be placed in the same series as Teiresias, Creon and, on the basis of a reconstruction of the background drama, Polybus and the unrecognized leader of the party encountered at the crossroads. These men belong together. They all have the mana of the father—the power and authority which Oedipus so much coveted that the recognition that someone else possessed them automatically aroused feelings of envy, competitiveness and hatred. Conceivably the Messenger and the Herdsman could fit into the series in other ways; for example, one or both of them might inherit the reverence and love which may be felt for the father, as the Ghost does in *Hamlet.* But in fact they do not function as fathers in any way. It does not matter in the least that they are old or that they have tried to help Oedipus in the past. The Messenger is just that—a person who brings news, most of which at first seems good and later bad. The Herdsman is a frightened servant from whom confirmatory and additional facts must be extracted. Both men appear upon the scene too late for their past services to be recognized. The information they give eclipses them and usurps Oedipus' entire attention.

No weakness is more widespread in the symbol hunting now so pandemic among English students or the symbolic criticism engaged in by those who teach them than the failure to distinguish between what *may* function symbolically and what in fact *does.* Thus the distinction being made here may be of general importance.

As I indicate in note 15, I believe that Schroeter's assumption that he can casually lay claim to the advantages of a number of critical approaches, even approaches for which he feels scorn, leads him to make other errors also. However, the errors do not nullify the many fine insights which stud his essay.

15. Eclectic criticism has undeniable advantages, and taken as a whole Schroeter's essay demonstrates this. However, the passage about punishment suggests that it has its dangers also, perhaps most especially when a critic lacks commit-

Oedipus has been finally forced to see who he is and what he has done and, before he could begin to digest the horror of this, has found his wife-mother dead—a suicide, it appears, but, as he must immediately feel, another victim, rather, of his misdeeds. To some extent both punishments must be a response to all that he now knows and feels, and it would be surprising if there were not close connections between them.

The sentence of exile may be a punishment for having settled down before he felt he had earned a right to—before he knew who and what he was and could reasonably hope to assume a place in society without uneasiness. At a deeper and more concrete level it may express the wish to undo his having settled down as King of Thebes and husband of the previous king's widow—in the haven which was no haven. Perhaps he feels he should have wandered always, or at any rate until he knew himself. There is something congruous between not knowing who or what one is and being a homeless wanderer, though it is a congruity hard to define in words.

Among other things, Oedipus' self-blinding expresses his shame. We must credit his repeated statements that he feels unworthy to look upon his city, his people, his children, or, when he dies, his father and mother. To an even greater extent the act expresses his need to punish himself for his failings and transgressions. Self-blinding is a condign punishment for Oedipus' failure to see while he had the gift of sight. Perhaps as early as during the first scene with Jocasta, when Oedipus expressed the fear that the blind seer had eyes, he was comparing himself invidiously with him. Now in any case he is ready to accept the taunt Teiresias hurled at him—that though he has the gift of sight, he has been blind all his life. Oedipus is also punishing himself for the taboos he violated during his "blindness."[16] Psychoanalytic studies show that blindness is a displaced and disguised equivalent of castration. Thus the mutilation Oedipus inflicts on himself is also a condign punishment for the interrelated crimes of parricide and incest, the talion punishment the unconscious would demand. Oedipus' choice of punishments is over-determined.

ment. The passage reflects no awareness of the close connection, genetically and dynamically, between incest and parricide, no awareness of the concept of over-determination, and, though Schroeter invokes the word "madness," no awareness of the way the mind works under emotional stress, to say nothing of madness.

16.   At some deep level Oedipus may even know that there was a connection between his "Oedipal" desires and his blindness—that his initial failure was his refusal to face and try to subdue those desires.

Even while Oedipus feels compelled to punish and maim himself, the vitality, sturdiness and intransigence which are part of his character do not entirely desert him. They assert themselves, in negative fashion, in his refusal to sentence himself to death, though this too would be an appropriate punishment, though in some respects, as the Chorus observes, it is a more tolerable one, and though the model for it is before him as he gazes upon Jocasta hanged. The qualities which distinguish Oedipus even as he errs assert themselves also in the punishments he does inflict upon himself. The physical punishment expresses other unconscious wishes besides the need to injure himself. After cutting the dangling noose, he tears away the brooches which fasten Jocasta's robe, thus baring the body of the woman from whose womb he was born. May not one faintly discern here a stubborn wish for physical union with the mother, though the wish must immediately travesty itself, since Jocasta is dead, and must be immediately atoned for by Oedipus' self-mutilation?[17] The wish to be reborn—to undo the whole shameful life he has led, to be granted a second chance—makes itself felt more obviously. In using Jocasta's brooches to gash out his eyes he is reconstituting as best he can the condition he was in when he came from her womb: he is once again weeping and blind, weak and helpless. The wish to start afresh could scarcely be better pantomimed with the scanty and dreadful materials available to him.

The sentence of exile dovetails with the self-blinding. As Mark Kanzer has pointed out, "in giving up his kingdom and his eyesight Oedipus [is renouncing] the gratification of his drives in the outer world. . . ."[18] We have seen that both punishments are admixed with an expiatory wish—the wish to be granted a second chance. Perhaps a more specific wishful element also lurks under Oedipus' blinding of himself: the hope that, once he is blind, he, like Teiresias, will be granted the gift of sight—more specifically, insight, the self-knowledge he has hitherto resisted rather than sought. As an alternative to suicide, exile has the advantage of permitting the fulfillment of such hopes. And in the great sequel to the play, *Oedipus at Colonus*, as Dr. Kanzer has brilliantly shown, some of the hopes which impelled Oedipus to cling to life are realized. Though he never acknowledges his guilt, he achieves a degree of understanding, gives up his selfishness and dependence on his infan-

17.   This wish is fulfilled in attenuated and sublimated fashion in *Oedipus at Colonus*, where Antigone can be viewed as a surrogate for the mother.
18.   "The 'Passing of the Oedipus Complex' in Greek Drama," *International Journal of Psycho-Analysis*, 29, part 2 (1948). Reprinted in Hendrik M. Ruitenbeek, ed., *Psychoanalysis and Literature* (New York, 1964).

tile sense of omnipotence and belatedly makes his peace with a surrogate father and with the customs and values which alone can safeguard society from a wholesale repetition, generation after generation, of the transgressions of which he has been guilty in *Oedipus the King*.

❀ Act One, Scene One, of *Lear*

FOR every interpretation which goes to the heart of a literary work and explains its basic substance, there seem to be a hundred which focus on superficial and tangential aspects or misinterpret the work, in whole or in part. Yet I believe that as we read we understand almost any imaginative work which is not beyond our level of intellectual and emotional sensibility.

Enjoyment of a work is an almost certain indication that we have understood it. This or that detail may have eluded us, or even been misunderstood, but if the work as a whole was incomprehensible, it probably gave us little pleasure. Would we enjoy *Hamlet*, for example, much less admire it, if we did not sense what keeps Hamlet from doing what he has unhesitatingly covenanted to do, avenge his father's death? If we think of Hamlet as a bungling man who spends half his time verifying his mission and then executes it in bungling fashion, or if we see him, as T. S. Eliot did, as "dominated by an emotion which is . . . in *excess* of the facts as they appear," and are unable to surmise the hidden basis of that emotion, it is doubtful if we would find the play of which he is the hero absorbing or adjudge it great. No satisfactory explanation of Hamlet's delay was offered until Freud achieved that breakthrough in *The Interpretation of Dreams* (1900). By "satisfactory" I mean consistent with—if not explanatory of—most other major aspects of the drama, for example, the inclusion of the Laertes and Fortinbras plot strands and Hamlet's self-castigation, melancholy, feeling that he is evil, and treatment of Gertrude and Ophelia. Yet *Hamlet* has been enjoyed and esteemed by countless spectators and readers since its first performance in 1602, including mil-

Reprinted from *College English*, November 1970.

lions of people in our century who have never read either Freud or the excellent exposition and further development of his ideas by Ernest Jones. One can only conclude that all or nearly all of those who found reading or viewing the play a richly satisfying experience must have intuitively grasped the nature of the inner resistances inhibiting its hero.

The point holds more obviously and dramatically for such a story as Hawthorne's "My Kinsman, Major Molineux." If we did not unconsciously understand why Robin laughs at his illustrious relative at the climax of the tale, we would find his behavior offensive, and the story poor, perhaps even repulsive.

If the premise that the enjoyment of literature depends upon understanding is correct, the basic cause of misinterpretations or attention to secondary meanings is not incomprehension, incomplete understanding, or misunderstanding, but *the difficulty of retrieving and verbalizing what we ourselves have intuitively grasped as we read*. This conclusion, which I think is inescapable, suggests that the first and probably most important task of the critic is one which has either escaped notice or appeared too obvious and routine to be worthy of notice: it is retrieval. The critic must devote much of his effort and energy to recapturing his own understanding and responses to whatever work he proposes to deal with. Such an undertaking may have hardly seemed worth specifying until our century, for understanding was equated with conscious understanding. It was also assumed—and to this day the assumption appears to underlie most of the teaching of literature—that our understanding is largely verbal or, if not, easily susceptible of being verbalized.

In fact, very little of our understanding is conceptualized and put into words. This is so most obviously because neither the speed with which a staged play or a movie glides by nor the rapid pace at which we choose to read works we find absorbing leaves much time for such an activity. But there is a more important and intransigent obstacle: the task is so difficult that it intimidates most readers, and few of those who attempt it succeed in recapturing and verbalizing more than a small portion of what they understood during and after reading. A significant proportion of our response—a proportion which tends to increase with the complexity and value of the literary work—is unconscious. Though it may seem redundant to say so, it must be stressed that those things which are understood unconsciously are meant to be understood unconsciously. They are usually implied or hinted at so delicately that we need not take conscious note of them; and because conscious awareness of them would lead to pain, anxiety, and displeasure, we choose to understand them subliminally. To an unappreciated extent, moreover, literature partakes of the nondiscursive character of the visual arts and music. In consequence, most of our preconscious and even many of our conscious responses to literature are extremely difficult to verbalize. Obvious examples are our feelings about formal qualities, including style, or the ambience of various scenes, or the tone of a work, individual parts of it or the distinctive manner of speech of various characters. It may be safely said that through the centuries relatively few readers have even attempted to formulate their responses to such aspects of literature, or often even simpler ones, in words. Indeed, tell it not in Gath, but many critics are clearly daunted by such tasks; and many errors are made in performing them, especially when a critic neglects or fails to recapture his emotional responses and relies entirely on a cerebral post-reading analysis.

It is not easy to describe what is involved in the actual process of recapturing one's responses. If my experience is typical, a direct attack is nearly always futile. One must cultivate a kind of openness, and this involves not only achieving a state of relaxation, even regression, but something not easy to combine with this, a selective alertness, so that when intuitive perceptions and responses come to mind unbidden, as they will, not even the most soft-spoken or far-fetched of these—*particularly* not these, for they are usually the most valuable—will go unnoticed. None of this is meant to suggest that these hard-won emotional reactions are sacrosanct. They must of course be checked carefully against the text. While some reactions may be correct and/or suggest insights and questions of great heuristic value, others will prove palpably mistaken and have to be discarded. The latter portion of the act of criticism, which involves not only reality testing but rounding out one's understanding, is largely cerebral. It is not likely to be very successful, however, if it is not based upon and informed by one's emotional responses.[1]

Although the task of recapturing what one understood and felt during and after reading is the indispensable foundation of the act of criticism, it cannot be regarded as a function of criticism. However, it is clearly in the service of the main function, the one that does more than any other to justify criticism. That function, assuredly, is illumination—the capacity of an insightful piece of criticism to open our eyes to meanings and excellencies of a literary work which, though perhaps felt to be present, have not been captured by previous critics in the recalcitrant medium of words.

Many students of literature may feel that evaluation is an equally im-

1.   For a related discussion of this view see my article, " 'Sailing to Byzantium'— Another Voyage, Another Reading," especially section 5, *College English*, January 1967. (See p. 128, this volume.)

portant or more important function of criticism. Perhaps it is, but it does not seem to require much, if any, special attention. A thorough study of a literary work is seldom undertaken unless the writer feels that it has merits which will repay study, and the writer's estimate can usually be inferred both by what he says and the very care he lavishes upon his exegesis.

2

This discussion of the importance of retrieval in the critical process is included here to explain my surprise that the observations to be made about the first scene of *Lear* have not been made many times before. Two or three observations of the same general character were made by Coleridge, but then in effect disavowed by the statements that the scene is improbable and, if some summary of what occurs in it could be otherwise conveyed, expendable.[2] While a visiting professor at Smith in 1967–68, Christopher Ricks, now of the University of Bristol, gave a speech at the University of Massachusetts in which he made a number of the points I shall make.[3] I feel justified in writing only because I had already formulated those points and others akin to them. So far as I can ascertain, except for the overlap with Coleridge and Professor Ricks, the points are new.

I cannot believe, however, that many of the observations to be made are *really* new; more probably they have been sensed but not expressed. The failure of more previous critics to make them is due almost entirely, I suspect, to their inability to recapture their responses as readers or spectators. As we shall see, some of the sources of the behavior of Lear and Cordelia are unconscious, hence not readily accessible. But most of the sources are not deeply hidden. Nearly all responsive readers of the play can—and, I believe, do—understand why Lear and Cordelia act as they do, though it must be stressed again, they might find it difficult to verbalize their understanding.

An understanding of the first scene in general and the interplay be-

2. In specifying what must be conveyed, Coleridge writes: ". . . let it only be understood that a fond father had been duped by hypocritical professions of love and duty on the part of two daughters to disinherit the third, previously, and deservedly, more dear to him. . . ." As I shall try to show, Coleridge was mistaken in assuming that Lear was duped by his two older daughters. *Lectures on Shakespeare, Etc.* (London and New York, 1937). The quotation is from p. 126.
3. In addition, Professor Ricks made a number of astute remarks about the political aspects of Lear's decision to divide his kingdom, some of them based on Harry V. Jaffa's fine article, "The Limits of Politics: An Interpretation of *King Lear*, Act I, Scene I," *American Political Science Review*, 51 (1957). Reprinted in abridged form in Helmut Bonheim, ed., *The King Lear Perplex* (San Francisco, 1960).

tween Lear and his daughters in particular rests upon the kind of elemental knowledge of the heart which we begin to acquire as infants and share with all human beings by the time we are grown-up. It rests also upon commonplace knowledge about what goes on in that most commonplace of all institutions, the family. For example, anyone who has grown up with brothers and sisters knows that by the time they reach marriageable age, if not long before, they have taken one another's measure. (Only children are also aware that this is so. They pick up the knowledge in various ways—for example, from friends who have siblings.) Similarly, everyone realizes that parents and children know one another reasonably well, though they are also aware that there is more room for wishful thinking, guilt, concealment and deception in this relationship. It is generally known too that the youngest girl in a family is likely to be the special favorite of the father.

To an astonishing extent our comprehension of the first scene of *Lear* is based on knowledge as elementary as this. Moreover, this kind of knowledge is brought into play automatically and effortlessly as we read fiction, as it is for that matter when we watch movies or television, or try to understand friends or relatives. In reading we couldn't very well disregard the knowledge if we wanted to. Of course, if we scorn such knowledge we could—and probably would—disregard it in the subsequent and cerebral task of analyzing a literary work and writing about it.

3

As so many who have written about *Lear* have perceived, the first scene of the drama has overtones of myth, ritual, fairy tale. Freud is among those who brilliantly discuss the ceremonial aspects of the scene.[4] But he was primarily concerned with deciphering the choice-among-three motif and illustrating its use in myths and fiction generally. When late in this essay he returns to *Lear*, it is in effect to ask whether its overpowering impact is not due to this motif rather than to "two prudent maxims" inculcated by the play. Of course there are still other possibilities. If Freud's focus had been on *Lear*, I am convinced that he would have discussed other aspects of the play. (As we shall see, he did so many years later.) I find it easier to accept his omissions than the contention of Russell Fraser, the editor of the Signet Classic edition of *Lear*, that what Shakespeare is up to here is dramatizing an idea: "the proposition that plainness is more than eloquence." I find myself even less sympathetic to Fraser's further contention that since the scene is "symbolic," it is not to

4. "The Theme of the Three Caskets," *Collected Papers*, vol. 4 (London, 1948).

be questioned in whole or in part. For example, we are not to ask why Cordelia loves and is silent. Evidently Professor Fraser believes that there is some irreconcilable strife between "symbolizing" and "meaning." He admonishes us in particular "to avoid the rationalization of conduct, on realistic grounds." "Rationalization" is of course a question-begging word; the very use of it suggests that any realistic interpretation of the scene would be unacceptable to Professor Fraser—an esthetic lapse, if not a moral misdemeanor.[5] But what if, however unwittingly, we do see a sound realistic basis for everything that happens in the first scene? As we know, even Coleridge, whom Fraser cites, explains some of the action and reactions of characters in this scene in realistic terms. To be sure, he in effect recants later on and he makes several other errors, of commission and omission. The "Notes on *Lear*" suggest that Coleridge is fallible too when he tries to convey his understanding of literature in words, most especially when he works in haste, as I believe he did in this instance.

As Coleridge read, I am convinced, he sensed the basis of the entire fabric of action and interaction in Scene I—as I believe responsive readers generally always have. We intuitively realize why each character behaves as he does. Towards the end of the scene Cordelia tells her sisters, "I know you what you are. . . ." By that point we also know Lear and his daughters, and Kent also, for what they are—and sense their knowledge of, and feelings for, one another. The exchange between Goneril and Regan at the end of the scene may add a little to our knowledge; it tells us what we should and may have surmised, that Lear has never been given to looking inward and has acted rashly on previous occasions. In the main, however, it simply confirms and makes explicit what we have already perceived. In addition, of course, it gives the scene a bitter edge by letting us know that Goneril and Regan are as keenly aware of the irrationality and stupidity of Lear's behavior as those who have been hurt by it.

5. In a perceptive essay for which in general one can feel nothing but admiration, "Shakespeare's Rituals and the Opening Scene of *King Lear*" (*Hudson Review*, 10, 4, 1957–58), William Frost also argues that it is necessary to choose between the mythical nature of Shakespeare's original material and motivation: ". . . the question of motive would . . . undermine dramatic effect in advance." I don't think this holds even for good fairy stories, much less for *Lear*. On the contrary, I would maintain that the opening scene owes much of its power to the way the firmly realistic substance reinforces the ritualistic performance. Our conscious attention is focused on the stately yet relentless ceremony; unconsciously we empathize with the participants and intuit the reasons for their behavior. . . . A brief selection from Frost's essay is included in *The King Lear Perplex*, op. cit.

Personally, I am so happy when I can recapture any kind of under-standing, certainly including realistic understanding of the characters, that I cannot forego the pleasure of trying to share it with others. I am particularly loath to make the sacrifice in the present instance because, unlike Coleridge, I feel that much would be lost by omitting the opening scene. So rich and compressed is this scene that much of the entire play lies coiled up in it. And much of the pleasure the play gives comes from perceiving the events already dimly foreseen at this early point actually unfold, taking a form which in general satisfies our expectations though, in accordance with Robert Louis Stevenson's formula, it surprises us too.

I have only one misgiving about proceeding: I would not want my surmises about the realistic aspects of the scene to detract in the slightest from its mythic, fairy-tale overtones. Those overtones are there, and they add significantly to the resonance and power of the scene. But I am not deeply worried about this danger. Like Professor Fraser I feel that the action of the scene deserves to be called symbolic, but it seems to me that when we invoke this word we wish to suggest a narrative element so rich in significance that it conveys more than one meaning.

4

What is basically being enacted in Act I, Scene 1, of *Lear* is an unwritten play. The play has no function in terms of the political purposes of the ceremony. The division of the kingdom, the redistribution of power and Lear's own plans, have all been decided upon in advance. The intention of announcing all these decisions in the course of a play is evidence of the assurance felt by its author, Lear, that it would be performed as planned, that everyone would accept and enact the role assigned him— or, more accurately, *her*. Other than Lear himself, the only characters in the drama he has composed in his mind are his daughters. Kent is an unwelcome intruder.

In terms of state purposes the play is a foolish way for Lear to make his decisions known. But for Lear himself the play has functions of the utmost importance. The king is an old man who, as he himself points out, is preparing for death. As part of that preparation he is doing some-thing which at some level he knows to be dangerous: he is surrendering his power, wealth and state functions to his daughters and their hus-bands, retaining for himself only the title and honors of a king and a small retinue of knights to attend him. He is in effect throwing himself on the mercy of his daughters and their husbands. Moreover, there is every reason to believe that he knows two of these daughters to be cold-blooded, calculating and untrustworthy. As the first speech of the play tells us, he also has, or has had, reservations about the Duke of Cornwall, Regan's husband. Lear is a frightened man. The despotism he displays later on may be in part a way of denying this and proving to himself that he still has authority and power. It is certain that he desperately needs the reassurance his play has been planned to elicit. We of course, whether readers or spectators, can see as Kent does that it is a poor way of eliciting reassurance upon which he can depend.

Intermixed with this need is an equally powerful desire for praise and love. They are of course the proofs Lear seeks that though he is surrendering his prerogatives he need not be afraid—reassurance against feared or already-present feelings of impotence and defenselessness. But we should not overlook his quasi-independent need to be flattered. This need too is understandable. We speak of extreme old age as a second childhood, and it is in childhood that narcissism is strongest. The regressive influence of age adds to Lear's need to be admired.

5

The burden of satisfying all of these needs—for reassurance, praise and love—falls almost entirely upon Cordelia. She is the heroine of Lear's play. She is given the climactic position in it, and is clearly intended to give a speech which outshines her sisters' speeches in substance and eloquence, a speech which is at once sincere, yet warm, even extravagant, in its declaration of love and approbation. The thirds into which the kingdom is divided are not exactly equal, any more than the halves into which a grapefruit is cut usually are. Cordelia's portion, Lear suggests, is "more opulent" than her sisters'—and really superior to theirs in some small way, I would suspect. It should be stressed, however, that the superiority of her portion is slight. We have every reason to believe Lear's statement that he is making and announcing the division of the kingdom at this time to prevent future strife; and the opening lines of the scene tell us that the portions going to Albany and Cornwall are so well equalized that neither duke will have cause for envy. We can assume that Lear would not jeopardize his goal of avoiding future war by giving Cordelia a portion notably superior to the others.

The early parts of Scene 1 prepare us for the recognition that Cordelia is Lear's favorite, if not the only daughter he loves. Though he calls his second daughter "Our dearest Regan," both his charge to her to speak and his earlier charge to Goneril are matter-of-fact. There is scarcely a wasted word. Moreover, though both daughters praise him fulsomely, his responses are perfunctory; indeed, both responses give the impression of having been memorized, or composed in a general way, before the ceremony. The text does not support Coleridge's view that Lear was "duped by [Goneril's and Regan's] hypocritical professions of love and duty. . . ." On the contrary, it is evident—probably even to Goneril and Regan—that Lear is gliding over this part of the ceremony as quickly as possible to get to the part for which the rest is preparation: his favorite's avowal of admiration and love. From "our joy" at the beginning to the hardly impartial suggestion at the end that Cordelia speak in such a way as to merit a "more opulent" third than her sisters, the invitation to her to avow her love has a different ring than the preceding ones.

Though we may be no better prepared than Lear to recognize it, the very fact that his expectations are focussed so completely upon Cordelia has its dangerous side. She is the daughter whose avowals can quiet his fears, but by the same token she is the one who can disappoint and hurt him most.

This obvious danger is compounded by two others. The first stems from the fact that Cordelia is Lear's youngest—and because he does not want to be reminded of his age may be thought of as more of a child than she is. Though Lear's bid to Cordelia to speak is longer than the bids to Goneril and Regan taken together, it is only three and a half lines in length. Yet in this brief speech Lear twice refers to Cordelia's youth. We may sense that his emphasis on this causes him to think of Cordelia as more obedient and pliant than her sisters, thus heightening the expectations based upon love and his assurance that the love is returned.

The very intensity of Lear's feeling for his youngest daughter is the second factor that makes his situation so dangerous. Unconsciously we may have already sensed that there is a not wholly desexualized—a repressed incestuous—element in Lear's feeling for Cordelia. There is additional evidence of this incestuous element later in the opening scene and elsewhere in the tragedy. For the light it throws upon this element and other feelings of Lear's, what he says when he is most enraged—disappointed and angry at Cordelia and further infuriated by Kent's intervention in her behalf—is particularly revelatory.

Most significant are some blunt words at the very beginning of his tirade against Kent:

I loved her most, and thought to set my rest
On her kind nursery.

"Set my rest" may mean not only "find my rest," but also, on the basis of usage in an Elizabethan card game, "stake my all." These words confirm some of the things we have sensed about Lear's feelings toward all three of his daughters. They tell us of course that Cordelia was his favorite and that he wanted to spend all his remaining days with her, but they just as clearly show that he had no confidence in the kindliness of his older daughters. We may feel that if Lear had been in better control of himself, he probably would have spoken less frankly. But the decision referred to should not be dismissed as the product of anger: it was evidently made when Lear was thinking carefully and objectively about his future course.

Like the phrase "set my rest," the word "nursery" may tell us more about Lear's feelings than he consciously intended to reveal. By Shakespeare's time, the Oxford English Dictionary tells us, the word had already acquired the significance of "relationship by having acted as nurse or foster mother to" as well as the meaning of "upbringing, breeding, nursing." The mother is of course the original incestuous object. A wife is often selected after her pattern, and a daughter may be her successor. The word "nursery" suggests that Cordelia has become the heiress to the feelings of love and attachment originally felt for the mother. It is not without significance, I believe, that neither Lear nor Gloucester, the analogous figure in the subplot, has a wife. One reason may be that the play is over-peopled, but it is difficult to resist the conjecture that at some level Shakespeare was aware of the incestuous nature of Lear's love for Cordelia and sensed that this feeling would be more unpalatable if Lear's wife were living.

Later in this outburst there is another remark which in indirect fashion suggests the strength of Lear's love for Cordelia:

So be my grave my peace, as here I give
Her father's heart from her!

The words "So be my grave my peace" seem to imply a comparison—probably to some such words as "and not my stay in my youngest daughter's 'nursery'." The pessimism of the words tells us again that Lear had never expected any kindness from his older daughters.

Considered closely, Lear's rage at Cordelia's refusal to accept the part assigned her in his play and his disinheritance of her are also evidence of his love: his fury and punitive behavior stem chiefly from the frustration of hopes too dear to be renounced. More technically, Cordelia's unanticipated behavior thwarts a whole cluster of unconscious, or at any rate unacknowledged, desires. Lear has evidently not even faced his dependency on his youngest daughter, much less specified the needs he expected her "performance" to satisfy. As we shall see, moreover, some of the things Cordelia says in her third and, ironically, most conciliatory speech give it the character of a sexual rejection. A metaphor Lear uses a little later in this outburst suggests that he

has understood the speech, or perhaps the entire pattern of her behavior, in this way: "Let pride, which she calls plainness, marry her."

After disinheriting Cordelia, Lear speaks harshly about her to the
king of France. However, the opening words of France's reply provide
further evidence of the intensity of Lear's affection for his youngest
daughter just before this turnabout:

> This is most strange,
> That she whom even but now was your
> best object,
> The argument of your praise, balm of
> your age,
> The best, the dearest . . .

The exchanges between Lear and Burgundy and Lear and France
dramatically expose the incestuous element in Lear's love. It is perfectly
clear that he no longer wants either Burgundy or France to marry
Cordelia. His anger is certainly a factor, but his attitude also suggests
that, while he was willing to share his favorite daughter with a husband,
he is reluctant to let another man possess her to the exclusion of himself. His position is hardly consistent with his disinheritance of his
daughter, but he is now dominated by a part of the psyche little concerned with consistency.

In 1934, some twenty years after writing "The Theme of the Three
Caskets," Freud read J. S. H. Bransom's *The Tragedy of King Lear* (Oxford,
1934) and became aware of the incestuous element in the love both Lear
and Cordelia felt for one another. In a letter to Bransom he tells him that
he is right, that "the repressed incestuous claims on the daughter's
love" is "the secret meaning of the tragedy." (This, surely, is too broad a
statement.) Then he adds, "Enough of that attitude has been retained in
actual life of the present day; in the unconscious these ancient wishes
remain in all their force."

Though what Freud proceeds to say is a little premature in terms of
our discussion, it is worth noting here. Bransom's supposition, he continues, also "illuminates the riddle of Cordelia. . . . The elder sisters have
already overcome the fateful love for the father and become hostile to
him; to speak analytically, they are resentful at the disappointment in
their early love. Cordelia still clings to him; her love for him is her holy
secret. When asked to reveal it publicly she has to refuse defiantly and
remain dumb. I have seen just that behavior in many cases."[6]

Towards the end of the first scene there is testimony from an unex-

6. Freud's letter is quoted in full in Ernest Jones, *The Life and Work of Sigmund
Freud*, vol. 3 (New York, 1957), pp. 457–58.

pected quarter of Lear's special attachment to Cordelia. We might suppose that Goneril and Regan would be hurt by the fact that their father prefers their younger sister to them. Actually, they are sufficiently cold-blooded and detached to note the fact indifferently and to comment on how foolish he was to cast her off.

Later in the play, when Lear has been subjected to the cruelty of his older daughters and is experiencing the fury of the storm, he speaks again in passion—passion born not only of his anger toward them but also, it may be surmised, toward himself. His last speech before his wits begin to turn shows that incest is very much on his mind. It is the second crime he specifies, and its placement gives it more emphasis than the one mentioned first.

> Let the great gods
> That keep this dreadful pudder* o'er our
> heads
> Find out their enemies now. Tremble,
> thou wretch,
> That hast within thee undivulged crimes
> Unwhipped of justice. Hide thee, thou
> bloody hand,
> Thou perjured,* and thou simular* of virtue
> That art incestuous. (III.ii.49-55)

When Lear and Cordelia are briefly reunited late in the play, his love—their love—reappears in its original intensity, if not in heightened intensity. As John Donnelly has observed, Lear's speech to Cordelia in V. iii., after their capture by the victorious British forces, is more like the speech of a lover to his beloved than that of a father to his daughter.

6

Why does not Cordelia, who loves her father, give him the praise and assurances he so obviously needs and is so obviously beseeching? We can perceive several interlocking factors that combine to inhibit her and set her on a mistaken course she can never correct, though she clearly feels a mounting need to assure her father of her love. She is furiously angry at him, we realize, for staging this farcical pageant, which puts a premium on hypocrisy. More obviously she is overcome by hatred of her unscrupulous sisters. She feels that she cannot compete with them in lying and does not want to participate in such a competition. She is re-

*pudder—termoil; perjured—perjurer; simular—counterfeiter

volted by play, players, and author—this last despite her love for her father. She is too completely in the grip of anger and revulsion to think clearly or to serve her own interests. Her initial refusal to say anything when it is her turn to speak is not simply a rebuff but a reprimand, and intended as one.

Her hatred of her sisters noticeably influences her behavior. Her tendency throughout to understate, to confine herself to minimal statements of her love, is clearly born in part of her desire to disassociate herself from her sisters, to show how different she is from them, and, by so doing, to convey her disapproval of them. But her course—it cannot be called a strategy since it is not rationally decided upon—hurts herself, not her sisters. As Lear perceives her behavior, her over-scrupulousness must make her seem dutiful at best, and patently unloving.

Indeed, everything Cordelia does here turns out wrong. Despite her rejection of the part she senses her father wants her to play, she does try to communicate with him. In particular, she tries to remind him of the cold-bloodedness and insincerity of Goneril and Regan, though this is neither necessary nor an acceptable substitute for what Lear wants from Cordelia. Probably because she is angry at him, moreover, her efforts are half-hearted and not well calculated to succeed. In responding to her father's second effort to induce her to speak, she makes a fugitive attempt to explain her recalcitrance. But the very placement of the words, "Unhappy that I am," causes them to be glided over and robs them of emphasis. She hopes that her tight understatements will call attention to the fulsomeness of her sisters' avowals of love. But such comparisons as Lear is capable of making are all to her disadvantage. Her speeches—in particular her "I love your Majesty/According to my bond, no more nor less"—seem meager and devoid of affection.

To be sure, her next speech (97–106) is longer and warmer. Moreover, she is here directly comparing herself with her sisters and more openly trying to warn her father of their hypocrisy. Though she couches what she says about her sisters in interrogative form, she all but declares: "They don't mean what they say. Their protestations to you aren't even consistent with their marriage vows." Cordelia's decision to bring up the conflict between a daughter's obligations to husband and father is not accidental. It is of course on her mind since she senses that she will suffer more than ordinarily from this conflict because of the unspoken demands her father makes upon her. The main determinant of her allusion is her unconscious awareness of the excessive, incestuous element in her father's love. Her fear is intensified, the entire pattern of her behavior suggests, by a more deeply buried realization that she must also be on guard against her love for him. The need she feels to defend herself against the over-strong attachment to her father has a pervasive influence upon her behavior. It is a major cause of her initial refusal to speak and all her subsequent mistakes. Unfortunately, no consideration she could have advanced to explain and justify her behavior could have been more detrimental in its effects. The point she is driven to insinuate does not escape her father. On the contrary, it has a greater impact upon him than is objectively warranted. The way she words her point must also wound Lear. The idea that the man she marries "shall carry/Half my love with him, half my care and duty" is intolerable to him. The word "half" is probably not meant literally, but this makes no difference: Lear cannot brook the idea of there being any limit on his favorite's love for him.

It is inappropriate to appraise Cordelia's conduct in moral terms. On the other hand, it can and should be noted that, allowing for the stress she is under, she behaves like a child, even a spoiled child, during her father's play. If we did not sense this, if we did not perceive that at times both she and Lear act like infants, we could not accept the suffering which they, and we, are later called upon to endure. That Cordelia is capable of acting more maturely and defending her own interests is shown a little later in this scene (225–34) when, while apparently asking her father to limit and specify the offenses responsible for his disfavor, she very effectively clears herself. Here she is buoyed by France's spirited defense and avowal of confidence in her. Earlier her poise had been undermined by the behavior of her father and sisters. When she acts childishly, she is in the grip of such primitive emotions as anger, resentment, and fear—and, what is perhaps more disturbing still, anxiety born of the feeling, in which her own love is a factor, that her father is making inappropriate demands upon her. Nevertheless, the sulkiness and recalcitrance she displays under these pressures are a part of her too and cannot be disregarded. Had she been more comfortable about her own feelings for her father, which however strong were under firm control, and had she been able to face his love for her consciously and calmly, she would have realized that it would never lead to demands she could not readily and guiltlessly satisfy. What her father needed was to be bathed in a protective affection which would obliterate the feeling that he was old and powerless. Cordelia could have avowed her love—avowed it as extravagantly as she sensed her father wanted her to. Facing her own repugnance for the ceremony, and even any slight hypocrisy of which she might be guilty, she could have given Lear the reassurance he so desperately needed. But of course if tragic characters were as rational and controlled as this, and as capable of compromising, they would not be tragic characters and there would be no tragedy.

7

Lear's daughters know him no less well than he knows them. There is no reason to doubt some of what Goneril and Regan say about him in private. We feel no disposition to question either Regan's statement that he has never sought to know himself or their judgment that what he has just done shows how old age is exacerbating his natural rashness. They are referring specifically to Lear's disinheritance of Cordelia and banishment of Kent, but what they say applies to the whole of his behavior, including his generosity to them. Lack of self-understanding is the key to everything Lear feels and does after Cordelia disappoints him and is a principal cause of the disappointment itself. Lack of self-control is also a factor in his behavior, but if he had had a fuller awareness of his own feelings, he would have had a much better chance of controlling them.

It seems unlikely that Lear ever acknowledged how much fear and anxiety he felt about giving up his power and prerogatives and going forth barehanded to meet death. It is still less likely that he apprehended the purposes of the play he had written in his mind. He seems blind to the intensity of his need for love and reassurance—and to the fact that the satisfaction of the need hinges almost entirely upon Cordelia. True, he has tried to be fair and has given all of his daughters roles in his play. But he is listening for one voice, one asseveration of love and esteem.

There is no indication that the speeches of Goneril and Regan have any emotional effect upon Lear. Paradoxically, it would have been better for Cordelia if they had buoyed his confidence: there would have been some diminution of the demands upon her. But what Lear wanted was an extravagant affirmation of esteem from Cordelia. We may suppose that he had composed innumerable speeches for her, each more satisfying than the one before in its affirmations of affection and approval.

Cordelia's actual behavior frustrates Lear's desperate need for love, praise and reassurance. The very real dangers of Lear's external situation do much to explain that need, but it is increased by unconscious factors. As has been mentioned, he is more frightened than he is willing to acknowledge—subject to innumerable vague and protean worries. An important function of the Fool—a splinter of Lear himself—is to name many of the anxieties, fears, and insights too painful for Lear to face. The Fool disappears when Lear himself begins to see more fully.

Cordelia denies her father the very things the ceremony was planned to provide. The impact of this is aggravated by other implications and effects of her behavior. First, it is experienced by her father as a rejection of *his* love. The distinction she draws between the love she owes father and husband is probably perceived as a bitter criticism of his love. Whereas acceptance of love, any kind of love, seems momentarily at least to justify it, rejection calls it into question, makes it seem dubious or evil. Cordelia's words and conduct probably make Lear subliminally aware of the not wholly desexualized nature of his feeling for her—and arouse guilt as well as anger. He feels that she is both scolding and rejecting him.

The independence and fastidiousness she displays hurt him for a second reason. They compel him to recognize that she is no longer baby or girl but grown woman. This in turn forces him to face something else he would prefer not to be reminded of, the fact that he is an old man. Her guardedness may also be wounding because it is the first sign of ambivalence he has permitted himself to recognize in someone he has thought of as loving him without reservation. Finally, as A. C. Bradley points out, Cordelia's behavior subjects Lear to public humiliation: he may feel that everyone present, Kent excepted, is aware of the lack of warmth and the criticism he senses in her words. His rage and need to lash out at her is fully understandable.

All the mistakes which account for Lear's later suffering are made while he is in the grip of this rage. He behaves like a child in a tantrum, striking out against those he loves, against his own self-interest, and against anyone who would remind him of the calamitous errors he is making.

Yet Lear knows that he has only one daughter who has a warm and generous nature and loves him. The fact that as he disowns her he invokes not only the sun but Hecate and the night suggests that he half realizes he is doing something evil. His refusal even to listen to Kent when he first tries to speak suggests even more forcibly that subliminally he knows that he is making a mistake.

We have seen how many constituents of Lear's next speech, the one which interrupts Kent's attempt to defend Cordelia, betray Lear's knowledge of the character of his daughters, of their feeling for him, and of his feeling for them. Yet in this very speech he proceeds to divide Cordelia's third of the kingdom between Cornwall and Regan, Albany and Goneril. His prerogatives are also divided between his sons-in-law. He retains only the titles and honors of king and a hundred knights, whom Cornwall and Albany, not he, must sustain. And he announces that he and his knights will divide their time between his older daughters and their husbands, moving monthly from one castle to the other.

His harshness to Kent once he is given a chance to criticize his sovereign's decisions shows us how determined Lear is not to acknowledge what on some level he assuredly realizes—that he has made a whole series of grievous mistakes. We may assume that Lear knows Kent almost as well as he knows his own daughters and is well aware that Kent has served him loyally and zealously and spoken sincerely. At this point Lear is astonishingly like Oedipus—determinedly blind and overcome by fright and anger when anyone tries to tell him what unconsciously or even preconsciously he already knows.

8

Though I have tried to support the interpretations suggested here by reference to the text, many of them were tentatively made before I consciously noted and marshaled all the relevant evidence. They were based in part on things intuitively understood—inferred in some instances. This requires no apology. Without the use of intuition and inference we could not penetrate below the surface of complex literary works, and reading would be a relatively unemotional and unrewarding activity. Inference requires considerable literary sophistication, and for that very reason the skill with which it is used is one of the things which distinguishes a good reader from a poor one. A timid reader or one blind to such things as symbolic reference, figures of speech, and irony can fail to perceive meanings which are fairly obviously implied. At the other extreme, some readers—including, alas, some critics—may force a passage hard to extract a meaning which supports a *parti pris* or an untenable interpretation. Despite these dangers, inference is an indispensable means of achieving understanding. Most great writers, whether or not they have formulated their knowledge, seem to realize that when a reader reaches out to grasp the significance of a work, a scene or a speech, what is understood has far more emotional impact than something explicitly stated. Without the use of inference we would miss many of the important meanings of such a work as *Lear*.

What is amazing is how much intuition and the disciplined use of inference add to our understanding of this play and Shakespeare's works in general. Is this because his characters, for example, have a life outside the play? A safe, but I fear somewhat dishonest and cowardly, answer would be, "No. They have a far richer life *inside* their play than lazy readers apprehend." This is true as far as it goes, but at the risk of antagonizing some readers and challenging them to re-examine a long-held conviction, I must confess my own conviction, which is that some Shakespearean characters demonstrably transcend their roles in a particular play, or plays, and come to have a quasi-independent existence in our minds. One thinks at once of Hamlet, Othello, Iago, Macbeth and Falstaff, as well as various characters in *Lear*.

The best explanation for this larger-than-art existence of certain characters has been advanced by J. I. M. Stewart, who depends in part upon Maurice Morgann and Coleridge. Like those earlier critics, Stewart bases his analysis upon an insightful and, I believe, fundamentally correct understanding of the creative process:

> . . . The artist does not get the essence of his characters from camera-work, as . . . [John W.] Draper would suppose; nor yet from a filing-cabinet of traditional literary types, which is the belief Professor Stoll constantly expresses with what softening word he can. He gets his characters from an interplay of these with something inside. And it is because he has a particular sort of inside, or psychic constitution, that he is obliged to get them. Falstaff and his peers are the product of an imagination working urgently from within. The sum of the characters is a sort of sum—nay, gives something like the portrait—of Shakespeare: a truth which Walter Bagehot realises in his essay, *Shakespeare—the Man*. . . .
>
> The inquiries of James and others into the phenomena of conversion, and of later investigators in the field of multiple and split personality . . . have shown how, in abnormal individuals not artistically endowed, either a co-presence or a succession of perfectly 'real' personalities can be a psychological fact. And a man writes plays or novels, I conceive, partly at least because he is beset by unexpressed selves; by the subliminal falling now into one coherent pattern and now into another of the varied elements of his total man—elements many of which will never, except in his writing, find play in consciousness. It is this that gives the characters their 'independence as well as relation'; their haunting suggestion of reality and of a larger, latent being unexhausted in the action immediately before us; their ability to beckon beyond the narrow limits of their hour. And here, too, we see how characters 'come alive'—how Falstaff came alive. It was not that Shakespeare took a traditional figure and clothed it with the spurious animation of a dazzling dress. It was that he took that figure and infused into it as much—and only as

much—of the Falstaff-being in himself as the exigencies of his design would admit. Of what more there was unused the bouquet, it may be, floats across the stage in those 'secret impressions' which Morgann felt. . . .

We have discovered, I think, why Morgann's essay is so much nearer to Shakespeare than Stoll's. Morgann better understands being creative. Stoll sees Shakespeare making his book as Stoll would make a book: knowing just what he would do, assembling his material from all available sources, and then constructing according to the best professional specifications of his age. But Morgann knows that nothing was ever born alive this way, and that despite all the artist owes to tradition and convention his is an inner travail still. That he draws from tradition is assured, and he will be the better, perhaps, for having before him the idea of the literary kind to which he would contribute. But *what* he contributes will be his own, or nothing in art. It will be radically his own, and not an old thing resurfaced. For the essence of his task is in exploring an inward abundance. When he does this in drama his characters, sympathetically received, will inevitably suggest to us a life beyond the limits of their rôle. And Shakespeare, from the vast heaven of his mind, expresses whole constellations of emotion in personative form. . . .[7]

I can think of no way of strengthening this explanation. I can only add that similar explanations could be advanced to explain the hold upon our minds of other elements in the plays, for example, certain situations, resolutions and inferred motivations. These may become so fixed in memory that we perceive examples of them not only in our own life but in things we hear and read about. We may also "analogize" on the basis of them, thus greatly extending their reference.[8]

9

All the rest of the tragedy is contained in embryo in the first scene. Mark Van Doren is certainly right in asserting that "the first scene . . . is a beginning, but all the rest is end."[9] To an astonishing extent it is all predictable end. This is particularly true in a negative sense. Though it is inconceivable, we realize, that the incestuous element in Lear's love for

---

7. *Character and Motive in Shakespeare* (London, New York, Toronto, 1950), pp. 121–22.
8. For a discussion of analogizing, a neglected but, I believe, highly valued aspect of our response to literature, see Simon O. Lesser, *Fiction and the Unconscious* (Boston, 1957; New York, 1962), pp. 242–47 and *passim*.
9. *Shakespeare* (New York, 1939; Garden City, N.Y., 1953), p. 204.

Cordelia could lead to a sexual advance, its presence makes it impossible that the play can end happily. The beloved is taboo. We do not know in detail how matters will work out, we do not anticipate the beneficent effects Lear's suffering will have upon him, but we do foresee that he and Cordelia will suffer as a result of the very intensity of their love and the mistakes they have made, and that the Fool, Kent, and anyone else who aligns himself with them will probably suffer too.

The exchange between Goneril and Regan when they are alone at the end of the first scene prepares us expressly for their mistreatment of their father. Their earlier exchange with Cordelia has shown that they are hard-hearted and not easily shamed or even discomposed. Now, even as we assent to some of their charges against their father, we feel uneasy: we sense that whether valid or invalid the charges are being advanced to justify already foreseeable ferocity in dealing with him. There is the beginning of a conspiracy to be strict with him and keep him in line. As appalling as anything they say is their lack of any feeling for their father or one another, their apparently inviolable cold-bloodedness.

The first scene also permits us to divine, though in a more general way, how the Gloucester subplot will work out. The exposition is brief and inconspicuous but deft.

Our first impression of Edmund is favorable, and we are later to see that he is not only intelligent and articulate but capable, virile and a natural leader. Here he must stand by silent while his father talks about his mother and Edmund's conception with a frankness, a lewdness and an undercurrent of boastfulness which must revolt him. But it seems to me that the way Gloucester talks has been given too much emphasis in many discussions of *Lear*. Nor is it clear that much importance should be attached to a factor on which Coleridge sets great store, the fact that Edmund had to do without "all the kindly counteractions to the mischievous feelings of shame, which might have been derived from co-domestication with Edgar and their common father . . ." (*Lectures* . . . p. 129). In view of what we see of Gloucester in this scene and learn of Edmund later, we have a right to feel skeptical about the way this co-domestication would have worked out. The factor of decisive importance, however, is Gloucester's treatment of Edmund in a far more important area. He interrupts the courtly exchange between his illegitimate son and Kent to remark, almost casually: "He hath been out nine years, and away he shall again." This exiling of a man of spirit and intelligence from home, country, position and, what may have been hardest of all to accept, any opportunity to use his abilities and prosper from using them, must have been a source of bitterness and relentless hatred of his father.

At the same time it would have exacerbated his competitive feelings toward Edgar and inspired deep feelings of envy. Inevitably Edmund would have thought that his legitimate brother was being unfairly favored. It is hard to resist the surmise that Gloucester's treatment of Edmund played an important part in warping his character.

Gloucester's treatment of his illegitimate son cannot have been without effects upon Gloucester himself. The guilt it caused helps to explain the ease with which Edmund gulls him, making reasonably credible what would otherwise be a creaky bit of melodramatic stage business. Gloucester is easily duped into thinking evil of his legitimate and loving son because he half fears, half knows, that he has treated his illegitimate son unjustly and feels a need to make restitution to him.

The symmetry of plot and subplot is not perfect. Though Lear's major blunder is his mistreatment of his favorite daughter, his suffering arises from a secondary mistake, the surrender of all his power, income, and possessions to Goneril and Regan and their husbands. Though Gloucester comes to mistreat his favored and better son, his suffering arises ultimately from his inhumane treatment of Edmund. Few readers are likely to be disturbed by this lack of symmetry. Gloucester's ill treatment of Edmund is mentioned so early and briefly that it probably has little impact and may not be noted. And there is no danger of mistaken expectations arising: the daughters of Lear and the sons of Gloucester are differentiated early and sharply. In a drama so concerned with the cruelty of children to parents and one another, however, the reader may fail to remark the extent to which *Lear* deals with the cruelty of parents toward their children. The action of both plot and subplot may be said to be initiated by a father's unwarranted mistreatment of a child.

10

Let me return briefly to the subject of the way the understandings set forth in this paper became known. To the best of my recollection, the most important of them occurred to me not during an *ex post facto* attempt to retrieve what I had grasped, as many if not most responses ordinarily do, but during a reading of *Lear*. Since it was a seventh or eighth reading, however, it is possible that some of the understanding had taken place between readings but did not announce itself until I reread the play. Since the reading in question was undertaken in preparation for teaching the play, it is also possible that it was atypical: it may have had as much in common with the kind of critical analysis teachers usually engage in after reading as with a reading undertaken for satisfaction and pleasure. As I recall, however, the reading was not relatively unemotional, as the later critical analysis of a work usually is, but exciting (perhaps in part because fruitful).

After the reading I tried to recapture other understandings and round out my understanding. Since I felt I now knew some of the motives for the behavior of Lear and Cordelia and was convinced that their behavior and the scene as a whole had a firm realistic basis, this proved relatively easy. Some ideas came to mind uninvited. Close study of the text yielded additional perceptions.

I hope that this formulation of my understanding of the opening scene and description of the way the understanding was reached will serve as a mnemonic device and help some readers to recall that they had some of these perceptions, or similar ones, or additional perceptions of the same general character, as they read or analyzed the scene—this whether or not the perceptions were ever formulated in words.

❀ Reflections on Pinter's
The Birthday Party

ONE cannot, and probably should not, write about Pinter without facing his similarity to Kafka and his acknowledged indebtedness to him.[1] In the course of telling stories which are apparently objective and up to a point even pretend to be realistic, both writers tap subjective concerns, many of which go back to infancy. Both deal with experiences which at first glance seem commonplace, even paltry, but which turn out to be battles for high stakes—sanity, for example, or sometimes life itself. Both share a conviction that the essential aspects of experience are ambiguous if not unknowable, yet both write simply and lucidly. Both achieve drama and poetry, without too many departures from colloquial speech and material that may appear to lack depth. Pinter is the more colloquial of the two, in part of course because he is a dramatist but also because a larger proportion of his characters are inarticulate or barely articulate and he has a sure ear for the diction of these characters, including their vulgarisms, neologisms, and slang.

Another similarity is too important to ignore: both men are preoccupied with our fears—our anxieties really—rather than our hopes. This is even more true of Pinter than of Kafka, one of whose two great novels is concerned with man's aspirations and strivings. Curiously, we are less

Reprinted from *Contemporary Literature*, vol. 13, no. 1. Copyright © 1972 by the Regents of the University of Wisconsin, pp. 34–43.
1. "Pinter, who acknowledges the influence of Kafka and Beckett, is, like these two writers, preoccupied with man at the limit of his being." Martin Esslin, *The Theatre of the Absurd,* revised ed. (Garden City: Doubleday, 1969), p. 255. See also Esslin's recent book, *The Peopled Wound: The Work of Harold Pinter* (Garden City: Doubleday, 1970), p. 29, for a statement of Pinter's sense of affinity with Kafka and Beckett.

likely to become aware of this preoccupation with anxiety than we are with one of its qualities, its abstractness. It is this abstractness which gives almost any situation in a Pinter play the effect of ambiguity, but this word is here scarcely adequate. In addition to permitting the viewer or reader to interpret the presented situation in an almost infinite number of ways, the abstractness provides a mold into which each reader can pour his own expressive content, in particular his free-floating anxieties, the kind which are intolerable precisely because they can be mobilized by so many different things. A further advantage of the abstractness is that the anxieties do not have to be specified even as one reexperiences them and tries to cope with them. The word "overdetermined" is also inadequate to describe a work which evokes this kind of response: it conveys a work's openness to multiple interpretations but not its power to impel a reader to become a covert coauthor. Whatever name one gives this quality, it does much to explain both the breadth and intensity of the appeal of Pinter's plays. In *The Angry Theatre* John Russell Taylor writes: "The ambiguity . . . not only creates an unnerving atmosphere of doubt and uncertainty, but also helps to generalize and universalize the fears and tensions to which Pinter's characters are subject."[2] It achieves this effect of generalizing and universalizing, paradoxically, by permitting the reader to individualize the content.

Some of Pinter's borrowing from *The Trial* in *The Birthday Party* must have been deliberate. Like *The Trial,* the play opens on the hero's birthday and it ends with two men taking him away—but the next day, not a year less a day later—perhaps to put him to death. Here a difference between Kafka and Pinter asserts itself. We know that K. is put to death; we witness his execution. We expect that Goldberg and McCann, who in effect abduct Stanley, are going to exploit him in some way for their own purposes—and we feel that they would not balk at murder. But we are not certain about either of these things and can only surmise what their exact plan is. Are they going to kill Stanley as a way of getting hold of some money he possesses, perhaps without being aware of it? Do they plan to put him in a corrupt and run-down rest home, where he will have scant chance of recovering, in order to divert some income to which he is entitled to their own pockets? Or do they have some quite different plan or motive for taking him away? We do not know. A Pinter play is like a Thematic Apperception Test. On the basis of scanty, obscure, and ambiguous evidence—a picture in the case of a TAT, puzzling dialogue and hazy glimpses of more puzzling people in the case of the play—we must decide the exact nature of the story being told: in this way also we are

2. *The Angry Theatre* (New York: Hill & Wang, 1962), p. 238.

put in the author's chair. And specifying the story being told, we find, is just a warmup for the more arduous task of deciphering its meaning.

Like Kafka, Pinter is apparently candid. The setting of *The Birthday Party* is a shabby living room in a seaside town in England, a room too appallingly real to question. Both the shabby woman who takes care of this establishment, Meg, a woman in her sixties, and her husband, Petey, a deck chair attendant, seem firmly, indeed inescapably, moored in the world of everyday being. Both speak about commonplaces in a dreary, flat, usually hackneyed way. Despite these reassuring indications, before long we find that we are in a strange world, a world where there are no signposts, where nothing is clearly defined. In some respects Pinter's plays are more continuously puzzling than Kafka's stories. In the end there is no significant difference: eventually in Kafka also one thing melts into another and everything dissolves into mystery and uncertainty. But provisionally Kafka may develop a character or a place with great solidity. Pinter weaves more loosely. He carefully—determinedly, it sometimes appears—leaves everything vague and fluid. Situations never assume a definite shape; either their outlines are left hazy and obscure or we are given two flatly contradictory versions of something and never told which one (if either) is correct. The development of the situations is no less enigmatic. We seldom feel that we have a sure grasp of the "what-ness," much less the significance, of the happenings in a Pinter play. Of course, much of this holds for Kafka also. The similarities between the two writers are more important than the differences. And one feels that the similarities were there to begin with, that the British Jewish dramatist apprehended reality in very much the same way that the Central Euro-pean Jewish novelist did and that Pinter, however unconsciously, was searching for someone like Kafka. If this is so, his appropriation of Kafka was not a matter of emulation but of seizing upon something helpful in defining and rendering his own vision of the human situation. This may explain the fact that, clear as the debt to Kafka is, not even *The Birthday Party*, Pinter's first full-length play, seems derivative. It is like Kafka but different. It bears Pinter's special stamp and, we feel certain, expresses his own vision.

It seems peculiarly difficult to specify the meaning of *The Birthday Party* primarily or largely in psychological terms.[3] In this respect it differs

---

3. It may be significant that Dr. Abraham Franzblau, who advanced a perceptive psychological interpretation of *The Homecoming*, was far less successful in my judgment in discussing *The Birthday Party*. See the *Saturday Review,* 8 Apr. 1967, and 3 Oct. 1967. One of the three interpretations of the play Esslin advances in *The Peopled Wound* is also psychological: "*The Birthday Party* might also be seen as an

both from most of Pinter's other plays and Kafka's stories. In *The Birthday Party* Pinter appears to be using psychological devices to make some melancholy comments on our society. A social reading will come to grips with more facets of the story and explain the play more comprehensively, I believe, than any of the interpretations advanced thus far.

From one point of view the play's six characters constitute a microcosm of society. In particular, they mirror the fundamental economic division in society, the division between exploiters and exploited. Goldberg and McCann are of course the exploiters—symbols both of the anonymous forces that control life and the managers, operators, and decision makers who understand those forces well enough to use them for their own ends. The reference is chiefly to economic forces, but the men's purposiveness, authority, and strength are vaguely enough defined to symbolize power in any form or area.

Despite—or because of—the kempt façade under which the power lies hidden, it is as cruel and remorseless as that of any primeval despot. Goldberg's bromides and moral platitudes help make him menacing: we feel defenseless before him because he has appropriated the decencies on which we thought we could rely for protection and perverted them to his own purposes—thus our pity and fear for Stanley, the borderline psychotic who in one day's harassment Goldberg and McCann are able to drag over the line, in all probability irreversibly. Without pity, but with some vague apprehension, we observe that the cruelty of the exploiters is not confined to the exploited group. When McCann shows the slightest trace of insubordination, Goldberg makes him say "Uncle." Dog eats dog.

At a still deeper level Goldberg and McCann may be responded to as surrogates for or agents of the father—the male who has first claim on the mother and seems almost omnipotent to a little boy, hence is hated, envied, and feared. The evidence for this is inferential but persuasive. Before Goldberg and McCann appear, we learn that Stanley regarded the "they" who blocked his second concert as agents of retribution for his failure to invite his father to his first concert, and this supposition is significant whether the concerts were pure fantasy or had some basis in reality. Moreover, from the time Meg mentions the fact that she is expecting two new roomers, we see that Stanley fears them. It seems rea-

---

image, a metaphor for the process of growing up, of expulsion from the warm, cozy world of childhood" (p. 84). This interpretation is invalidated, I believe, by the fact that at the end of the play Stanley is psychotic and the captive of the two men who have destroyed his sanity. There is little prospect that he will regain his sanity, much less grow up.

sonable to suppose that a feeling that the newcomers are also emissaries of the father is the ultimate source of this fear—and of the hostility which quickly manifests itself once the men appear.

Pinter's constellation of the exploited provides if anything a still sadder commentary on our society. As we have seen, one member of the group is completely unqualified for life: by his entire pattern of behavior Stanley is pleading *nolo contendere*. Meg is not much more competent or effective. Intellectually, she is a cretin, either illiterate or not up to the strain of reading. She is disregarded and treated contemptuously by her husband, Petey, and hardly seems to notice much less contest this. She thinks she has been well served if her husband condescends to read her a juicy item or two from the tabloid he always carries to hide in. Still, she feels his lack of love. Her libidinized though mainly maternal love for Stanley is born, we feel, of her desperate loneliness and lack of love. The exploited, Pinter is saying, for all their economic and emotional poverty are sometimes capable of giving. Even though Stanley is not all there and grumbles a great deal, he is aware of Meg's love and, in one of the most moving moments of the play, shows that he returns it.

Lulu, the girl next door but hardly the cleanly girl next door of American movies and situation comedies, is also capable of love. Lulu is Sex, she has been around, she is clearly there to satisfy sexual needs and to have her own needs satisfied. It might seem that she could be placed with the exploiters as well as with the exploited, and during the birthday party which climaxes the play she pairs off with Goldberg. But even the sexual practices to which he introduces her do not corrupt her, and we feel that nothing can. While she is far more sensual—and real—than Dostoevsky's Sonia, she shares her impregnable innocence. Her limitations must be noted, but they are in a sense, if not her virtues, her defenses against corruption. She is not much brighter than Meg; perhaps by the time she is as old as Meg she will be equally dull. She is not interested in, and probably not capable of understanding, anything which is even slightly abstract. But in part because she is simpleminded, she refuses to notice that Stanley is ill. With the slightest encouragement, we feel, she could love him. She is kind to him, helpless as he is, until the party, when, lacking even the ability to discriminate immediately between good man and bad, she responds to Goldberg. But once she knows him, revulsion follows swiftly. Lulu will not join the exploiters unless she becomes corrupted and she will not become corrupted. She sleeps with Goldberg, but we feel sure she will not stay with him.

At first meeting, Petey, who completes the exploited group, is far from prepossessing. He is without love, warmth, or purpose. He teaches us the saddening lesson that there is exploitation among the exploited as well as among the exploiters. In Act One, the furtiveness with which he transfers his earnings from one place to another suggests that he tells his wife no more than is good for her, gives her as little as possible, and stows away the rest for himself. And just as Meg retreats from life into infantile narcissistic daydreams, he, though better endowed, retreats from it into the meaningless but distracting jumble of his newspaper.

Nevertheless, in certain respects Petey is at the "desirable" end of the spectrum among the exploited group. (To be sure, it is a narrow spectrum.) He is the most alert representative of the group Goldberg and McCann must deal with and manipulate. Moreover, he possesses a measure of courage. He stands up to Goldberg and protests his appropriating control of Stanley. Goldberg quiets his first objection by assuring him that arrangements have been made to take Stanley to a doctor. When Petey intervenes again, just as Goldberg and McCann are preparing to leave with Stanley, Goldberg uses a variant of this same "don't you worry" formula. In addition, he puts down a bill that one feels is more than ample to cover his and McCann's overnight stay. After some hesitation Petey pockets the bill, as his previous handling of money made us expect he would, and his resistance subsides.[4] The exploited, Pinter

4.   Both this business about the bill and the earlier business about the stealth with which Petey handles his own money are evidently made before or during the New York performance of *The Birthday Party* in the 1967–68 season. There is no reference to them in the Grove Press edition of the play. To ascertain whether these changes and additions represented second thoughts of Pinter's or in any case had been approved by him, I wrote him a note of inquiry, to which he was kind enough to reply. Mr. Pinter has no memory "of Petey handling his money with stealth in Act One." And he feels that Petey's ultimate acceptance of the money Goldberg throws on the table as he leaves does nothing to characterize him. "I think your memory has misled you in your reference to the passing of money from Goldberg to Petey in the third act. It was intended in no way to be a reassurance or bribe. Actually I introduced this piece of business myself when I directed the play at the Aldwych in 1964 (I think!). What actually happens or should have happened was this: Goldberg makes his point about Monty to Petey and Petey falls silent, as always. Goldberg then simply places a bill or two onto the table, as a final courteous insult, if you like. Petey does nothing. The action continues. After they have all gone Petey, on his return to the table, automatically puts the money into his pocket. There's no point in his leaving it lying around. What has taken place is merely an added punctuation to the action. It has no further significance in my view—I mean to be applied to the character of Petey."

With all respect to Mr. Pinter, I must add that *after* seeing the bit of business about money in Act One, I could not help thinking that the money Goldberg left was immediately perceived to be more than enough to cover the overnight stay of himself and his hatchet man and thus that bribery, as well as reassurances and threat, helped to overcome Petey's resistance to his "guests" taking Stanley with

seems to be saying, accept their place in the pecking order without serious fuss. Those with a will to power do not experience too much difficulty either in seizing or remaining at the controls.

Meg has given Stanley a birthday present, which is lovingly wrapped.
It turns out to be a toy drum—bought, she tries to explain, to make up for
his not having access to a piano. Though nothing which is told us about
the characters is firmly established, it seems reasonably certain that at
one point Stanley at least felt that he was a promising pianist. The drum is
a well-intentioned but stupid present. If one does not have time to
foresee the effects it will have on Stanley, as soon as they appear one
feels one should have foreseen them. Stanley puts the drum around his
neck and begins to beat on it rhythmically, perhaps wanting to show his
appreciation to Meg and taking pleasure in once again making music. But
bitterness overcomes him: soon he is beating on the drum angrily,
vindictively. Music turns into cacophony as the first act curtain falls.

That evening there is a party, presumably to celebrate Stanley's
birthday, though it is still not certain that it is his birthday and he stead-
fastly denies it. A party means fun and games, and the group decides to
play blindman's bluff. No selection could have been more apposite for
symbolizing the cruelty inflicted upon Stanley during the "party" without provoking the attention of Meg and Lulu, much less any re-
monstrance from them. Only Petey is absent and this seems appropriate:
he is neither totally blind nor, except with Meg in certain areas, interested in deceiving others.

We have already seen Goldberg and McCann treat Stanley with the
utmost cruelty, subjecting him to a tattoo of questions and crazy accusations and insults which eventually make him scream in rage, terror, and
helplessness. Now when Stanley is blindfolded, McCann deliberately
snaps the frame of his glasses and then puts the drum before him so that
he steps on it, stumbling and breaking it. At intervals Goldberg and Lulu
embrace and kiss, quite openly. We are not surprised when Stanley
breaks down completely. Nor are we surprised at the first indication of
this—he tries to strangle Meg. We have seen that he is too easily irritated
by her stupidity and slovenliness and at some level have even sensed the
underlying source of his hostility: his fear of the way Meg satisfies his
desire to be infantilized. Unconsciously he must realize that her babying
reinforces his reluctance to resume life as an adult. His act gives

---

them. The "intentional fallacy" is not at issue here. My reaction to the significance
of the money exchange in Act Three, which I assume was shared by some members
of the audience, was born of the earlier bit of business about money evidently
added by the director or producer.

Goldberg and McCann the excuse they have been looking for to also use physical force to subjugate him.

An unexplained blackout now occurs. McCann shines his torch, but it is knocked out of his hand, probably by Stanley. While Goldberg and McCann look for the torch, Stanley "picks up LULU and places her on the table" (stage direction). Shortly afterwards McCann finds his torch and "shines it on the table and STANLEY." The next sentence in the stage direction which ends Act Two reads: "LULU is lying spread-eagled on the table, STANLEY bent over her." Even a critic as astute as Martin Esslin is misled by this description—in particular, I suspect, by the word "spread-eagled"—and refers to Stanley's action as an attempt at rape.[5] But surely Stanley's treatment of Lulu is fueled chiefly by anger and jealousy arising from her behavior with Goldberg. Stanley may also be trying to show Lulu and himself, and possibly the other three people present, that he could be a good sexual partner also, perhaps a better one than Goldberg. But a spectator or reader has good reason to view such a claim with mistrust. It seems possible that Stanley is impotent. His Act One rejection of Lulu's invitation to go on a picnic with her provides firmer evidence that he is probably too shy to make a sexual advance to a woman, much less attempt rape. Moreover, anyone who had empathized with Stanley during the torment which is the party as he experiences it must sense that he is at low ebb and feels little inclination for sex. What lies under your dreary social occasions, Pinter seems to be asking throughout this second act, but eroticism and aggression? But Goldberg's complacent and sometimes insulting replies to Lulu's ingenuous expressions of admiration suggest that eroticism plays a minor role. The act ends with cruelty firmly in the saddle: Goldberg and McCann are again converging upon Stanley.

We never learn the exact nature of the going-over Stanley was probably subjected to that night, but the next morning the brutal McCann is loath to return to Stanley's room and even Goldberg is edgy. Eventually McCann does fetch Stanley, who is now clean-shaven and dressed for departure. Once again Goldberg and McCann subject him to an unendurable rapid-fire verbal barrage. But it is superfluous. Stanley's will to resist has vanished and he can only make meaningless sounds.

The Birthday Party does not promise Stanley, or any of the rest of us, a happy year or a happy life. The ending of the play provides no catharsis for the pity and fear it has aroused. It is more depressing than the ending of The Trial, largely because the conclusion of the play does not terminate our thinking about Stanley. This is not to minimize the grimness of

5.   The Peopled Wound, p. 77.

the ending of *The Trial*. It will be recalled that K. suffers a cruel death at the hands of the two executioners he awaits on the eve of his thirty-first birthday, though he has had no notice of their coming: while the hands of one of the men are at K.'s throat, "the other thrust the knife deep into his heart and turned it there twice."[6] But Kafka does much to soften this ending. He has prepared us throughout the novel for the probability that K. will ultimately surrender to his guilt and become reconciled to the need for punishment. Moreover, K. is reminded of his guilt in the concluding scene: he glimpses Fraulein Burstner, though it "was not quite certain that it was she."[7] It does not matter: K. acquiesces to the sentence of death. The ceremonial quality of the scene and the pervasive suggestion that it is a subjective experience also help to make the scene palatable.

So does the relative definiteness of the ending. In contrast, the ending of *The Birthday Party* is provisional. Since Stanley has been pushed over the line into psychosis and is completely at the mercy of the men who inflicted this injury, no happy ending is conceivable, but the involved reader or spectator is likely to extrapolate and supply some ending, or endings. Since whatever particulars he supplies are the work of his imagination, they are likely to be especially vivid and moving. No matter what shape the ending takes, it is likely to be hard to accept.

Amazingly, inexplicably, *The Birthday Party* does not suffer seriously from the failure to supply any information or use of form which would reconcile readers or viewers to what lies ahead for Stanley. To the contrary, for a long time the play—in particular, the ending and the surmises the reader or viewer supplies to round out the ending— has continued to haunt anyone whom *The Birthday Party* has put under its distinctive spell.

6.   *The Trial,* definitive ed. trans. by Willa and Edwin Muir, rev. and with additional materials trans. by E. M. Butler (New York: The Modern Library, 1956), p. 286.
7.   *Ibid.,* p. 282.

❀ *Macbeth*: Drama and Dream

WITH the exception of *Hamlet*, and perhaps *King Lear*, more may have been written about *Macbeth* than any other play, yet some of the most significant aspects of the drama have gone unremarked—or noted too casually to provoke curiosity and analysis. Consider the many loose ends and apparent inconsistencies in the play, for example. Lady Macbeth speaks of having "given suck," but Macbeth has no son and no further reference is made to his wife's child, or children. Although Macbeth sees apparitions even before the murder of Duncan and, in general, seems unsure of his course and plagued by guilt, it is his strong-willed wife who breaks down first; though it is he who feels that "all great Neptune's ocean" cannot wash Duncan's blood from his hand and balks at returning the daggers, it is his wife who returns them and belittles the deed. It is she who futilely tries, while walking in her sleep, to rid her hands of the smell of blood. Or consider all that is made of the fact that Banquo has a son who may become king and father to a line of kings. For a time Macbeth regards Banquo and Fleance as the obstacles to the content he expected to feel as king and he steeps himself more deeply in blood to have them killed. Though Fleance escapes and the prospect that Banquo's descendants will rule is visualized during Macbeth's second visit to the weird sisters, nothing further is made of this plot thread. It is Duncan's older son, Malcolm, who is to be crowned king as the tragedy ends.

Even among the critics who show some awareness of *Macbeth's* defects, few conclude that the play is badly flawed. This is a more remarkable

Reprinted from *Literary Criticism and Psychology*, Joseph P. Strelka, ed., The Pennsylvania State University Press, University Park, Pennsylvania, 1976.

tribute to the play than it may seem, for, as I shall try to show, some of its strengths have also gone unremarked. Shakespeare does such a superb job of storytelling in *Macbeth* that we read it in an almost trancelike state and refuse to be distracted by this or that apparent flaw. To be sure, this is true to some extent of all of Shakespeare's plays and for that matter all competently written imaginative literature. Fiction is usually read with a willing suspension of disbelief, or to put Coleridge's insight into the language of our century, with a suspension of the vigilance normally exercised by the ego. But it is inadequate to regard Shakespeare's achievement in *Macbeth* as merely quantitative. Here as in some other cases a quantitative difference becomes qualitative—and of decisive importance. In most instances the extent and number of the departures from realism which occur in *Macbeth* would cause a reader to withdraw the trust he has provisionally granted the drama and to begin to read it detachedly and critically. Shakespeare does not permit this to happen. He induces a regression so deep that we read *Macbeth* as though it were an account of a dream.

More accurately, it is an account of a *series* of dreams, fantasies, and thoughts—a chain of mental speculations, mostly of the "What if . . . ?" kind. "What will happen if my valor comes to the attention of Duncan?" "What if he rewards me by making me one of the most powerful men in the land?" "What if he were to die and by some series of events I become king?"

It is remarkable that *Macbeth* can provide this sense of being privy to its hero's most secret thoughts and dreams, for drama is the most objective of all genres and may seem to have no devices save soliloquies and asides, which are somewhat awkward for taking a reader inside the mind, where thoughts and dreams are born. Shakespeare not only surmounts this difficulty with ease; he simultaneously accomplishes something which some might say is impossible in a drama: he tells his story largely from what today would be called the point of view of one of its characters. Macbeth's dreams are the basic subject of the play, and we see those dreams taking shape not only when he is on stage but often even when he is not. In scenes in which Macbeth plays a part, other characters—to say nothing of witches and apparitions—often talk and act as if they were enactments of Macbeth's dream-and-thought-fabric. More amazingly, when Macbeth is not physically present, other characters sometimes behave as if they were acting out his dreams. *Macbeth* may seem to be written in the same fashion as the other tragedies, but a close look reveals that it is not. Whole scenes, or crucial parts of scenes, are dramatized, not objectively (as they are, for example, in *Hamlet, King Lear,* and *Othello*) but *as Macbeth would imagine them.* Present or absent, he dominates almost the entire action. *Macbeth* is developed by what might be called, anachronistically, an objectified stream-of-consciousness technique.

Another important difference between *Macbeth* and Shakespeare's other plays, a formal one, is still less likely to be noted. To an astonishing extent *Macbeth* is written in the language of our dreams and daydreams, in what Freud calls the language of primary process thinking.[1] This is appropriate, but I am not sure it was deliberate. It would be my guess that Shakespeare let things well up from the unconscious to an exceptional degree while writing *Macbeth,* and that—allowing for the cuts, interpolations and loose ends, discontinuities and other changes believed to have been made by others—this is the main factor responsible for blemishes.

Whatever the genetic explanation may be, extensive use of primary process thinking in *Macbeth* contributes to an achievement of the highest order. It gives the play an organic quality it might otherwise lack. It lulls us into a state of relaxation in which we not only brush off inconsistencies, many of which, we sense, are only apparent or unimportant, but also understand the play much better and more easily than we would if we were more alert. It is largely responsible for our reading the play subliminally as a tissue of Macbeth's dreams, fantasies, and thoughts as well as an objective drama—this without becoming aware of the many violations of objectivity. Finally, it is responsible for the fact that we feel no need to choose between these two ways of apprehending the play. The shift back and forth between them is unconscious and effortless be-

1. Primary process thinking is largely in the service of the id, secondary process thinking in the service of the ego. It is easiest to understand the first mode of thinking by comparing it with the second, the kind of thinking dominant most of the time in maturity. Secondary process thinking is "ordinary, conscious thinking." It is "primarily verbal" and it follows "the usual laws of syntax and logic."

In contrast, primary process thinking "is characteristic of those years of childhood when the ego is still immature." This helps to explain its characteristics. Since it is initially the mode of thought of the preverbal child, it makes relatively little use of verbal representation, often substituting "visual or other sense impressions" for words. It shows no concern with time and makes no use of "negatives, conditionals and other qualifying conjunctions." It permits opposites to replace one another and mutually contradictory ideas to "coexist peacefully." It makes frequent use of "representation by allusion or analogy . . ." and may employ "a part of an object, memory or idea . . . to stand for the whole, or vice versa. . . ." In addition to dominating our dreams and fantasies, primary process thinking plays a considerable though subordinate role in the thinking of adult life—in jokes and slang, for example, and also in such a highly esteemed activity as the creation of poetry. I have here mainly relied upon and often paraphrased Charles Brenner, *An Elementary Textbook of Psychoanalysis* (Garden City, N.Y.: Anchor Books, 1955). The quotations are also from this valuable book, pp. 52–55.

cause the two ways of viewing the material of the play reinforce and enrich one another. At points the objective confirmation of some dream or desire is synergistic in its effects.

The claim that almost every scene of *Macbeth* can be experienced as a dream and an event dramatized, not objectively but from the hero's point of view, can be illustrated by glancing at the first three scenes. These fall into a pattern of increasing complexity. Other scenes will also be discussed, but the consideration of the opening three should show how almost any scene of the play can be understood simultaneously as dream and as event.

Perhaps Macbeth's second encounter with the weird sisters (IV. iii) is the scene which can most obviously be read as a dream. Until the appearance of Lennox at the end, the only characters besides Macbeth are witches, who are easy to see as embodiments of Macbeth's thoughts, and apparitions, whose claim to existential reality is more tenuous still. The fact that Macbeth does not even have to voice his questions to the apparitions confirms the impression that he has evoked them into being, and other characteristics of the scene help to establish its dreamlike quality.

Only a little less obviously, the first scene of the play is also a dream of Macbeth's, or a fragment of a dream: the witches are planning a meeting with him. What they will propose—that is, the exact nature of the desires stirring in Macbeth—is undefined; but the fact that the proposals are projected onto witches shows that they are felt to be evil. The "Fair is foul, and foul is fair" motif applies, not to those desires, but to Macbeth's battles, which are not only lost and won, but have evil as well as good effects.

It is not easy for a modern reader also to perceive the scene as objective. However, most Jacobean spectators evidently did not have this difficulty. They found it relatively easy to accept the existence of witches, perceived as embodiments of the evil in the world. As a corollary to this, they apparently found it no more difficult than the Greeks to think that such spirits would be concerned with mankind and individual people. The three witches in *Macbeth* are clearly concerned with the play's hero: this one touch suggests that the play is not wholly objective but often developed from Macbeth's point of view. Modern readers too, I believe—if not at the beginning at any rate by the time they are under the spell of the play—provisionally accept the existence of the witches as incarnations and agents of evil. This does not interfere with their perception of them as externalizations of the evil gestating in Macbeth.

The second scene is more easily read as objective; indeed, readers are seldom aware of having understood it in any other way. Unconsciously, the scene is read as a classic wish-fulfilling dream. Evidently Macbeth's desire to have his valor praised by everyone, and recognized and rewarded by the king, involves no conflict or self-reproach. In his dream, his exceptional bravery is not only brought to the attention of the king but singled out for special praise by the captain. Duncan asks a question which couples his generals, but his only other interruption of the captain's account is to praise Macbeth. And the scene ends happily, as a wishful dream should, with Duncan dispatching Ross to inform Macbeth that he has been named Thane of Cawdor—and praising him once again.

The very factors which make the scene so satisfying to read as a dream tilt the scene so far in Macbeth's favor that, if we were not already in a quasi-trancelike state, we would be dissatisfied with it. Evidently Banquo is also an able and courageous general. If we were more alert, the desire for both justice and formal symmetry would make us feel that he should be accorded more praise and that there should be some indication that he too will be rewarded. (So far as we are informed, he never is.)

Scene iii reads equally well as dream or as objective but actually Macbeth-dominated dramatization. The most obvious basis for apprehending the scene as a dream is the reappearance of the witches. This together with Macbeth's immediate reference to "foul and fair" may make us think of the scene as a continuation of the dream begun in scene i. Subliminally, we may also be struck by the close correspondence between the material in this scene and what Macbeth would be thinking at this very time.

We know that he is walking to see his sovereign and if, as I believe, we are by now inside his mind, we know that one of the things he is thinking about is how he will be rewarded for his valor and his victories. We even know what Macbeth has dreamed but perhaps momentarily forgotten, that one of his rewards has been decided upon. And we have no doubt that it is Macbeth's dream which is unfolding. The first part of the scene tells us that it is Macbeth the witches are awaiting. When he and Banquo appear, Banquo addresses them at length, but it is Macbeth they respond to. Not only the substance of what they say but the incantatory way they express themselves show that it is Macbeth they are thinking of—or projections of his thoughts.

Even Banquo may be part of Macbeth's dream fabric. If Macbeth were walking alone to see his sovereign and speculating about how he is to be rewarded, it would be natural for him to think of his fellow general. Banquo is a rival claimant for the recognition and honors for which Macbeth longs. Moreover, Macbeth fears Banquo. One of his fears is alluded to in the scene: Banquo has a son who may someday rule Scotland; Macbeth has no son. The second fear is not mentioned until III.i, an example of the extent to which the play follows primary process logic. (In other instances explanation also follows thought or act—or is not given at all.)

Much of I.iii revolves around two prophecies the witches make to Macbeth: they call him Thane of Cawdor (this may be no more than an announcement), and promise him he will be king "hereafter." We may assume that both statements express wishes of Macbeth. No explanation of either wish is offered, and I will postpone discussion of speculations about the motives afforded by the play. What should be noted without delay is that the scene can also be read as a dramatization of actual events; though here, perhaps to a greater extent than in scene ii, the occurrences are presented as Macbeth would imagine them. This is obviously true up to line 50. Banquo, beginning with his second speech, acquires substantiality. He alerts us to Macbeth's reactions to what the witches tell him, as he does later to Macbeth's reactions to what he learns from Ross and Angus. Banquo also induces the witches to notice him and prophecy to him. The prediction is interesting to Macbeth and Banquo, who does not hesitate to warn Macbeth of the dangers latent in the prophecy that Macbeth will become king. Each general confirms the prediction made to the other, as though neither can quite believe what he has heard.

With the entrance of Ross and Angus the scene acquires additional substantiality. Here also, however, developments are dramatized from Macbeth's point of view and/or the focus is on him. The news the emissaries bring (I.iii. 89–107) is all to obviously presented as Macbeth would imagine it. Although Banquo is present he is given neither praise nor a share in the king's bounty; indeed, he is utterly ignored. A critically alert reader would realize that this part of the scene would be embarrassing to all four participants. But being so completely under the spell of the play, the reader does not engage in reality testing. Shakespeare further protects the material by displacing our attention from the news Ross and Angus bring to its connection with the prophecies of the witches.

This scene illustrates Shakespeare's ability to induce the reader to slip back and forth between the two ways of apprehending the play. The first fifty lines of the scene are probably understood as being predominantly a part of Macbeth's dream-thought-fabric and, as mentioned, the Second Witch's speech, "All hail, Macbeth! Hail to Thee, Thane of Cawdor!"[2] is apprehended as an expression of his wish. In contrast, the king's emissaries seem to be real visitors from a real world. Ross's news that Duncan has actually named Macbeth Thane of Cawdor is such a startling coincidence that even Banquo is profoundly affected by it. To Macbeth the news is like a sign from fate. It seems to validate—and legitimatize—his most secret dreams, the whole pattern of desire of which becoming Thane of Cawdor is a part. It casts shadows beyond itself, appearing to sanction even the wish to become king. Macbeth's first words after Angus explains the fate of the previous thane tells us it has had this magical significance for him: "Glamis, and Thane of Cawdor:/ The greatest is [to follow]."

The coincidence may make a modern reader think of a similar incident in a great nineteenth-century work of fiction—the apparently chance discovery by Raskolnikov that at precisely seven o'clock the next evening Lisaveta will be absent from her sister's apartment—a discovery that makes him feel he must go through with a murder which up to that point has seemed dreamlike and unreal. Shakespeare uses another conjunction of this sort in the very next scene of Macbeth. Duncan's decision to visit Inverness is interpreted by both Macbeth and Lady Macbeth as a sign that they should proceed with the terrible act they are contemplating. However, whereas it is a clear "go" signal to Lady Macbeth, it simultaneously imposes another constraint on her husband—and reminds him of all the other arguments telling him to abstain from the unjustified murder. But this attempt to strengthen his defenses is ineffectual. What he wants appears within easy reach and his scruples are overcome, or lost sight of, in a matter of minutes.

Shakespeare's double vision of almost every scene of Macbeth may have been inadvertent. Since he had two potential male heroes, he probably felt a need to emphasize Macbeth so that Banquo would simply be a foil to him, not a rival claimant for our interest. The emphasis was also necessary to induce audience identification with Macbeth.

The half-"real," half-dreamlike world Shakespeare conjures up in Macbeth is so enthralling that we feel no disposition to choose between alternatives, to decide on a single attitude toward the play, which would break its spell. It is helpful of course that Macbeth dominates both ways of perceiving the story, so that the gap between them is not great. Each kind of reality, or unreality, that of dreams, that of the actual, comes to suffuse the other. Thus we are not even taken aback when, in IV.i, Mac-

2.   This and all other quotations from Macbeth are from the Signet Classic edition, ed. Sylvan Barnet (New York: New American Library, 1963).

beth asks Lennox, "Saw you the weird sisters?" But we could wonder how Lennox even knows what Macbeth is talking about.

The deep suspension of disbelief with which we read helps to explain our refusal to pay much attention to other slips, gaps, inconsistencies, and the presentation of material in apparently illogical sequence. We do not question the primary process language and we tend to be uncritical even in thinking about the play after reading or viewing it. To accept I.iii as realistic would involve provisional belief either in witches or in the rare psychological occurrence of *folie à deux*. Few readers, or critics, seem troubled by such considerations.

The only casualties of our uncritical reading of the play are parts of it which do not admit of double vision and whose single strand of reference takes us away from Macbeth for what seems a considerable time. Parts of scenes which seem wholly objective—for example, II.iii up to the appearance of Macbeth—do not suffer, for they are swiftly traversed. Nor do objective, highly dramatic scenes which introduce appealing characters; the scene at Macduff's castle (IV.ii) will serve as an example. It is only when a scene is objective and takes us away from Macbeth for an extended period that our interest tends to flag. The scene in which Malcolm tests Macduff's loyalty (IV.iii) is perhaps the only good example. We may explain our dissatisfaction on some other basis, such as lack of realism, but its chief source, I believe, is our impatience to return to Macbeth.

Since *Macbeth* appears to have been written in a state of regression, it is not surprising that there are delayed explanations and numerous omissions. In particular, little attention is paid to motivation, even in Macbeth's case, despite the fact that we are often inside his mind. We are never told, for example, why Macbeth dreams of being named Thane of Cawdor. Nor are we told why Macbeth wanted to be king. Some of the immediate determinants of the desire are fairly easy to surmise. From dreaming of being rewarded by the king to dreaming of becoming king is but a short and pleasant step. The skill and courage Macbeth displayed in the battles, which in a sense begin the tragedy, influence him in a more direct way. They may make him think of himself, probably with warrant, as preeminent on the fields of battle. Why not then preeminent during peacetime also? Almost certainly, Macbeth's victories bolster his sense of his own worth, make him feel that his countrymen in general will now esteem him more. This in turn makes the idea of higher station seem a realistic possibility. In a sense the criminal dreams which undo Macbeth are born of success. But as we shall see, that is not their ultimate source.

It is important to note that this first intimation that Macbeth will become king arouses fear rather than satisfaction. There could be no better evidence that the idea of murdering Duncan is already gestating in his mind. A little later he does face the need for this murder—only to be overcome by such fears that he falls into a trance in which he becomes oblivious to the presense of Banquo, Ross, and Angus. He shies away from the idea of killing Duncan with the wish that chance will crown him, but it seems that neither the reader nor Macbeth has any faith in this solution. Before his crime is named, Macbeth begins to suffer from guilt. The crown is not golden even in anticipation, but mottled and tarnished.

The most strenuous objection to the way of reading *Macbeth* being developed here will come, I suspect, from those who believe that Lady Macbeth is a stronger character than her husband and maintain that she dominates him and the action of the early part of the play. Of course, she is not a stronger character or she would not collapse completely before her husband—and for that matter the play would not be called *Macbeth*. The failure to understand the nature of the interaction between Macbeth and his wife must stem in part from failure to read the work with sufficient care or to recall all we sensed as we read, in part from ignorance of ourselves and human nature generally—or temporary lack of access to what we know.

If we read the play carefully and have some experience of life and knowledge of ourself, it seems to me we can hardly fail to perceive that, far from Lady Macbeth dominating her husband, Macbeth skillfully enlists and uses his wife's help. In I.iv Macbeth encounters an apparently new obstacle to his desire with far less fear and ambivalence than he showed in the preceding scene. At the same time, before we so much as meet Lady Macbeth, he diagnoses the weakness in himself which may make it impossible for him to attain his desire:

> The Prince of Cumberland! That is a step
> On which I must fall down, or else o'erleap,
> For in my way it lies. Stars, hide your fires;
> Let not light see my black and deep desires:
> The eye wink at the hand; yet let that be
> Which the eye fears, when it is done, to see.

(I.iv. 48–53)

What Macbeth is hoping for is some way of outwitting conscience—or to use the language of twentieth-century depth psychology, the superego. His attempt to secure his wife's help is the most ingenious of the devices he employs, and her goading and participation reduce his guilt to the point where he can go through with the murder. Still, he is just barely able to do so; and after the first murder his efforts to circumvent or mollify his conscience are still less successful. To be sure, his superego does not stop him from murdering Duncan or others, but it does prevent him from deriving any satisfaction from the murders. Even this formulation is inadequate: as we have seen, Macbeth is tormented by guilt and anxiety before the murder of Duncan—even before the crime has assumed definite shape in his mind. At the time he plans the murder of Banquo and Fleance, he deliberately tries to harden himself in order to be impervious to the stings of conscience. Although he does in fact become harder and his sensibility dulls, this stratagem is no more successful than the others. He is guilt-ridden when he reluctantly enters the combat with Macduff which ends with his death. He goes to his grave without having achieved any satisfaction or even respite from self-reproach from his career of crime. Each murder augments his guilt, increases his self-condemnation, deepens his depression, and intensifies his fear of, and even desire for, punishment.

The fact that Macbeth has a severe superego must be stressed in order to correctly understand the play. Macduff and his other enemies talk of him as a devil, but they do not know him from the inside, as we do. Shakespeare does not want us to accept their judgment without important qualifications. I have no wish to extenuate, much less excuse, Macbeth's crimes, but he is a murderer of the Brutus or Raskolnikov kind, not the Richard III kind. The killing of the grooms perhaps excepted, he is never able to murder cold-bloodedly. He is never able to deceive himself by justifying his crimes.

Despite his inability to distort reality, it seems that his ego is crippled in some respects. It behaves like the ego of a person suffering from an obsession or compulsion. Otto Fenichel writes: "In all psychoneuroses the control of the ego has become relatively insufficient. . . . In compulsions and obsessions, the fact that the ego governs motility is not changed, but the ego does not feel free in using this governing power. It has to use it according to a strange command of a more powerful agency, contradicting its judgment. It is compelled to do or think, or to omit certain things; otherwise it feels menaced by terrible threats."[3] The hypothesis that Macbeth's ego is impaired in some such way as this helps to explain the anomaly of a man with a conscience like his being able to murder. The hypothesis also explains the feeling the play gives

3. *The Psychoanalytic Theory of Neurosis* (New York: Norton, 1945), p. 268.

that the agonizing inner struggle Macbeth undergoes is between id and superego, with practically no mediation by the ego. As a result of its weakness, he is victimized by both of the opposed and never reconciled parts of his psyche: he yields to his impulses but is lashed before, during, and after each surrender.

Macbeth realizes that he must do everything he can to deceive his conscience, and, immediately after expressing the vain wish to be blind to his own acts, he writes to his wife. Although sequence is not always a reliable guide in *Macbeth*, it does occasionally help in establishing causal connections. One does not have to examine Macbeth's letter searchingly to see that one of its aims is to induce his wife to persuade him to murder Duncan. If she persuades him, Macbeth believes he can claim that the idea comes from outside and he can deny his own responsibility. The ending of the letter is seductive in tone. It tries to recruit his wife not simply as a helper but as an accomplice in crime, and twice offers her an incentive for giving him her support. "This have I thought good to deliver thee, my dearest partner of greatness, that thou mightst not lose the dues of rejoicing, by being ignorant of what greatness is promised thee. Lay it to thy heart, and farewell" (I.v. 11–15).

Macbeth wants to create the illusion that external forces are impelling him onward. The attempt to secure his wife's involvement is of a piece not only with his later use of hirelings to commit his crimes; it squares also with his tendency to externalize temptations, wishes, and fears in the forms of witches and apparitions.

The mechanism Macbeth hopes to take advantage of in enlisting the help of his wife must be older than marriage—as old as continuing close relationships of any kind between two people: a person communicates something to a confidant in order to provoke an anticipated and desired response.[4] Often a person wants encouragement to do something which he wants to do but which arouses so much conflict that it cannot be done without outside support—or support which appears to come from outside. Alternatively, help may be desired in resisting a course of action which is tempting, but which is perceived to be wrong and/or likely to lead to trouble.

Macbeth's situation and procedure fall into a common pattern. His

4. For a wonderful example of this mechanism in contemporary fiction, see *To the Lighthouse*, "The Window," ch. 7—the account of the way Mrs. Ramsey musters her energies to provide the sympathy and reassurance she senses her husband needs.

desire to be king is so overpowering that he is *almost* willing to kill Duncan to attain his goal, though he recognizes he has no justification for such an act. He acquaints his masculine, aggressive, not overly scrupulous wife with his dilemma on the assumption that she knows him well enough to identify his dominant wish and to give him just the kind of encouragement and active assistance he needs to gain it. (He is right about this, though it seems to me that Lady Macbeth never recognizes the basis of her husband's hesitancy as clearly as his speeches permit us to recognize it.) Whether his reasoning is conscious or, as is more likely, unconscious, Macbeth must feel that the letter is an important step in doing what he senses to be necessary—overcoming the inner resistances which keep him from killing Duncan. Meanwhile, the very act of sharing his tempting but frightening dream with his wife may somewhat reduce his guilt feelings.

Once aroused Lady Macbeth does such a vigorous job of persuasion we may forget that it was her husband who enlisted her support. The intensity of her desire that he become king may be a surprise to him and to Lady Macbeth herself. In the great invocation in I.v, which begins, "Come, you spirits/that tend on mortal thoughts, unsex me here . . ." she appears to be summoning strength from reserves never before tapped. There can be no questioning of Lady Macbeth's wifely devotion. She mobilizes all her strength to play the role she feels she must play to bring happiness to her husband and herself.

It is necessary to ask why Macbeth should want to kill Duncan, whom he cannot find fault with as a man or king and who has been particularly gracious and generous toward him. Neither Macbeth nor, interestingly, Lady Macbeth ever makes an attempt to extenuate, much less justify, the murder. But if we did not feel that there was an adequate explanation for what Macbeth does, we would not have a high opinion of the tragedy.

Perhaps Macbeth is actuated by unconscious hostility. Some psychoanalytic interpretations of the drama have been based on this hypothesis: Macbeth is seen as a bad son acting out some unextirpated hatred for the father upon a surrogate. But apart from the fact that Macbeth at no point seems to be a son figure, unless the murder of Duncan itself admits of no alternative explanation, there is no trace of such hatred, either before or after the crime. When at the end of the superb after-the-murder scene with Lady Macbeth, he exclaims to the unknown person knocking at the gate, "Wake Duncan with thy knocking! I would thou couldst!" we have no doubt that he means it. There is more reason to suspect his public comment on Duncan's death in the next scene (II.iii.93–98), since he is here trying to make himself one with the others lamenting the murder, but I believe that, ironically, the occasion provides a welcome opportunity to say something he deeply feels; and his prognosis of his own situation is uncannily accurate.

What circumstances, what motive or motives, could drive a man like this to kill when there is no excuse for killing? As we have seen, it was success which crystallized and gave urgency to the desire to be king; and rewards stemming from success, such as being named Thane of Cawdor and being visited by Duncan, seemed like signs from fate that he should act to attain his desire. But Lady Macbeth's reaction to her husband's letter—her lack of surprise as much as what she says—indicates that unrest and amorphous ambition antedate the action of the play.

Those feelings were born of failure, not success. Macbeth went through with an act for which he knew himself unqualified and killed a man he loved because he was an unhappy, discontented, even desperate man, who found life sterile and empty. And because he was desperate, he nurtured the absurd, groundless hope that being king would somehow change everything. When the play begins, Macbeth is already a thane of Scotland and a renowned general; but he is also middle-aged, childless, friendless, and loveless. Moreover, though an intelligent man, he is without any interests which might make his life seem meaningful.

The claim that Macbeth is loveless seems to be contradicted by his closeness to his wife during the early part of the play, but it is possible, even likely, that their partnership in crime brought them closer together than they had been for a long time, or perhaps ever before. The crime offered the vaguely defined but alluring promise of curing their discontents, of making their lives more fulfilling. During the planning of the murder of Duncan, as G. Wilson Knight points out, they are "in evil with" one another, just as Antony and Cleopatra are in love with one another. Even during this period of closeness, however, though Lady Macbeth is loyal and devoted to her husband and each of them is dependent to some extent on the other, there is no indication of passionate love, past or present, on either side. It is possible that Macbeth has had no children by his wife because he is impotent. His complaint about the "barren scepter" (III.i.62) the weird sisters have put in his grasp may include this second meaning. There are more definite indications that his marriage, like so many middle-aged marriages, has deteriorated into a kind of business partnership. Perhaps it had never been more than that.

If these speculations are correct, Macbeth is susceptible to the dream of becoming king because for a long time before the play opens he had been oppressed by a discontent so profound that he felt almost any change would be for the better. Perhaps Macbeth's willingness to court death was born of desperation, of a feeling that matters might as well be either better or worse. He fights Macduff with the same fury at the end of the play when he is not only desperate but hopeless. Interestingly, two of the murderers Macbeth enlists to kill Banquo and Fleance, the First Murderer in particular, express the very psychology I am describing as they accept their assignment:

> And I another
> So weary with disasters, tugged with fortune,
> That I would set [risk] my life on any chance,
> To mend it or be rid on't.
>
> (III.i.111–14)

Later there is firmer evidence that Macbeth was impelled to his first crime by discontent. He reminds his wife that the purpose of killing Duncan had been to gain their peace, but the statement, the most explicit the play offers, is embedded in a speech of such eloquence ("We have scorched the snake, not killed it . . .") that, bewitched by its beauty, we may not take in the plain sense of much that is said:

> better be with the dead,
> Whom we, to gain our peace, have sent to peace,
> Than on the torture of the mind to lie
> In restless ecstasy [frenzy].
>
> (III.ii.19–22)

The placement of the revelatory phrase, "to gain our peace," may also keep it from attracting the attention it deserves.

Just before Macbeth's entrance, his wife had soliloquized: "Nought's had, all's spent,/Where our desire is got without content." This too suggests that the hope for something like peace, a feeling of satisfaction and well-being, gave birth to the desire of Macbeth and his lady to become king and queen.

The still more famous "She should have died hereafter" passage (V.v.17–28) also may be evidence of this motive. The passage is usually viewed as a set piece, with no important relationship to the play as a whole, but I believe that the feelings of the emptiness, sterility, and meaninglessness of life it expresses are feelings Macbeth was trying to combat from the very beginning. To be sure, now that his wife is dead and the mistakenness of his course is becoming more apparent with each new development, the feelings are being reexperienced with greater poignancy.

Even with goading from his wife, Macbeth proceeds with the murder of Duncan only with great difficulty. With the hysteric's facility for converting thoughts and feelings into somatic or external terms, he conjures up a dagger, and a little later sees it covered with gouts of blood. Not only these hallucinations, but various things he says show that he is already tormented by guilt: yet his crime is still "but fantastical." In I.iii, once he began sensing what he would have to do to become king, he took refuge in wishful thinking:

> If chance will have me King, why, chance may
> crown me,
> Without my stir.

Although he now realizes that this is a vain hope, he has not otherwise made much progress. He is still hoping that the "sure and firm-set earth"—and by this I think he means the gods and destiny, not simply the human beings at Inverness—will remain ignorant of his deeds. Revelatory also is the phrase, "I go, and it is done." He glides over, is unwilling to visualize, the murder itself.

What he tells his wife in II.ii makes it clear that during or immediately after the murder—here as elsewhere time indications are uncertain—his guilt deepened further. Even more significant is the way his unconscious desire to be caught and punished discloses itself in the very execution of his crime: he has forgotten to smear the grooms with blood and to leave their daggers near them, and he has brought the daggers to his own chamber. Now he is so overwhelmed by guilt that he cannot return them and bloody the grooms. It is Lady Macbeth who undertakes these repugnant errands. His speeches when he hears the knocking confirm the intensity of his guilt: he is continuing his self-punishment and clearly plans to punish himself further.

Macbeth again receives desperately needed help from his wife after the murder of Banquo. But after killing Duncan, Macbeth never again *asks* for her help. It is important to observe what causes this turnabout. His own inner feeling is the primary factor. He had unjustifiably hoped that his wife's help would enable him not only to go through with a wanton murder, but to kill his king-benefactor-cousin-guest with little or no guilt. Instead he is flooded with guilt. His disappointment may make him realize that he has been unrealistic in his expectations and that his wife cannot give him the escape from self-reproach he had hoped for. After III.iv, he no longer gives her his full confidence, and the reader feels that some of his endearments are perfunctory. He thinks of her less and less thereafter. Once it is committed, the crime that was to bring them together and make their marriage more fulfilling isolates them further.

The banquet scene (III.iv), the last scene in which Macbeth speaks with his wife, or imagines himself doing so, may also be understood as a dream. Indeed, if we had not by this point abandoned reality testing we could scarcely accept it in any other way. It is hard to explain how the banquet guests could fail to note Macbeth's conversation with the First Murderer, harder still to explain how they could avoid overhearing the exchange between Macbeth and his wife, whose second speech to him (61–69) makes it plain that he is the murderer of Duncan.

We do not see Lady Macbeth again until the sleepwalking scene (V.i), and that is the last time we see her. In V.iii, the doctor gives Macbeth a report of her illness, and in the final speech of the play we learn that she may have killed herself. The sleepwalking scene does not seem to be part of Macbeth's dream fabric, but rather something which took place after he became so immersed in his anxieties that he seldom thought of his wife. It is possible, however, that, preoccupied as he was, he had become aware of his wife's disturbed and depressed state of mind and even of her sleepwalking. In that case Macbeth could have dreamt that sleepwalking scene to deal with the anxiety he felt about others learning of his wife's condition—and, what was more frightening still, learning of his crimes from what she said and did while in a somnambulistic state.

Although Macbeth has become separated from his wife, it seems to me that his responses to the news of her illness and the news of her death both show that he feels deep sympathy for her. His response to the account of the "thick-coming fancies/That keep her from her rest" is rich in feeling. It is obvious here (V.iii.39–54) and in the speech he makes when he learns of her death that some of the regret he expresses is for himself. He is in fact confusing his wife's situation and his own. Nothing could show more clearly that the tie with her is still not severed. To be sure, the second speech seems dry and impersonal, but its tone is a defense against feeling. Although Macbeth is controlled and detached, what he says expresses regret and self-reproach, for such separation as has occurred between him and his wife, for the futility and meaninglessness of their crimes and their lives, and for her suffering and disappointment no less than for his own.

Certain parts of the group of scenes we have been considering—the Porter's soliloquy and exchange with Macduff and Lennox, and the exchange between Ross and the unnamed Old Man—do not seem to be products of Macbeth's mind. They lack resonance in consequence. Here and throughout the play the most intense scenes seem to be both parts of Macbeth's thought fabric and accounts of events. Their intensity derives in large part from the fact that they are apprehended in both ways.

Although Macbeth renounces the idea of using his wife a second time to deceive his superego, he tries to achieve the same end by different means. He never ceases to hope that, should he have to kill, he can find some way of doing so without being crushed by guilt.

In the final speech of the conversation with his wife which follows the planning of the murder of Banquo and Fleance, he invokes "seeling night" to "scarf up the tender eye of pitiful day." I think he is also expressing the wish that *he* may be blindfolded. Although the ambiguous "bond" he wants night to "cancel and tear to pieces" almost certainly refers to the prophecy that Banquo's sons will someday rule Scotland, it may also refer to *his* bond to his fellow general and to mankind.

Indirectly and obscurely Macbeth is expressing the old wish that he can be blind to his own acts and he reverts to it once more in III.iv.140–41. Nevertheless, it seems unlikely that he still has any real faith in this possibility. As we know, however, he has employed three murderers to get rid of Banquo and Fleance, and he appears to hope, in this way, to reduce or eliminate his own feeling of responsibility. He tries to prove his innocence to the Ghost of Banquo by claiming that he had not killed him. But the very fact that he conjures up the Ghost, whether in a hallucination or a dream, shows how ineffectual this new stratagem is in evading guilt.

In III.ii and again, more sharply, in III.iv, he expresses the wish that by deliberately hardening himself, by immersing himself more deeply in evil, he can make himself impervious to guilt:

> My strange and self-abuse
> Is the initiate fear that wants hard use.
> We are yet but young in deed.

(III.iv.143–45)

At the time Macbeth makes this speech he is evidently already contemplating the murder of Macduff. By this point he has coarsened a great deal, and he coarsens further before our eyes in IV.i as a result of the rage and fear he feels when he learns that Macduff has fled to England. He again employs murderers, this time to do away with Macduff's family. But the combined effects of these mechanisms for hoodwinking the superego or becoming indifferent to its reproaches is nil. Whatever his actions may suggest, he never achieves cold-bloodedness and indifference to conscience. We learn this from Macbeth's first comment to Macduff on the battlefield before Dunsinane:

> Of all men else I have avoided thee.
> But get thee back! My soul is too much charged
> With blood of thine already.

(V.viii. 5–7)

Although against his will, Macbeth is a moral man to the very end of the tragedy, and this is his real problem: the source of his efforts to deceive conscience and keep himself in ignorance of his own deeds. Those efforts are foredoomed to failure. He is unable to keep any aspect of his behavior from awareness; he is compelled to perceive not merely his acts, but their wrongness and their consequences. From the time he subterraneously reaches the decision that murder is not too high a price to pay for being king (in the play seen as an action), his situation is probably hopeless. Certainly it is hopeless from the moment when, against the dictates of his own mind and heart, he goes through with the crime. He commits a murder for which he knows there is no excuse, and his punishment, whether "actual" or imagined, is Dantesque: he becomes a murderer.

His situation is irremediable and he knows it. The scorpions which have taken possession of his mind are an integral part of his punishment: he is plagued incessantly by self-reproach and the feeling that, to achieve a sense of security, he must murder again and again. The death he finally achieves is a release as much as a punishment. Two speeches in V.iii, 19–29 ("Seyton!—I am sick at heart . . .") and 39–45 ("Cure her of that . . ."), corroborate what the very tonelessness of the "She should have died hereafter" speech tells us more subtly: for some time he has been ready to welcome death.

Macbeth's feeling that he must do away with Banquo and Fleance may easily be perceived as another part of his dream fabric. His rivalry with Banquo and fear of him can be sensed in I.iii and is of course expressed explicitly in III.i. His fear of Banquo's descendants is unmistakable even in the earlier of these scenes and is heavily emphasized in lines 57–72 of the later scene. In dreams no less than in real life, even if he finally succeeded in killing Duncan and Banquo, he would continue to worry about the prophecy that Banquo's descendants would eventually rule Scotland.

Act IV, scene i, can be read like an account of an actual dream. Shakespeare had to be deeply inside the mind of Macbeth to write the scene; in addition to flowing like a dream and dealing with the worries which preoccupy Macbeth at this point, the scene expresses them in the logic and images Macbeth would fall into. If Macduff is not a friend, then he is an enemy. Thus the apparition of the Armed Head, which expresses his fear of Macduff.

We might suppose that at this point the dreamwork would attempt to provide reassurance against the warning. If so, the attempt is unsuccessful. It is ominous to begin with that Macbeth conjures up a Bloody Child. We know that as early as I.iii he feared the Crowned Child he is soon to see. The Bloody Child extends this fear to a still-to-be-born or just-born child; it must seem to Macbeth that he must fear all children, even those not yet conceived. At the same time the Bloody Child represents the retributive fears he has as a result of the murder of Banquo and the attempt to murder Fleance; and, equally, of the consequences of the "strange things" taking shape in his mind which crystallize at the end of the scene—the decision to kill Macduff's wife and children.

Nor do the words of the Bloody Child succeed in reassuring Macbeth. The way its promise is phrased—"none of woman born/shall harm Macbeth"—seems calculated to allow for loopholes. As we read, we notice this, if at all, only subliminally, but Macbeth's response shows clearly that his fear has not been quieted:

> Then live, Macduff: what need I fear of
> thee?
> But yet I'll make assurance double sure,
> And take a bond of fate. Thou shalt not live;
> That I may tell pale-hearted fear it lies,
> And sleep in spite of thunder.   (IV.i.82–86)

The image of "a Child Crowned, with a tree in his hand" condenses Macbeth's deepest and most terrifying fears. From the beginning the realization that some other man's child would succeed him has galled him, making him aware of his childlessness and perhaps his impotence, and it has intensified his guilt by making his crimes seem selfish and futile. The tree the child has in its hand is a fertility symbol, contrasting with Macbeth's "barren scepter." Inevitably, the apparition calls to mind the promise the witches have made to Banquo. He asks the apparition about this just before it disappears; and it paves the way for the heartbreaking image of the eight kings and Banquo—the "family tree" which the weird sisters show him immediately afterward. In an only slightly hidden way the apparition also voices Macbeth's growing fear of "conspirers." At some level he realizes that he is creating the coalition of forces which will ultimately destroy him.

We may become consciously aware of the hedged nature of the promise that Macbeth shall not be vanquished until "Great Birnam Wood to high Dunsinane Hill/Shall come against him." It is not until the play is analyzed that we are likely to realize how natural it is that Macbeth, a general used to sizing up terrain and developing strategies of attack and defense, should have thought of the trick which later occurs to Malcolm. The connection between the tree the child carries and fertility gives another implication to the moving wood, which later exposes the futility of Macbeth's hopes and leads to his death. Shakespeare wants us to feel that a sterile and death-oriented man like Macbeth cannot prevail for long against life-affirming forces.

Just as the news Ross and Angus brought after Macbeth's first encounter with the witches seems to confirm his hopes and justify the terrible act he is considering, so Lennox's news that Macduff has fled to England confirms his fears and is seized as an excuse to proceed with murders more wanton and useless still. I have had to scant the artistry of *Macbeth.* The formal symmetry of I.iii and IV.i is another example of how pervasive it is. The artistry is all the more remarkable if, as I suspect, *Macbeth* was written while Shakespeare was in a distraught state.

To a greater extent than any other drama I know, *Macbeth* is "written" in the language of what Freud calls primary process thinking, the language of the unconscious. This would perhaps be more apparent if the play were less concerned than it is with Macbeth's anxieties and fears. Primary process thinking is usually under the sway of the pleasure principle; its common function is to provide the hallucinatory gratification of desires. But there are anxiety dreams and fantasies as well as wish-fulfilling ones. Even when Macbeth seems preoccupied with his anxieties, numerous characteristics of primary process thinking are clearly in evidence.

If Shakespeare were less of an artist, gross content elements would make us aware of the extent to which primary process thinking prevails in *Macbeth.* Readers not only accept, but quickly begin to take for granted the strange world the play conjures up. In this world the prophecies of supernatural creatures and apparitions often correctly foreshadow and even seem to bring about events. Prophecies hinge upon such things as a wood moving or a person being vulnerable to someone born of a Caesarian operation, but not to someone born in the ordinary way. Our credulity is explained in part by our intuitive ability to understand primary process language—in particular, to perceive the subjective meaning of something apparently objective.

Other things besides unrealistic story elements suggest the extent to which *Macbeth* is written in the language of the unconscious. Like our fantasies and dreams the play is a rebus in which cause often follows effect and explanation often follows act. Equally significant is the almost complete disregard of time. Psychoanalysis has taught us that the idea of time does not exist in the unconscious. Similarly, in *Macbeth* there are practically no clues to the passage of time, though this plays an important part in the Holinshed account upon which Shakespeare drew. Not only have we no idea of how long a period of time the play covers; we seldom have a sure idea of how much time elapses between any two scenes. Such references to time as appear are often vague or careless. In the banquet scene Macbeth refers to charnel houses and graves sending "those that we bury back," but in fact when he speaks there would not have been time to bury Banquo.

Perhaps more significant still is the extent to which a tendency to picture everything manifests itself in *Macbeth*. Wishes, fears, means, and guilt feelings (the bloody dagger, the Ghost of Banquo) are externalized, often personified, shown, and/or voiced. Figures of speech abound, pour out in such profusion that more than one metaphor seems mixed, more than one speech incoherent. As Cleanth Brooks shows, however, the images and symbols which run through the play are (like many of our dreams) better organized than they appear to be.[5] Moreover, the more we penetrate the surface of the play, the more unified and understandable they become.

As we have seen, *Macbeth* can be read as a tissue of its protagonist's dreams, fantasies, and thoughts. Even when viewed as a dramatization of events, those events are often shown as they would be imagined by Macbeth: to some extent nearly every scene reflects his wishes or fears. Thus there is really little difference between the two ways of apprehending the play, and we feel no disposition to choose between them. Moreover, the play is written to an exceptional extent in the language of our dreams and fantasies. Although *Macbeth* has rivals in our century, for example, *Six Characters in Search of an Author*, it may remain the most subjective play ever written. We read it in a state of relaxation, in much the way we read fairy stories in childhood. However it is apprehended, we accept it primarily, I believe, as a dramatization of psychic reality.

5.   "The Naked Babe and the Cloak of Manliness," in *The Well-Wrought Urn* (New York: Reynal and Hitchcock, 1947).

Still, Shakespeare brings off the miracle of persuading us provisionally to accept *Macbeth* as an account of "real" events. A priori, nothing seems more improbable than the idea that a man with such an unrelenting conscience as Macbeth's would embark on a career of crime. Yet Shakespeare makes a play based upon such apparently irreconcilable plot elements believable. However understood, *Macbeth* is among other things one of the world's greatest cautionary tales. Even a person of probity and strong conscience might *dream* of committing an unjustified murder to obtain something desperately desired. Moreover, even such a person might find it impossible to relinquish the dream. Against his will he might find himself returning to it night and day, embellishing it, visualizing ways and means, imagining this or that vicissitude and contingency until, to his horror, a whole series of crimes had been thought through from beginning to end. As Shakespeare has shown, however, what would be uppermost in the mind of such a person is not the crimes or their rewards but the punishment to be endured. Again and again the dreamer would in effect be telling himself, "Only evil and suffering would come of this." The result, if not the purpose, of the dream-thought-fabric would be to pare down the temptation and emphasize its consequences, so that the feared impulse could be controlled. In most cases only the dreamer would profit from this, but when the dream fabric is embodied in a work of art, readers and spectators share in the benefits.

Considered as a dramatization of actual occurrences, *Macbeth* is probably a still more effective cautionary tale. When events seem less contingent and more real, tragedy has its maximum impact on us—though the events are experienced vicariously. The vicarious gratification of impulses, which plague us no less than Macbeth, would make them less urgent and hence more amenable to control, especially if the gratification was apparently real. The emphasis, or overemphasis, on punishment would remind us of the terrible price the gratification entails and hence provide a constraint against yielding to desire.

It is of the utmost importance that Macbeth's first crime, which is the one that fathers all the others, is the murder of his sovereign, who is important in his own right and is the symbol of order in the state. Moreover, it is a murder he knows to be unjustified. No crime could better symbolize what might be called the sacred crimes, the violations of the primeval taboos upon which civilization rests. Nor could any crime better illustrate the strength and tenacity of our anarchistic desires. Many of those desires and the tendency to put the satisfaction of the desires above everything else go back to childhood, but neither the desires nor this tendency is ever completely relinquished; they may still be trouble-some when we are grown-up. In our minds and hearts we have all ex-perienced the temptation to which Macbeth was subjected, or tempta-tions analogous to it, and at one time or another we have yielded to them, in thought if not in deed. The fact that *Macbeth* has this reference to a wide range of our most primitive desires and conflicts helps to ex-plain its unshakable hold on the imagination of mankind.